HERBAL DRUG TECHNOLOGY

FROM PLANT TO MEDICINE

RAO MURALIDHAR RAO

Made with ♥ on the Notion Press Platform
www.notionpress.com

Dedication

I dedicate this book, Herbal Drug Technology: From Plant to Medicine, to the memory of my beloved father, **Akkaladevi Venkat Rajaiah**. His passion for plants, his love for family, and his unending dedication to helping those in need have been a constant source of inspiration for me.

As a graduate of B.Sc. Agriculture and a former Assistant Director of Agriculture, my father was a true champion of the natural world. His deep appreciation for the healing properties of plants was matched only by his unwavering commitment to helping others. Whether it was through his work in agriculture or his tireless efforts to assist those in need, my father always put the needs of others first.

It is with great pride and love that I dedicate this book to my late father, who taught me the importance of pursuing my passions, following my dreams, and helping others along the way. May his memory continue to inspire us all to appreciate the natural world and to make a difference in the lives of those around us.

Dr.Muralidhar Rao Akkaladevi

Hyderabad

27-01-2023

Contents

Herbal Drug Technology: From Plant To Medicine

By

Dr A Muralidhar Rao

Published by Notion Press

Notion Press Media Pvt Ltd,
#7, Red Cross Road,
Egmore, Chennai, Tamil Nadu 600008

Email ID: publish@notionpress.com

Prologue

Herbal medicine has been used for centuries as a primary source of healing and treatment for various ailments. It has a rich history and diverse cultural roots that have influenced the way it is practiced today. The field of herbal drug technology has evolved rapidly in recent years, thanks to advances in science and technology that have allowed us to better understand the therapeutic properties of plant-based medicines.

This book, Herbal Drug Technology: From Plant to Medicine, is a comprehensive guide that explores the complex world of herbal medicine. Each chapter provides a detailed overview of the various aspects of herbal drug technology, with a focus on the science behind the medicine.

Throughout this book, readers will gain a deeper understanding of the ways in which plants have been used to treat a wide range of health conditions, and how modern technology has helped us to refine and improve these treatments. The book also covers important topics such as quality control, drug formulation, and regulatory issues, providing readers with a holistic view of the herbal drug technology industry.

As the world continues to seek out natural and alternative forms of medicine, Herbal Drug Technology: From Plant to Medicine is an essential resource for anyone interested in the fascinating and rapidly evolving field of herbal medicine. Whether you are a student, researcher, or healthcare practitioner, this book will help you to better understand the science behind the medicine, and the ways in which plant-based medicines can be used to promote health and wellness.

I

Herbs as Raw Materials

Introduction

Herbs have been used for medicinal purposes for thousands of years in traditional medicine systems such as Ayurveda and Chinese medicine.

Herb

An herb is defined as a plant or plant part that is used for medicinal, aromatic, or culinary purposes. Herbs can include leaves, flowers, fruits, seeds, roots, and bark, and can be used in various forms such as teas, tinctures, capsules, and ointments.

Herbal medicine

Also known as phytotherapy, is the use of plants or plant extracts for the treatment or prevention of disease. It has been used for thousands of years in many cultures around the world.Herbal medicines can be used alone or in combination with other therapies, and can be administered in various forms such as capsules, tablets, teas, tinctures, and ointments.Fungi, bee products, and animal parts are also commonly used in herbal medicine. For example, mushrooms like reishi and cordyceps are used for their immune-boosting properties, while bee products like honey and propolis have antibacterial and anti-inflammatory effects. Animal parts, such as deer antler and tiger bone, have also been used in traditional Chinese medicine for centuries.Herbal medicine can also include complex chemical compounds, such as alkaloids and flavonoids, which are found in plants and have specific medicinal effects.Dosage forms of herbal medicine include teas, capsules, tinctures, and ointments. Herbal extracts, which are concentrated forms of the active ingredients in a plant, are also commonly used.

Herbal medicine may also have cultural or traditional significance, and can be used to treat and prevent illnesses in the traditional or cultural context.Herbal medicine is not only limited to the usage of dried plant material but also includes the usage of the whole plant like leaves, stem, root and even the seeds.

Herbal medicines can be used in different forms like teas, infusions, decoctions, syrups, tinctures, capsules, tablets, and creams.Overall, herbal medicine can be a valuable addition to a healthcare regimen, but it's important to use caution and consult with a healthcare professional before using any herbal products.

Herbal medicine differs from conventional medicine in several ways:

1. Herbal medicine uses whole plants or plant extracts, while conventional medicine uses isolated chemical compounds. This means that herbal medicine contains a complex mixture of compounds, some of which may have synergistic effects that enhance the medicinal properties of the plant.
2. Herbal medicine is often used to treat the whole person, rather than just the specific symptoms or disease. Herbal medicine aims to restore balance and harmony to the body, rather than just treating symptoms.
3. Herbal medicine is usually less expensive than conventional medicine.
4. Herbal medicine is often associated with traditional or cultural medicine, and can be used to treat and prevent illnesses in the traditional or cultural context.

5. Herbal medicines are not always regulated in the same way as conventional drugs, and there may be variation in the quality and potency of herbal products. Therefore, it's important to use reputable sources when purchasing herbal products.

Not all herbal medicines have been extensively studied for safety and effectiveness, and some may have potential side effects or interactions with other medications. Therefore, it's important to consult with a qualified healthcare professional before using any herbal medicine.

Unlike conventional medicine, herbal medicines have no standard dosage, administration and frequency, the dosage, administration and frequency of herbal medicines are often based on traditional usage, and may vary depending on the preparation method, the plant species and the individual patient.

Herbal medicine often focuses on preventative measures and promoting overall wellness, while conventional medicine tends to focus on treating illnesses and diseases once they have already developed.

Herbal medicinal products

Also known as herbal supplements or phytomedicines, are defined as products that are made from one or more herbal ingredients and are intended to be used for the treatment or prevention of disease. These products can be found in various forms such as capsules, tablets, teas, tinctures, and ointments.Finished herbal products are ready-to-use products that are manufactured according to good manufacturing practices (GMPs). They can include teas, capsules, tablets, and syrups. These products are usually standardized, meaning they contain a consistent amount of the active ingredient(s) in each dose.Powdered herbal drugs are dried, ground plant parts that can be used to make teas, capsules, and tablets. They can also be added to food or used as a topical treatment. Powdered herbal drugs can vary in quality and potency, so it's important to use reputable sources when purchasing them.

It's important to note that the safety and effectiveness of herbal medicines may vary, and some can interact with other medications. It's always recommended to consult with a qualified healthcare professional before taking any herbal medicine.

Herbal medicinal products should be stored according to the manufacturer's instructions to ensure potency and safety.Herbal medicinal products should be avoided during pregnancy, breastfeeding or if you have any chronic illness unless recommended by a qualified healthcare professional.Herbal medicinal products should be avoided with prescription medications, as they can interact with them.

Herbal drug preparations: These are substances made from various parts of plants, such as leaves, roots, flowers and seeds, that are processed to extract the active ingredients. These preparations are made through different methods like extraction with various solvents, purification, concentration and other processes. These preparations can come in various forms, including powders, extracts, and juices. These are used in the pharmaceutical and health industry as alternative medicine.

Herbs and medicinal plants play a vital role in the healthcare system, providing raw materials for various industries and serving as a source of traditional medicine for many people. With the increasing demand for natural and organic products, the use of herbs as raw materials is expected to continue to grow in the future.According to a study by the World Health Organization (WHO), 80 percent of the population in developing countries rely on traditional plant-based medicines for their healthcare needs. India and China are the two major producing countries, accounting for 40 percent of global biodiversity and a significant number of rare species. These countries are known for their medicinal and aromatic crops, which provide raw materials to a variety of industries, including pharmaceuticals, cosmetics, fragrances, and flavors.

The global market for medicinal plants has always been large, and it has been on the rise in recent years. Trade data shows that the export of medicinal plants from India alone is estimated at Rs. 550 crores. This highlights the significance of herbs as raw materials in various industries and the potential for economic growth in this sector.

It is important to note that while herbal medicine has been used safely and effectively for thousands of years, not all herbs or herbal products are safe for consumption. Some herbs can interact with prescription drugs, and some can cause adverse reactions in some individuals. Therefore, it is crucial to seek the guidance of a qualified healthcare professional when using herbal medicines, and to use high-quality, properly sourced and processed herbal products.

Sources of Herbs

Herbs can be sourced from two main ways:

wild harvesting and cultivation.

Wild harvesting

It refers to the collection of herbs from their natural habitat, such as forests, meadows, and mountains. This method of sourcing herbs has been used for thousands of years and is still used today in traditional medicine systems. Wild harvesting is considered as the traditional method of collecting herbs, it is often more expensive and labor-intensive than cultivating herbs. It also has a higher risk of contamination from pollutants, chemicals and pests. However, wild harvesting can lead to over-harvesting and depletion of certain herb populations, which is why it's important to practice sustainable harvesting methods.

Cultivation

It refers to the growing of herbs in gardens, fields, or greenhouses. This method of sourcing herbs allows for control over the growing conditions and can ensure a consistent supply of herbs. Cultivated herbs can also be grown using organic or biodynamic farming methods, which can increase the quality of the herbs. The importance of sustainability in herb collection is vital for the preservation of plant species and their habitats, as well as for maintaining the purity and quality of herbs. Cultivation of medicinal and aromatic plants involves the intentional growing and harvesting of the plants in controlled conditions. The main advantage of cultivation is that it allows for better control over the quality of the harvest, as well as the ability to grow plants in large quantities. Additionally, cultivation can reduce the pressure on wild populations of the plant, and make the plant more accessible for people to use.

However, there are also several disadvantages to cultivation. One of the main disadvantages is that cultivation can require a significant investment of resources, including land, water, and labor. Additionally, cultivation can require the use of synthetic fertilizers and pesticides, which can have negative impacts on the environment. Cultivation can also be difficult to manage pests, diseases and weather conditions which can affect the yield and quality of the plant.

Herbs that are commonly used in Indian herbal medicinal products

Neem (Azadirachta indica): used for various health conditions such as diabetes, skin diseases, and as an anti-inflammatory and antipyretic.

Turmeric (Curcuma longa): used for anti-inflammatory effects, to treat various health conditions such as pain, cancer and depression, and as an antioxidant.

Holy basil (Tulsi, Ocimum sanctum): used as an adaptogen, to help the body cope with stress, as well as to treat respiratory and fever.

Guggulu (Commiphora mukul): used to lower cholesterol and triglyceride levels, and to treat arthritis and other inflammatory conditions.

Shankhapushpi (Convolvulus pluricaulis): used as a brain tonic, to improve cognitive function and memory, and to treat anxiety and depression.

Amla (Emblica officinalis): used as a natural antioxidant and for various health conditions such as diabetes and high blood pressure.

Licorice (Glycyrrhiza glabra): used to treat ulcers, respiratory conditions, and as an anti-inflammatory and expectorant.

Vidanga (Embelia ribes): used to treat various health conditions such as worms, indigestion and as an antipyretic.

Vidanga (Embelia ribes): used to treat various health conditions such as worms, indigestion and as an antipyretic.

Guduchi (Tinospora cordifolia): used as an immune-booster, to treat various health conditions such as fever, diabetes and as an anti-inflammatory.

Selection, Identification, and Authentication of Herbal Materials

The selection, identification, and authentication of herbal materials is crucial in ensuring the safety and effectiveness of herbal medicinal products.This is a critical quality assurance process that ensures that the herbal products we use are safe and effective, and that they contain the correct plant species.There are several methods used for the identification and authentication of herbal materials, and one of the most important is the taxonomic method. This method involves the use of morphological and microscopical characteristics of the plant, such as leaf shape, flower color, and cell structure, to identify the plant species.

The morphological method is based on the macroscopic examination of the plant and its parts, such as leaves, stem, root, and seeds, and it is the most traditional method of identification. While, Microscopical method is based on the microscopic examination of the plant's cells, tissues and spores. The main advantage of this method is that it allows to identify the plant even in the absence of flowers and fruits.

In India, there are several institutions involved in the authentication of herbal materials. The Indian government has established the Ayush (Ayurveda, Yoga and Naturopathy, Unani, Siddha and Homoeopathy) Quality Control of Herbal Medicines Laboratory under the Ministry of Ayush, which is responsible for the quality control and standardization of Ayush medicines. The Central Council for Research in Ayurvedic Sciences (CCRAS) also conducts research on Ayurvedic medicines and their standardization.In addition, there are several other organizations and research institutes that focus on the identification and authentication of herbal materials, such as the National Medicinal Plants Board, the Indian Institute of Herbal Medicine, and the Rajiv Gandhi Centre for Biotechnology.

It's important to note that the identification and authentication of herbal materials is a complex process that involves the use of various methods and the collaboration of multiple institutions. However, by following a proper identification and authentication process, we can ensure that the herbal products we use are safe, effective, and of the highest quality.

Criteria for selecting high-quality herbs

Proper botanical identification: The correct botanical identification of the plant is essential to ensure the safety and effectiveness of the herb. Misidentification can lead to the use of an herb that is toxic or ineffective. Therefore, it is important to use a combination of traditional knowledge, scientific methods, and reference materials such as herbarium specimens, monographs, and floras to ensure the correct identification of the herb.

Harvesting at the right time: Herbs should be harvested at the correct stage of growth, as the chemical composition of the herb can change depending on the stage of growth. For example, some herbs may have higher levels of medicinal compounds at certain times of the year, while others may be toxic if harvested at the wrong time.

Sustainability: It is important to source herbs from sustainable sources to ensure the long-term survival of herb populations and to protect the environment. This includes using sustainable harvesting methods and ensuring that the herbs are grown using organic or sustainable farming practices.

Purity: The herbs should be free from contaminants such as pesticides, heavy metals, and microorganisms.

Techniques for identifying and authenticating herbal materials

Macroscopic and microscopic examination: This technique involves the examination of the physical characteristics of the herb, such as shape, color, and texture, as well as the examination of the herb under a microscope.

Chromatographic analysis: This technique involves the separation and identification of the chemical compounds present in the herb, such as alkaloids, flavonoids, and terpenes.

DNA barcoding: This technique involves the use of genetic markers to identify the herb, which can be useful in cases where the herb is difficult to identify using traditional methods.

The ability to authenticate herbal drugs is particularly important when dealing with drugs that are commonly substituted or contaminated with other varieties that are indistinguishable based on their morphological or chemical properties. Unfortunately, many herbal drugs in the market today cannot be identified or authenticated based on their physical or histological characteristics. The use of incorrect drugs can not only be ineffective but may also worsen a person's condition.

It's important to note that while these techniques can be useful in identifying and authenticating herbal materials, they should be used in conjunction with other methods, such as traditional knowledge, to ensure the correct identification of the herb. Thus, the selection, identification, and authentication of herbal materials is crucial in ensuring the safety and effectiveness of herbal medicinal products. It's important to use a combination of traditional knowledge, scientific methods, and sustainable sourcing practices to ensure the correct identification and authenticity of the herbs used in medicinal products.

Processing of Herbal Raw Materials

Herbal materials can be considered as the starting materials and herbal preparations can be considered as intermediates in the production of finished herbal products. These herbal preparations are also used as herbal dosage forms for therapeutic applications.

Processing of herbal materials is a multi-step process that depends on the intended use of the final product.Primary processing of herbal raw materials refers to the initial steps taken to prepare the plant material for further use. This includes activities such as harvesting, cleaning, and drying the plant material.

During harvesting, the plant material is collected at the appropriate time, when it contains the highest concentration of active compounds. Cleaning involves removing any dirt, debris, or other foreign materials from the plant material. Drying is done to reduce the moisture content of the plant material, which helps to preserve it and make it easier to handle.Secondary processing of herbal raw materials involves further steps to prepare the plant material for use. This includes activities such as cutting, grinding, and powdering the plant material. Cutting and grinding reduce the size of the plant material, making it easier to handle and use. Powdering is done to reduce the particle size of the plant material, making it easier to mix with other ingredients and to extract the active compounds.Specialized processing of herbal raw materials refers to the more advanced techniques used to extract, purify, and concentrate the active compounds from the plant material. This includes methods such as maceration, distillation, chromatography, and centrifugation. These methods are used to extract the active compounds from the plant material, and purify and concentrate them for use in herbal medicinal products.

It's important to note that the specific processing methods used will vary depending on the plant material and the desired end product. Each step in the process must be carefully controlled to ensure that the final product is safe, effective, and of the highest quality.

In conclusion, primary processing of herbal raw materials includes activities such as harvesting, cleaning, and drying the plant material. Secondary processing includes cutting, grinding, and powdering the plant material. Specialized processing includes advanced techniques used to extract, purify, and concentrate the active compounds from the plant material. All these steps are important to ensure that the final product is safe, effective, and of the highest quality.

The processing of herbal materials

Collection of drugs: This refers to the process of gathering the raw materials from the source, whether it be wild or cultivated.

The collection of medicinal plants is an important task that can be undertaken by both casual, unskilled native labor or by skilled people. The season in which the plants are collected is of great importance as the amount and sometimes the nature of the active constituents is not constant throughout the year. For example, Rhubarb contains no anthraquinone glycosides derivatives in winter but contains anthranols which on arrival of warmer weather, are converted by oxidation into anthraquinones. The age of the plant is also important as there is increasing evidence that the composition of a number of secondary plant metabolites varies appreciably throughout the day and the night.

The most advantageous time of collection is during that period when the plant part constituting the drug is highest in its content of active constituents. An example of the importance of the suitable time of harvesting is Ephedra species, where the content of alkaloids is highly variable, and reaches the maximum in autumn. However, it is important to note that these are general rules for collecting the parts of the plants rich in the active constituents and may not apply to all plants. It is also important to concentrate on adverbal words and those that show the time exactly (e.g. after, before, at, late, etc.).

Roots and rhizomes are collected at the end of the vegetation period (i.e. usually in autumn). In most cases, they must be washed free of adhering soil and sand. Bulbs are collected in late autumn, best after the plant has flowered and fruited. Bark is collected in autumn after leaf fall, or spring before the development of the leaves. In spring, the cambium shows its maximum activity producing an abundance of undifferentiated cells that are still soft making stripping the bark, existing outside the cambium, easier. It is also approved to collect the bark after rain has fallen, as the bark will be damp and easy to be removed.

Leaves and herbs are collected at the flowering stage. It is preferred to collect the stems with the leaves and separate them from each other later. Collection in the morning is important in some cases as with Solanaceous leaves. Flowers are usually collected when fully developed. Collection should be in dry weather and towards the middle of the day, after dew has dissipated. In certain cases, as with cloves (Eugenia caryophyllata), the unopened flower is picked. Fruits and seeds are collected when fully ripe and grown, or nearly grown.

After the plants have been collected, the next step is the drying process. It is important to dry the plants in a well-ventilated area out of direct sunlight, using methods such as hanging them in bunches or laying them on screens. The drying time will vary depending on the weather and moisture content of the plants, but it can range from a couple of days to several days. Herbal materials are dried to reduce moisture content and preserve the active compounds.Drying is the process of removing moisture from the herb to prevent spoilage and preserve the chemical compounds in the herb.

Natural drying is the process of drying plant material using natural methods such as sunshine or shade drying. This method is widely used in the herbal industry as it is cost-effective, simple and it preserves the chemical constituents of the plant material.Sunshine drying is a method that involves exposing the plant material to sunlight to dry it. This method is widely used for herbs with high moisture content. The advantage of sunshine drying is that it is a fast method and it does not require any special equipment. However, it has a disadvantage that the herbs are exposed to high temperatures, which can cause damage to the chemical constituents of the plant material.Shade drying is another method that is widely used for drying plant material. This method involves exposing the plant material to indirect sunlight or in a shaded area. The advantage of shade drying is that the herbs are not exposed to high temperatures, which helps to preserve the chemical constituents of the plant material. However, shade drying is a slower method and it requires more space to dry the herbs.Chemical constituents such as tannins, alkaloids, flavonoids and essential oils are stable in dried plant material, but when exposed to high temperatures, they may degrade or volatilize. Therefore, shade drying method is recommended for herbs that are rich in these chemical constituents such as digitalis, senna, and clove.

Different drying methods, such as air-drying, shade-drying, and machine drying, can be used depending on the herb and the desired final product.

Drying is an important process in the preservation of medicinal plants. It serves to rapidly remove water, which in turn stops enzymatic activity, eliminates degradation of active components, and reduces external attack by fungi. Generally, drying is done at relatively high temperatures to ensure quick drying. The chosen temperature should guarantee quick drying, while also being suitable for many components that are sensitive to heat.

Many fresh drugs contain a considerable amount of water (60-90%), and all moist drugs are liable to develop mold, so they must be dried as soon as possible. If enzyme action is to be encouraged, slow drying at a moderate temperature is necessary. If enzyme action is not desired, drying should take place as soon as possible after collection.

In dry climates, arrangements for drying may be carried out under the cover of sheds, at night, or through sun-drying, as long as the active components are not adversely affected. Drying by artificial heat is more rapid than open air and is often necessary in tropical countries where the humidity is very high.

Fairly rapid drying helps flowers and leaves to retain their color and aroma, but if leaves and other delicate structures are over dried, they become very brittle and tend to break. As a general rule, leaves, herbs, and flowers may be dried between 20 and 40 degrees Celsius, while barks and roots should be dried between 30 and 65 degrees Celsius.

Freeze drying, also known as lyophilization, is a very mild method of drying. Frozen material is placed in an evacuated apparatus which has a cold surface maintained at -60 to -80 degrees Celsius. Water vapor from the frozen material then passes rapidly to the cold surface. The method requires a relatively complicated apparatus and is much more expensive than hot-air drying. Lyophilization is very important for drying heat-sensitive substances, such as antibiotics and proteins.

The aboveground parts of plants, including stems, can be dried by bundling them in small bunches that allow for adequate air circulation. Tie the bunches using string or rubber bands, which will adjust as water evaporates and the stems shrink. Hang the plants in a well-ventilated area out of direct sunlight. Cars with open windows can serve as an alternative drying space, especially in damp or poorly ventilated indoor spaces. String can be tied between the handholds above the windows and plants can be hung using paperclips bent to create hooks. Rubber bands or string can also be looped around the line. If weather permits, leave the windows open a bit for air circulation and park in the shade to avoid direct sunlight. Alternatively, leaves, flowers, stems, and bark can also be dried by laying them in baskets or on nylon screens.

Depending on the weather and moisture content, the herbs will dry completely in a couple of days to several days.

When drying roots, it is important to first wash off any soil. Use water that is not too hot as it can damage the roots. Slicing the roots with a knife while they are fresh and easier to cut is a good option, as it allows for better air circulation during the drying process. The sliced or whole roots can then be dried using various methods such as in baskets, on screens or in the oven, as described in the previous answer. It is important to ensure that the roots are dried in a well-ventilated area out of direct sunlight to preserve their medicinal properties.

Specific processing

This includes specific methods to extract, purify, and concentrate the active compounds.Specific processing refers to the methods used to extract, purify, and concentrate the active compounds in a plant. These methods are critical in ensuring that the final product is safe, effective, and of the highest quality.One of the most common methods used to extract the active compounds from a plant is maceration. This is done by soaking the plant material in a liquid, such as water or alcohol, for a period of time. This allows the active compounds to dissolve into the liquid and be separated from the plant material.Another method used to extract the active compounds from a plant is distillation. This is done by heating the plant material, causing the active compounds to vaporize. The vapor is then condensed back into a liquid, which contains the active compounds.Once the active compounds have been extracted, they must be purified. This is done by removing any impurities or other unwanted materials from the extract. This can be done by using various techniques such as chromatography, centrifugation, and filtration.The final step in specific processing is to concentrate the active compounds. This is done by removing any remaining solvent or water from the extract, leaving a concentrated form of the active compounds. This can be done by using techniques such as evaporation or spray drying.It's important to note that specific processing methods vary depending on the plant and active compounds being extracted. The methods used must be carefully chosen to ensure that the final product is safe, effective, and of the highest quality.

Time of collection

The timing of the collection is important as it can affect the quality and quantity of the raw materials.In general, it can affect the potency and effectiveness of the plant. Aboveground parts of plants, such as leaves, flowers, stems, and bark, are best harvested during the full moon, while roots are best harvested during the new moon. This is due to the shifting energy of the plant affected by the lunar cycle. The ideal time for harvesting aboveground parts is in the spring and summer, before or during flowering, while roots are best harvested early in spring or late in the fall when the plant's energy is concentrated in its roots. The best time of day to harvest is after the morning dew has evaporated and before the full strength of the sun in the late afternoon. Clear and sunny weather is ideal for harvesting, as rain can wash away some of the beneficial constituents of the plant. It is also important to only take what is needed from each plant in order to preserve its health.

Harvesting

This involves the process of cutting, plucking or gathering the raw materials.

When gathering leaves, flowers, stems, and bark, it is important to select the most vital parts of the plant. This includes choosing healthy leaves that have not been damaged by insects. One method of harvesting is to pinch off the new growth, such as the top leaves and flowers or buds, which stimulates the plant's growth. Another method is to harvest the entire stem by cutting it close to the ground or just the top few inches. Having a sharp knife can assist in making precise cuts, which helps to minimize harm to the plant by avoiding pulling or tearing.

Roots are a potent source of medicine, but they should be harvested with respect as the plant must be killed in order to gather its root. It is best to harvest roots in the fall, after the plant has had time to flower and go to seed, to ensure more plants for the future. Some slower-growing roots can be harvested, and new growth or buds can be replanted after taking what is needed.

When harvesting roots, the earth around the plant should be loosened with a shovel or trowel to gently lift the entire root system out. Some plants with taproots may be difficult to harvest whole, as they may break before letting go of their hold, such as burdock. After digging the roots, it is important to fill the space back in with soil.

Garbling

Garbling is the process of removing impurities from a drug during its preparation. This includes removing extraneous matter such as other parts of the plant, dirt, and added adulterants. It is typically done after the drug is dried and before it is packaged. The European pharmacopoeia sets a standard that a crude drug should contain no more than 2% foreign matter. Specific actions may include removing stems from leaf drugs, using magnets to remove particles of iron, and using sifting or air currents to remove dirt and sand. This process is important as the presence of impurities such as sand in powdered plants can damage the machinery used in tablet production.

Packing

Herbal materials are packaged to protect them from damage and to maintain their quality.

The way drugs are packaged depends on their intended use. The packaging should protect the drug and be space-efficient. Leaf and herb materials are commonly compressed into solid, compact masses using power balers. Bales used for overseas shipment typically weigh between 100-250 pounds.

Storage: Herbal materials are stored in a manner that preserves their quality and stability.Dried herbs should be stored in airtight glass jars and kept in a dry area away from direct sunlight and extreme temperatures. Labeling the jars and bags is also important to avoid confusion. Herbs should generally be used within 6 months or a year and roots within 3 years, but ultimately it is suggested to rely on your own judgment and senses to decide if an herb or root still possesses its vital essence.

These steps are carried out under Good Manufacturing Practice (GMP) conditions to ensure quality and safety of the final product. The finished products can be in various forms such as decoctions, tea bags, granules, syrups, ointments or creams, inhalations, patches, capsules, tablets and pills, among others.

Proper processing of herbal raw materials is essential to ensure the safety and effectiveness of the final herbal medicinal product. This includes methods for drying, storage, and preservation of herbs, standardization of herbal extracts and preparations, and quality control measures.

Proper storage of dried herbs is essential to prevent spoilage and preserve the chemical compounds in the herb. Herbs should be stored in a cool, dry, and dark place, in airtight containers.

Preservation methods such as freezing, dehydrating, or vacuum sealing can also be used to preserve the herb and its chemical compounds.

Good Manufacturing Practices (GMP) should also be followed during the processing of herbal raw materials to ensure product safety and effectiveness. This includes implementing strict hygiene and sanitation protocols, using appropriate equipment and facilities, and maintaining accurate records and documentation.

In addition to the above methods, extraction and partitioning methods can also be used to separate and isolate specific compounds or groups of compounds from the plant material.

Extraction methods: Extraction is the process of separating the active compounds from the plant material. Different extraction methods, such as maceration, percolation, and distillation, can be used depending on the type of herb and the desired final product. The choice of extraction method can affect the yield and the quality of the extract.

Partitioning: Partitioning is the separation of different chemical compounds present in the plant material by using solvents with different polarities. This process can be used to isolate specific compounds or groups of compounds from the plant material.

It is important to note that GMP guidelines should be followed during the processing of herbal raw materials to ensure product safety and effectiveness. This includes implementing strict hygiene and sanitation protocols, using appropriate equipment and facilities, and maintaining accurate records and documentation.

Stability testing should also be performed to determine how the quality of the product changes over time under different storage conditions. It is important to note that different herbs may require different processing methods and formulations to ensure safety and efficacy. Therefore, it is crucial to consult with experts and follow established guidelines for the processing of herbal raw materials.

Safety management of toxic herbs is an important aspect of traditional medicine. While many herbs and their source medicinal plants have therapeutic benefits, some are known to contain toxic substances that can cause severe side-effects or even death. These toxic herbs and their preparations or dosage forms have a narrow therapeutic window between the effective dose and the lethal dose.

Examples of such toxic herbs include cardio-active preparations such as Powdered Digitalis and Digitalis Capsules. These herbs have therapeutic benefits as a cardio-tonic agent when taken in the proper dosages, but can be lethal when an overdose is taken. Therefore, it is important to have proper regulation, quality control and education about the safe use of these herbs. This includes proper labeling, dosage guidelines, and warning about potential side effects. It is also important to have proper training for healthcare providers and traditional practitioners who use these herbs in their practice.

In general, the safety management of toxic herbs requires the use of the appropriate dose, careful monitoring of patients and the use of appropriate delivery systems. It is important to be aware of the potential risks and benefits associated with these herbs, and to always use them under the guidance of a qualified healthcare professional.

II

Biodynamic Agriculture

Biodiodynamic agriculture is a holistic,sustainable farming method that emphasizes the interconnection of the farm ecosystem and the use of natural preparations and methods to enhance crop growth and health. It was first developynamiced in the 1920s by Rudolf Steiner, an Austrian philosopher and scientist, and is considered the fgren experimented with and implemented by farmers around the world.

Like other organic approaches, biodynamics emphasizes the use of manures and composts and excludes the use of synthetic fertilizers on sreultuicoil and plants. However, methods unique to the biodynamic approach include treating animals, crops, and soil as a single system, an emphasis on local production and distribution systems, and the use of traditional and new local breeds and varieties. Biodynamic agriculture also uses various herbal and mineral additives for compost additives and field sprays.

The World Health Organization (WHO) has developed a series of technical guidelines for the quality control of herbal medicines, including guidelines for Good agricultural and collection practices (GACP) for medicinal plants. These guidelines provide a framework for the cultivation, harvesting, and processing of medicinal plants to ensure their safety and effectiveness. Biodynamic agriculture aligns with these guidelines and focuses on using sustainable and holistic farming practices to produce high-quality medicinal plants.

In contrast to monoculture, sustainable agriculture practices include crop rotation and an assortment of animal life. Rotating crops from field to field and raising varied animal species, along with cover crops and green manures, encourages healthy soil, reduces parasites and controls weeds and pests.

Good agricultural practices (GAP) in the cultivation of medicinal plants describes general principles, including quality control measures, and provides technical details for the cultivation of medicinal plants. This includes:

➢ Identification/authentication of cultivated medicinal plants ➢ Selection of medicinal plants ➢ Botanical identity ➢ Specimens ➢ Seeds and other propagation materials ➢ Cultivation ➢ Site selection ➢ Ecological environment and social impact ➢ Climate ➢ Soil ➢ Irrigation and drainage ➢ Plant maintenance and protection ➢ Harvest ➢ Personnel

GAP ensures that the medicinal plants are grown, harvested and processed in a manner that meets the safety and quality standards set by the WHO. The adherence to these guidelines helps to ensure that the medicinal plants are safe, effective and of high quality for use in traditional and modern medicine.

Overview of Biodynamic farming principles and practicices

The principles of Biodynamic farming include the use of organic, non-toxic methods to grow crops and raise animals, a focus on soil health, and the use of crop rotation and companion planting to enhance biodiversity. The farm is seen as a self-sustaining ecosystem, with the use of composting, crop rotation, and other natural methods to maintain soil fertility.Holistic approach: Biodynamic farming takes a holistic approach to farming, viewing the farm as a self-sustaining organism. This approach includes considering the interactions between the plants, animals, soil, and environment, and striving to create balance in the ecosystem.

Animal husbandry: Biodynamic farming also includes the use of animal husbandry, such as the use of draft animals for plowing and composting, and the use of cow horns filled with cow manure and other natural preparations to improve soil fertility.

Community and social engagement: Biodynamic farming also emphasizes the importance of community engagement and social responsibility. Biodynamic farmers often participate in local farmers markets and engage with their communities to educate them about the benefits of sustainable farming practices and the value of consuming locally grown, organic foods.

Biodynamic certification: Biodynamic farming is recognized as a form of organic farming, and farmers can choose to be certified as Biodynamic by organizations such as Demeter International. This certification process includes inspections of the farm and the use of specific guidelines and standards.

Biodynamic farmers use a range of natural preparations to enhance plant growth and health, such as fermented herbal and mineral preparations, which are applied to the soil or sprayed on the plants. These preparations are believed to improve the health of the soil, as well as the plants, and to enhance the resistance of the plants to pests and diseases. Thus biodynamic preparations are a set of natural preparations that are used to enhance plant growth and health, and to improve soil fertility

Horn manure: Horn manure is a preparation made from cow manure that is packed into cow horns and buried in the soil over the winter. The horns are dug up in the spring and the contents are mixed with water and sprayed on the fields as a soil conditioner. This preparation is believed to improve soil structure and fertility.

Horn silica: Horn silica is a preparation made from finely ground quartz that is packed into cow horns and buried in the soil over the winter. The horns are dug up in the spring and the contents are mixed with water and sprayed on the fields as a foliar spray.

This preparation is believed to improve the health and vitality of the plants.

Preparation 500: Preparation 500 is a preparation made from fermented cow manure that is sprayed on the fields to enhance soil fertility and to stimulate microbial activity in the soil.

Biodynamic preparations are applied to the soil or sprayed on the plants, in extremely small amounts and following specific guidelines and timing.

Biodynamic calendar: Biodynamic farmers also use a specific calendar to determine the best times for planting, harvesting, and applying preparations to the plants. This calendar is based on the lunar and planetary cycles and is believed to enhance the health and vitality of the plants.The calendar includes specific dates for planting, harvesting, and applying preparations to the plants that are in tune with these cycles.

Flower, fruit, leaf, and root days: The calendar also includes specific days for planting different parts of the plants, such as flower, fruit, leaf, and root days. These days are believed to be the most favorable for planting specific parts of the plants, in order to enhance their growth and development.

Moon Phases: The calendar also takes into account the different moon phases, with the new moon and full moon being the most favorable days for planting, and the first and last quarter of the moon being the most favorable days for harvesting.

Astrological signs: The calendar also considers astrological signs, with certain signs being more favorable for planting and harvesting specific crops.

The calendar is also used to schedule the application of Biodynamic preparations, with certain days being more favorable for applying specific preparations.

It's important to note that the use of the Biodynamic calendar is optional and not all Biodynamic farmers use it.

In summary, the Biodynamic calendar is a tool that Biodynamic farmers use to schedule planting, harvesting, and the application of preparations, based on lunar and planetary cycles, flower, fruit, leaf, and root days, moon phases, and astrological signs. The calendar is believed to enhance the growth and development of plants, and is optional for Biodynamic farmers to use.

Good Agricultural Practices (GAP) in Cultivation of Medicinal Plants

Good Agricultural Practices (GAP) is a set of guidelines and standards for growing and producing agricultural products in a sustainable and responsible way. It is designed to protect the environment, improve the quality and safety of agricultural products, and promote fair trade.

The objectives of Good Agricultural Practices (GAP) are to ensure that agricultural products are grown and produced in a sustainable and responsible way, protecting the environment and promoting fair trade. The main objectives of GAP include:

Protecting the environment: GAP aims to reduce the use of synthetic pesticides and fertilizers, which can have harmful effects on the environment. It also promotes sustainable farming practices such as crop rotation, companion planting, and the use of beneficial insects to control pests and diseases. This helps to maintain the long-term health of the soil and reduce the impact of agriculture on the environment.

Improving the quality and safety of agricultural products: GAP includes guidelines for good hygiene and sanitation practices, which are essential for ensuring that agricultural products are safe and of the highest quality. This includes guidelines for the handling, storage, and transportation of agricultural products, as well as guidelines for the use of pesticides and other chemicals. This helps to ensure that the final products are free from contaminants and are safe for consumption.

Promoting fair trade: GAP promotes fair trade by ensuring that farmers receive a fair price for their products, and that consumers have access to high-quality products at a fair price. This helps to create a sustainable and fair market for agricultural products, and it ensures that farmers are able to make a living from their work.

Improving efficiency and productivity: GAP promotes sustainable farming practices that are more efficient and productive than traditional methods. This includes using modern technologies, precision agriculture and implementing best practices that are known to increase yields, reduce costs and minimize waste.

Increasing profitability: By implementing GAP, farmers can reduce costs associated with inputs such as synthetic pesticides and fertilizers, and improve the efficiency and productivity of their operations. This can lead to increased profitability for farmers and a more sustainable agricultural industry.

Conserving biodiversity: GAP encourages farmers to cultivate medicinal plants in ways that conserve biodiversity and protect wild plant populations. This includes practices such as crop rotation, agroforestry and intercropping, which can help to preserve local biodiversity and support a healthy ecosystem.

Providing safe and high-quality products: GAP ensures that the final products are safe and of the highest quality, which is essential for the medicinal plants industry. This includes guidelines for the handling, storage, and transportation of the plant materials, as well as guidelines for the use of pesticides and other chemicals.

Reducing environmental impact: GAP helps to reduce the environmental impact of agricultural practices, by promoting sustainable farming practices, reducing the use of synthetic pesticides and fertilizers, and conserving biodiversity.

In conclusion, the objectives of GAP are to ensure that agricultural products are grown and produced in a sustainable and responsible way, protecting the environment and promoting fair trade. By following GAP guidelines, farmers can improve the quality and safety of their products, increase profitability, and protect the environment. Consumers can also be ensured that the products they consume are safe, high-quality and sustainable. GAP is crucial for the medicinal plants industry as it helps to ensure that the final products are safe, effective, and of the highest quality, which is essential for the medicinal plants industry.

Key elements of Good Agricultural Practices (GAP)

Site selection and preparation: This is one of the most important key elements of GAP. Site selection involves choosing a suitable location for the cultivation of medicinal plants based on factors such as climate, soil type, and water availability. The location should be free from pollutants and other environmental hazards. Site preparation involves preparing the soil for planting by removing debris, tilling, and adding necessary nutrients and fertilizers.

Planting and growing: This key element involves selecting the appropriate plant species and varieties for cultivation, based on factors such as climate, soil type, and water availability. This includes providing the necessary care and maintenance such as irrigation, fertilization, pest and disease control, and pruning. Proper maintenance helps to ensure that the plants are healthy and will produce high-quality medicinal products.

Harvesting and post-harvest handling: This key element involves proper timing of harvest, handling and storage of the harvested plant material, and ensuring that it meets the necessary quality and safety standards. Proper timing of harvest ensures that the plant material is at its peak of maturity and contains the highest concentration of active compounds. Proper handling and storage of the harvested plant material is necessary to prevent spoilage, decay, or loss of quality. The harvested plant material should be dried and stored properly to preserve its chemical constituents.

It's important to note that each key element of GAP is interrelated and dependent on the others. Site selection and preparation provide the foundation for successful planting and growing, while harvesting and post-harvest handling ensure that the final product is safe, effective and of the highest quality. Adhering to GAP in the cultivation of medicinal plants ensures that the final product is safe, effective, and of the highest quality, and it also helps to protect the environment and promote sustainability.

In India, Good Agricultural Practices (GAP) for medicinal plants involve following the guidelines set by the Ministry of AYUSH (Ayurveda, Yoga and Naturopathy, Unani, Siddha and Homoeopathy) and the National Medicinal Plants Board.

In India, medicinal plants are grown in various regions with different agro-climatic conditions. Some of the specific guidelines for GAP of medicinal plants in India are:

Soil and Water Management:In India, medicinal plants are grown in a wide range of soils including red, lateritic, alluvial, black and mountain soils.

Adequate irrigation is necessary to ensure consistent growth and prevent stress on the plants.

Pest and Disease Control:Integrated pest management (IPM) strategies should be used to control pests and diseases, which involve using a combination of cultural, biological, and chemical methods.

Harvesting and Post-harvest Handling:Proper timing and techniques for harvesting medicinal plants are crucial for maintaining their quality and efficacy.

Plants should be harvested at the peak of maturity and handled carefully to avoid damage.

Proper storage and drying methods should be used to preserve the plants' active compounds.

Traceability:Traceability is essential for ensuring the safety and quality of medicinal plants.Each batch of plants should be traceable from the field to the final product, including information on the variety, location, and date of cultivation, as well as any treatments applied.

In addition to these guidelines, farmers are also encouraged to adopt organic farming methods for cultivation of medicinal plants to ensure their safety and quality. The National Medicinal Plants Board also provides support and training to farmers and entrepreneurs for the cultivation and value addition of medicinal plants.

Organic farming methods and principles: Organic farming is a method of growing crops and raising animals without the use of synthetic pesticides, fertilizers, or genetically modified organisms (GMOs). Organic farming methods include crop rotation, companion planting, and the use of natural fertilizers and pest controls. Organic farming also emphasizes the importance of soil health, biodiversity, and sustainability. Biodynamic farming is considered a form of organic farming as it follows similar principles.

Thus ,Organic farming is an integrated farming system that aims for sustainability, enhancement of soil fertility, and biological diversity as it prohibits the use of synthetic pesticides, antibiotics, synthetic fertilizers, genetically modified organisms, and growth hormones with rare exceptions. Organic agriculture is a production system that sustains the health of soils, ecosystems, and people. It relies on ecological processes, biodiversity, and cycles adapted to local conditions, rather than the use of inputs with adverse effects. Organic agriculture combines tradition, innovation, and science to benefit the shared environment and promote fair relationships and a good quality of life for all involved.

Organic farming can primarily be divided into two types: Pure organic farming and integrated organic farming. Pure organic farming involves avoiding all artificial chemicals, and every fertilizer and pesticide used are derived from completely natural sources such as blood meal or bone meal. Integrated organic farming involves integrating techniques aimed at achieving ecological requirements and economic demands, such as integrated pest management and nutrient management. This approach also allows for the use of some synthetic inputs, but only when deemed necessary for the health and well-being of the farm ecosystem and the farm production.

Nutrient management is an essential aspect of organic farming as it helps to maintain healthy soil and promote plant growth. Organic farming follows a healthy way of farming for both crops and consumers by using composted organic manure to provide nutrition to crops, which improves the organic content and fertility of the soil. Additionally, organic farming uses bacterial and fungal biofertilizers to enhance soil nutrients. These biofertilizers are made from natural microorganisms that help to improve the soil's structure, increase water-holding capacity, and promote nutrient cycling.The use of organic manures and biofertilizers in organic farming helps to improve soil health, increase crop yields and quality, and reduce the need for synthetic fertilizers. Organic farming also relies on crop rotation and intercropping to maintain soil fertility, as well as using cover crops to fix nitrogen and add organic matter to the soil.

Another important aspect of nutrient management in organic farming is the use of natural pest and disease control methods. This includes the use of beneficial insects, companion planting, and crop rotation to control pests and diseases naturally. This not only reduces the need for synthetic pesticides but also helps to maintain a balance within the ecosystem and promote biodiversity.

Importance of soil health and biodiversity in medicinal plant cultivation: Soil health and biodiversity are essential for the cultivation of medicinal plants. Healthy soil is rich in microorganisms and nutrients, which are necessary for the growth and development of plants. Biodiversity, on the other hand, is important for maintaining a balanced ecosystem and reducing the risk of pest and disease outbreaks.

Sustainability and ethical considerations in medicinal plant cultivation: Sustainability and ethical considerations are important in the cultivation of medicinal plants. This includes using sustainable farming practices that do not harm the environment or deplete natural resources, and sourcing medicinal plants ethically, ensuring that the plants are not harvested in a way that harms local communities or ecosystems.

Cover cropping: Organic farmers use cover cropping to improve soil health and fertility. Cover crops, such as clover, alfalfa, or rye, are planted between cash crops to protect the soil from erosion, to add organic matter to the soil, and to suppress weeds.

Composting: Organic farmers also use composting to improve soil health. Composting is the process of breaking down organic material, such as plant debris and food scraps, to create a rich, nutrient-dense soil amendment.

Crop rotation: Organic farmers use crop rotation to maintain soil health and to reduce the risk of pests and diseases. Crop rotation involves planting different crops in a specific order in the same field over time. This helps to improve soil health, suppress weeds and pests, and reduce the risk of disease.

Integrated pest management (IPM): Organic farmers also use Integrated Pest Management (IPM) methodologies to control pests and diseases, this includes monitoring pests and diseases, identifying the pests and diseases, and taking appropriate action to control them.

Pest and Pest Management in Medicinal Plants

Pests can cause significant damage to medicinal plants, reducing yield and quality of the final product. Common examples of pests include insects, mites, and diseases caused by microorganisms.

Pest and pest management in medicinal plants is an important aspect of organic farming as it ensures the safety and quality of the final product. Organic farming uses various techniques to control pests and weeds while maintaining soil fertility, such as crop rotation, mixed cropping, organic control, and hand weeding.

Crop rotation is the practice of growing different crops in the same field in a specific order to reduce pest and disease pressure. Mixed cropping is the practice of growing two or more crops together in the same field to reduce pest and disease pressure. Organic control methods such as the use of beneficial insects and natural predators are also used to control pests. Hand weeding is also an effective method of controlling weeds.

Sometimes, natural or other organically approved insecticides like neem pesticides are also used in organic farming. These pesticides are derived from natural sources and are less harmful to the environment and humans compared to synthetic pesticides.

Natural pest control: Organic farmers use a range of natural pest control methods, such as companion planting, trap cropping, and the use of beneficial insects and predators, to control pests and diseases. Organic farmers also use a range of natural pesticides, such as neem oil, pyrethrum, and Bacillus thuringiensis (BT) to control pests and diseases.

Identifying and preventing common pests and diseases in medicinal plants: Identifying and preventing common pests and diseases in medicinal plants is essential for maintaining healthy and productive crops. This includes monitoring plants for signs of infestation or disease, identifying the pests or diseases, and taking appropriate action to control them. Prevention methods include crop rotation, companion planting, and proper sanitation and hygiene practices in the field.

Identification: Identifying common pests and diseases in medicinal plants can be challenging, as many pests and diseases have similar symptoms. However, it is important to correctly identify the pest or disease in order to choose the most appropriate control method. This can be done by observing the symptoms of the plants, such as discoloration, wilting, or abnormal growth patterns, as well as by taking samples of the affected plant parts and observing them under a microscope or sending them to a lab for analysis.

Prevention: Preventing common pests and diseases in medicinal plants is often the most effective and least expensive method of control. Prevention methods include crop rotation, companion planting, and proper sanitation and hygiene practices. For example, crop rotation can help to reduce the buildup of pests and diseases in the soil, while companion planting can help to repel pests and attract beneficial insects. Proper sanitation and hygiene practices, such as removing and destroying infected plant parts, can help to reduce the spread of pests and diseases.

Cultural control: Cultural control methods include practices that can be used to prevent pests and diseases from occurring or to reduce their impact. These methods include crop rotation, companion planting, and proper sanitation and hygiene practices. Some cultural control methods include selecting resistant varieties, adjusting planting dates, and adjusting the pH of the soil.

Biological control: Biological control methods include the use of natural predators and parasites to control pests and diseases. For example, ladybugs are often used to control aphids, and parasitic wasps are used to control caterpillars.

Chemical control: Chemical control methods include the use of biopesticides and bioinsecticides, which are natural alternatives to synthetic chemical pesticides. These methods are used only when necessary, and in small amounts, to minimize the impact on the environment and human health

Biopesticides and bioinsecticides

Biopesticides are pesticides derived from natural materials such as animals, plants, bacteria, and certain minerals. These natural pesticides are often less toxic than synthetic chemical pesticides, and are less likely to harm beneficial insects, birds, and other wildlife. Some examples of biopesticides include neem oil, made from the seeds of the neem tree, and spinosad, derived from a soil bacterium.

Bioinsecticides are a subcategory of biopesticides, specifically designed to control insects. They are naturally occurring compounds or microorganisms that are toxic to certain insects or disrupt their growth and reproduction.

One advantage of biopesticides over synthetic pesticides is that biopesticides are derived from natural sources and are less harmful to the environment and non-target organisms.

Animals such as ladybugs and lacewings can be used as biopesticides, as they feed on common plant pests. Plants such as neem and marigold also have pesticidal properties and can be used to control pests.

Minerals such as diatomaceous earth and kaolin can also be used as biopesticides. Microorganisms, such as the spores of the bacteria Bacillus thuringiensis (Bt), can also be used as biopesticides to control insects.

In summary, pests can cause significant damage to medicinal plants. The use of biopesticides, which are derived from natural sources, can be an effective method of pest management, and include animals, plants, minerals, and microorganisms such as Bt spores.

Microorganisms that act as biopesticides include bacteria, fungi, and viruses. One of the most widely used biopesticides is Bacillus thuringiensis (Bt), a soil-dwelling bacterium that produces a toxin that is toxic to certain insects, such as caterpillars and mosquitoes. Bt is used as a spray or a dust to control pests on a wide range of crops, including fruits, vegetables, and ornamental plants.

Another example of a biopesticidal microorganism is the fungus Beauveria bassiana. This fungus infects and kills a wide range of insects, including beetles, moths, and ants. Beauveria bassiana can be applied as a spray or a powder to control pests on crops and in greenhouses.

Viruses can also act as biopesticides. For example, the baculovirus is a virus that infects and kills caterpillars and other lepidopteran insects. Baculovirus can be used to control pests on a wide range of crops, including fruits, vegetables, and ornamental plants.

Another example of biopesticide microorganisms is Trichoderma harzianum, a fungus that can inhibit the growth of plant pathogenic fungi and bacteria. Additionally, Streptomyces spp is a group of bacteria that produce a variety of secondary metabolites with pesticidal properties.

It's important to note that microorganisms used as biopesticides should be tested for safety and efficacy before they are used in commercial applications, as they may also causedamage to non-target organisms or have other negative impacts on the environment.

Microbial pesticides are pesticides that contain microorganisms, such as bacteria, fungi, or viruses, which attack specific pest species or entomo-pathogenic nematodes as active ingredients. These microorganisms are used as bio-insecticides to control insect pests and bio-herbicides to control weeds. They are considered a more environmentally friendly alternative to synthetic pesticides as they are derived from natural sources and have less impact on non-target organisms.

Plant-Incorporated Protectants (PIPs) are pesticidal substances that are produced in genetically modified plants or organisms (GMOs). These pesticidal substances are produced through the genetic material that has been incorporated into the plant. The protein and its genetic material are regulated by the Environmental Protection Agency (EPA) while the plant itself is not regulated. A common example of PIPs is the production of transgenic plants that express insecticidal endo-toxins derived from the soil bacterium. These PIPs are considered a more efficient and sustainable way to control pests as they are self-protective and reduce the need for additional pesticide applications.

Pheromones and semi-chemicals are substances that are naturally produced by insects to communicate with each other and are used in pesticides to disrupt their mating and reproductive cycles. Plant extracts are derived from plants and are used to repel or poison pests. Natural insect growth regulators are substances that mimic the natural hormones that regulate the growth and development of insects, and are used to disrupt their normal growth patterns.

Biochemical pesticides are considered to be a more environmentally friendly alternative to chemical pesticides as they are derived from natural sources and have less impact on non-target organisms. They are also less persistent in the environment and break down more quickly than chemical pesticides. Biochemical pesticides are considered to be an important tool in integrated pest management programs because they help to reduce the use of chemical pesticides and promote a more sustainable agriculture.

Advantages: Biopesticides and bioinsecticides have several advantages over synthetic chemical pesticides, including: they are often less toxic to humans and other non-target organisms; they break down more quickly in the environment; they are less likely to lead to the development of resistance in pests; and they can often be used in conjunction with other pest control methods to enhance their effectiveness.

Bio pesticides: Examples include Bacillus thuringiensis (Bt), which is used to control caterpillars, and Neem oil, which is used to control a variety of insects and mites.

Microbial pesticides: Examples include Beauveria bassiana, which is used to control a variety of insects, and Metarhizium anisopliae, which is used to control a variety of pests.

Biochemical pesticides: Examples include pheromones, such as the sex pheromones of moths which used to attract and trap them, and natural insect growth regulators, such as chitin inhibitors which are used to disrupt the growth and development of insects.

Plant-Incorporated Protectants (PIPs) : Examples include genetically modified Bt cotton which contains a toxin derived from Bacillus thuringiensis that kills certain insect pests and genetically modified soybeans that are resistant to herbicides.

Limitations: Biopesticides and bioinsecticides also have some limitations, including: they are often less effective than synthetic chemical pesticides; they can be more expensive to produce; and they can be less stable and less consistent in their effectiveness than synthetic pesticides.

Integrated Pest Management (IPM) is a comprehensive approach to managing pests that combines a variety of strategies, including biopesticides, to effectively control pests while minimizing negative impacts on the environment.

The principles of IPM include

Prevention: Preventing pests from becoming a problem by identifying and eliminating the conditions that allow them to thrive.

Monitoring: Regularly monitoring crops to detect pests early, so that action can be taken before they cause significant damage.

Acceptable levels of pests: Setting a threshold for the acceptable level of pests, so that action is only taken when necessary to prevent damage to the crop.

Crop sanitation: Maintaining clean and healthy growing conditions to prevent pests from thriving.

Mechanical control: Using physical methods to control pests, such as traps and barriers.

Biological control: Using natural predators, parasites, and pathogens to control pests.

Chemical control: Using pesticides as a last resort, when other methods have failed to control the pest population to an acceptable level.

The concept of basic IPM system includes:

Identification of pests, their damage and life cycle.

Setting action thresholds for pests.

Monitoring and record keeping.

Implementation of cultural, physical, biological and chemical control measures.

Evaluation of the effectiveness of the measures taken.

Continual improvement of the system.

List of some natural plants that can act as pesticides include:

Neem (Azadirachta indica)

Pyrethrum (Chrysanthemum cinerariaefolium)

Nicotine (Nicotiana tabacum)

Rotenone (Derris elliptica)

Marigold (Calendula officinalis)

Eucalyptus (Eucalyptus globulus)

Peppermint (Mentha piperita)

Garlic (Allium sativum)

Tomato (Solanum lycopersicum)

Identification of pests, their damage, and life cycle is an important step in the Integrated Pest Management (IPM) process.

This involves identifying the specific pests that are causing damage to the crop, understanding their biology and behavior, and determining the best control strategies to use.

To identify pests, it's important to examine the crop regularly for signs of damage and to look for the pests themselves. The damage caused by pests can take many forms, including holes in leaves, wilted or discolored plant tissue, or distorted growth. By examining the damage, you can often identify the type of pest that is causing it.

Once the pest has been identified, it's important to understand its biology and behavior. This includes information such as the life cycle of the pest, its preferred host plants, and the environmental conditions that it thrives in. Understanding the pest's biology and behavior can help to determine the best control strategies to use.

For example, if the pest is a caterpillar, it's important to know the stage of its life cycle when it is most vulnerable to control measures, as well as what kind of food plants it feeds on. If the pest is a fungus, it's important to know the ideal humidity and temperature range for its growth.

It's also important to understand the damage caused by the pest and the impact on the crop yield and quality. For example, if the pest is a leaf miner, the damage will be visible on the leaf surface, but the plant will be able to recover from it. However, if the pest is a stem borer, the damage will be inside the stem and the plant will not recover from it.

Setting action thresholds for pests.

Setting action thresholds for pests is an important step in the Integrated Pest Management (IPM) process. Action thresholds refer to the point at which pest populations have reached a level where they are causing economic damage to the crop and need to be controlled.

Determining the action threshold for a particular pest depends on several factors, including the crop being grown, the stage of crop development, and the economic value of the crop. For example, a higher action threshold may be acceptable for a pest on a crop that has a low economic value, while a lower threshold may be necessary for a pest on a high-value crop.

To set action thresholds, it's important to monitor the crop regularly to detect pests early and to determine the population size of the pests. Different pest monitoring methods can be used, such as visual inspections, sticky traps, and pheromone traps.

Once the pest population has reached the action threshold, control measures can be implemented. These measures can include cultural controls, such as crop rotation and proper sanitation, physical controls, such as trapping and barriers, biological controls, such as using natural predators and parasites, and chemical controls, such as using pesticides.

It's important to note that action thresholds should be regularly reviewed and updated, as pest populations can change over time due to factors such as changes in weather and crop management practices.

Monitoring and record keeping

Monitoring and record keeping are essential components of Integrated Pest Management (IPM). Regular monitoring of the crop allows pests to be detected early, before they cause significant damage, and allows for timely implementation of control measures.

There are various methods of monitoring pests, depending on the crop and the pest in question. Some common monitoring methods include visual inspections, sticky traps, pheromone traps, and sweep nets. These methods can be used to detect the presence of pests, as well as to estimate population sizes and to monitor changes in pest populations over time.

Record keeping is an important aspect of monitoring. It's important to keep detailed records of the monitoring data, including the date, the location, the pest species, the number of pests detected, and the control measures taken. This information can be used to track the effectiveness of the control measures and to make informed decisions about future control strategies.

Record keeping can be done through various methods such as paper-based records, spreadsheets, or specialized software. It's important to keep the records in a safe and accessible location, and to ensure that the data is accurate and complete.

Implementation of cultural, physical, biological and chemical control measures

Implementation of cultural, physical, biological and chemical control measures is an important step in the Integrated Pest Management (IPM) process. These measures are used to control pests and to minimize negative impacts on the environment.

Cultural control measures include practices such as crop rotation, proper sanitation, and proper irrigation and fertilization. These practices can help to create a healthy growing environment that is less conducive to pest growth and reproduction.

Physical control measures include methods such as trapping and barriers. Traps can be used to capture pests, while barriers can be used to keep pests out of the crop area. Physical controls are often used in combination with other control measures to provide an integrated approach to pest management.

Biological control measures include using natural predators, parasites, and pathogens to control pests. Examples of biological control measures include using ladybugs to control aphids, and using a fungus to control caterpillars.

Chemical control measures include using pesticides as a last resort when other methods have failed to control the pest population to an acceptable level. It's important to use pesticides carefully and responsibly, following the label instructions and taking steps to minimize negative impacts on the environment.

It's important to note that the selection of control measures will depend on the specific pest, the crop, and the environmental conditions. It's also important to implement the measures at the right time, when the pest is most vulnerable, to ensure the most effective control.

Thus, Implementation of cultural, physical, biological and chemical control measures is an important step in the IPM process. These measures are used to control pests and to minimize negative impacts on the environment. Cultural measures include crop rotation, proper sanitation, and proper irrigation and fertilization. Physical measures include trapping and barriers, biological measures include using natural predators, parasites, and pathogens and chemical measures include using pesticides as a last resort. The selection of control measures will depend on the specific pest, the crop and the environmental conditions. It's important to implement the measures at the right time for the most effective control.

Continual improvement of the system

Continual improvement of the system is an important aspect of Integrated Pest Management (IPM). It involves regularly reviewing and evaluating the effectiveness of the pest management strategies and making adjustments as needed to improve the overall effectiveness of the system.

Evaluation of the effectiveness of the pest management strategies can be done by comparing the pest population levels before and after the control measures were implemented. It's also important to evaluate the impact of the control measures on the crop yield and quality. This information can be used to make informed decisions about future control strategies.

It's important to keep records of the pest management strategies that have been implemented, as well as the results of the evaluations. This information can be used to identify trends and patterns in pest populations, and to identify areas where the pest management system can be improved.

The pest management system can be improved by:

Reviewing and updating the action thresholds for pests.

Adopting new pest management strategies, such as new biopesticides or cultural practices, as they become available.

Refining the monitoring methods to make them more accurate and efficient.

Developing an emergency plan in case of an unexpected outbreak of pests.

Biodynamic Agriculture and Medicinal Plant Quality

The impact of Biodynamic farming on the quality of medicinal plants: Biodynamic farming is a holistic and ecological approach to agriculture that emphasizes the use of natural inputs, such as compost and biodynamic preparations, to improve soil health and plant growth. Biodynamic farming also emphasizes the importance of biodiversity, crop rotation, and other sustainable farming practices. These practices can lead to higher quality medicinal plants, with a higher content of medicinal compounds, as well as a better taste, aroma, and appearance of the plant.

The role of Biodynamic preparations in improving plant growth and health: Biodynamic preparations are a unique aspect of Biodynamic farming. These preparations are made from natural materials, such as cow manure, quartz, and yarrow, and are used to enhance plant growth and health. The preparations are applied to the soil, seeds, or plants, and are thought to work by promoting microbial activity in the soil and by improving plant'sIn summary, Biodynamic Agriculture and Medicinal Plant Quality emphasizes the use of natural inputs, such as compost and biodynamic preparations, to improve soil health and plant growth. Biodynamic farming also emphasizes the importance of biodiversity, crop rotation, and other sustainable farming practices. These practices can lead to higher quality medicinal plants, with a higher content of medicinal compounds, as well as a better taste, aroma, and appearance of the plant. The use of Biodynamic preparations is also considered to be a unique aspect of Biodynamic farming, which can be used to enhance plant growth and health, by promoting microbial activity in the soil and by improving plant's resistance to pests and diseases.

The benefits of Biodynamic agriculture in the cultivation of medicinal plants

The benefits of Biodynamic agriculture in the cultivation of medicinal plants: Biodynamic agriculture is a holistic and ecological approach to agriculture that emphasizes the use of natural inputs, such as compost and biodynamic preparations, to improve soil health and plant growth. This approach can lead to higher quality medicinal plants, with a higher content of medicinal compounds, as well as a better taste, aroma, and appearance of the plant. Biodynamic farming also emphasizes the importance of biodiversity, crop rotation, and other sustainable farming practices, which can reduce the environmental impact of farming and promote a more sustainable food system.

The importance of continued research and development in Biodynamic farming practices for medicinal plants: The field of Biodynamic agriculture is still relatively new and there is a need for continued research and development in order to better understand the principles and practices of Biodynamic farming. This includes research on the effectiveness of Biodynamic preparations, the impact of Biodynamic farming on soil health and plant growth, and the potential for Biodynamic farming to be integrated into larger-scale food production systems.

III

Preparation and Standardization of Ayurvedic Formulations

Definition of Ayurvedic Formulations: Ayurvedic Formulations are preparations made from natural ingredients such as herbs, minerals, and metals, according to the principles of Ayurveda. These formulations are used to prevent, manage and treat various illnesses and are available in various forms like tablets, capsules, syrups, oils, ghee, etc.

Importance of preparation and standardization in Ayurveda: Ayurvedic Formulations are an integral part of the Ayurvedic system of medicine. They are considered safe and effective when prepared and standardized according to the principles of Ayurveda. However, the quality of Ayurvedic Formulations available in the market varies widely, and there is a need for proper preparation and standardization to ensure safety and efficacy.

Proper preparation of Ayurvedic Formulations involves the correct selection of ingredients, their appropriate processing, and the use of standardization techniques. This ensures that the final product contains the desired active ingredients in the correct quantity and is free from contaminants.

Standardization of Ayurvedic Formulations involves the use of various techniques such as Chromatography, Spectrophotometry, and HPTLC to ensure that the product contains the desired active ingredients in the correct quantity. This also ensures the quality and safety of the final product.

Proper preparation and standardization of Ayurvedic Formulations are essential for the safety and effectiveness of Ayurvedic Formulations. It ensures that the final product is of high quality and is free from contaminants, thereby reducing the risk of adverse reactions and increasing the chances of therapeutic success.

Moreover, preparation and standardization of Ayurvedic Formulations are important for the credibility and scientific validation of Ayurveda, which will help in the integration of Ayurveda with modern medicine and increase its acceptance globally.

Principle of Preparation

Importance of Quality Control in Ayurvedic Formulation Preparation: Quality control is a crucial aspect of the preparation of Ayurvedic formulations. It ensures that the formulations are safe, effective and consistent in their quality. Quality control measures are implemented throughout the entire process of preparation, from the selection of ingredients to the final product.

Standardization Techniques in Ayurvedic Formulation Preparation: Standardization is the process of ensuring that the Ayurvedic formulations are consistent in their quality and meet established standards. The following are some of the standardization techniques used in Ayurvedic formulation preparation:

Physical examination: Physical examination is used to check the appearance, texture and color of the formulation.

Chemical analysis: Chemical analysis is used to check the presence of active ingredients, impurities and contaminants in the formulation.

Microbial analysis: Microbial analysis is used to check the presence of microorganisms in the formulation.

Heavy metal analysis: Heavy metal analysis is used to check the presence of heavy metals in the formulation.

In-vitro analysis: In-vitro analysis is used to check the bioactivity of the formulation.

In-vivo analysis: In-vivo analysis is used to check the safety and efficacy of the formulation.

It's important to note that, these techniques are used to ensure that the Ayurvedic formulations meet established standards, and that the final product should be evaluated by a qualified Ayurvedic practitioner to ensure safety and efficacy.

Proper storage techniques for Ayurvedic Formulations: Proper storage is essential for ensuring the stability and shelf-life of Ayurvedic formulations. The following are some recommended storage techniques:

Store Ayurvedic formulations in airtight containers to prevent contamination and moisture.

Keep the formulations in a cool, dry place away from sunlight and heat.

Avoid storing Ayurvedic formulations near strong odors as they may absorb the odor and lose their potency.

Label the containers with the name of the product, expiry date, batch number and any other relevant information.

Shelf life and stability of Ayurvedic Formulations: The shelf life and stability of Ayurvedic formulations depend on several factors such as the ingredients used, the storage conditions, and the preparation method. Proper storage can extend the shelf life of Ayurvedic formulations, but it's important to pay attention to the expiry date. The expiry date can vary depending on the formulation and its ingredients, but it's generally around 2-3 years for most Ayurvedic formulations if stored properly.

It's important to note that, Proper storage is crucial for maintaining the safety and efficacy of Ayurvedic formulations, so it's important to follow the recommended storage techniques and pay attention to the expiry date.

Marketed preparations

Overview of Ayurvedic Formulations available in the market: There are a wide variety of Ayurvedic formulations available in the market, including herbal supplements, herbal teas, herbal oils, herbal powders, and herbal tablets. These formulations are used to treat a wide range of ailments such as allergies, asthma, arthritis, diabetes, and many more. Some of the most popular Ayurvedic formulations include Chyawanprash, Triphala, Guggulu, Shankhpushpi, and Ashwagandha.

Quality control and standardization of marketed Ayurvedic Formulations: Quality control and standardization are crucial for ensuring the safety and efficacy of marketed Ayurvedic formulations. The following are some of the quality control and standardization measures that should be taken for marketed Ayurvedic formulations:

Selection of ingredients: The ingredients used for the preparation of marketed Ayurvedic formulations should be of good quality and should be free from contaminants. The ingredients should be obtained from reputable suppliers and should be checked for quality before use.

Standardization: Marketed Ayurvedic formulations should be standardized by determining the physical, chemical and biological properties. The pH should be between 6.5-7.5, and the specific gravity should be between 1.2-1.5.

Microbial analysis: Marketed Ayurvedic formulations should be tested for the presence of microorganisms before and after preparation. The total viable count of microorganisms should be less than 10^3 cfu/g.

Heavy metal analysis: Marketed Ayurvedic formulations should be tested for the presence of heavy metals before and after preparation. The heavy metal content should be within the permissible limits as per WHO guidelines.

Loss on ignition: Marketed Ayurvedic formulations should be tested for the loss on ignition which is an indication of the purity of the product. The loss on ignition should be less than 10%.

Fineness: Marketed Ayurvedic formulations should be tested for the fineness which is an indication of the particle size of the product. The fineness should be more than 90%.

It's important to note that, these values can vary slightly, depending on the ingredients and recipe used, and that the final product should be evaluated by a qualified Ayurvedic practitioner to ensure safety and efficacy.

It's also important to note that, proper storage techniques should be used to ensure the stability and shelf-life of marketed Ayurvedic formulations. The product should be stored in airtight containers and kept in a cool, dry place.

The importance of preparation and standardization in Ayurveda cannot be overstated as it is crucial for the safety and effectiveness of Ayurvedic formulations. Proper preparation and standardization of Ayurvedic formulations ensure that they are safe to consume and that they contain the appropriate ingredients and dosages to effectively treat the intended condition.

Standardization of Ayurvedic formulations

It is a process of ensuring that the formulation is consistent in its composition and quality. This is done by determining the physical, chemical and biological properties of the formulation. This ensures that each batch of the formulation is of the same quality and contains the same active ingredients in the same quantity.Proper preparation of Ayurvedic formulations is also essential for their safety and effectiveness. The ingredients used in the preparation should be of good quality, free from contaminants, and obtained from reputable suppliers. The preparation method should be followed correctly, and the formulation should be prepared under clean and hygienic conditions. The finished product should be checked for any impurities and microorganisms before being packaged and labeled.

Quality control is also an important aspect of preparation and standardization. It is essential to check the formulation for its physical, chemical, and biological properties before and after preparation. This ensures that the product is safe for consumption and meets the required standards.

Aristas and Asawas

Overview of Aristas and Asawas in Ayurveda: Aristas and Asawas are traditional Ayurvedic preparations that are used to treat various illnesses. Aristas are liquid preparations that are made by boiling the ingredients in water, while Asawas are solid preparations made by boiling the ingredients in ghee or oil.

Aristas

Aristas

Aristas are traditional Ayurvedic preparations that are made by boiling the ingredients in water. They are used to treat various illnesses and are available in various forms like syrups, decoctions, and infusions. The preparation of Aristas involves the correct selection of ingredients, appropriate processing, and the use of standardization techniques.

Principle of preparation: The principle of preparation of Aristas is based on the concept of extracting the active principles from the ingredients by boiling them in water. The boiling process causes the ingredients to release their active principles, which are then dissolved in water to form the final liquid preparation.

Method of preparation: The method of preparation of Aristas involves the following steps:

Selection of ingredients: The correct selection of ingredients is crucial for the preparation of Aristas. The ingredients should be fresh, clean, and free from contaminants.

Cleaning and washing of ingredients: The ingredients should be cleaned and washed thoroughly to remove any dirt or dust.

Soaking and grinding of ingredients: Some ingredients may require soaking before boiling to soften them and make them easier to grind. The ingredients are then ground to a fine powder to increase the surface area and facilitate extraction of active principles.

Boiling of ingredients: The ingredients are then boiled in water for a specified period. The boiling process causes the ingredients to release their active principles, which are then dissolved in water to form the final liquid preparation.

Straining and filtration: After boiling, the mixture is then strained to remove any solid particles, and then filtered to obtain the final liquid preparation.

Parameters affecting preparation:

Temperature: The temperature at which the ingredients are boiled plays an important role in the preparation of Aristas. The boiling temperature should be appropriate for the ingredients being used to ensure that the active principles are extracted efficiently.The boiling temperature should be between 80-90 degree Celsius, to ensure that the active principles are extracted efficiently.

Fermentation time: The fermentation time also plays an important role in the preparation of Aristas. If the ingredients are fermented for an appropriate period, it will increase the bioavailability of active ingredients.The fermentation time depends on the type of ingredients used, but it can range from 1-7 days.

Type of containers: The type of containers used for boiling the ingredients also affects the preparation of Aristas. The containers should be made of appropriate materials such as glass or stainless steel to prevent contamination of the final product.

Preparation conditions: The preparation conditions such as lighting, ventilation, and cleanliness of the area should be appropriate to prevent contamination of the final product.

Precautions:

The ingredients should be fresh, clean, and free from contaminants.

The preparation and standardization of Aristas should be done by qualified Ayurvedic practitioners or under their guidance.

The containers used for boiling the ingredients should be made of appropriate materials such as glass or stainless steel to prevent contamination of the final product.

Proper storage techniques should be used to ensure the stability and shelf-life of Aristas.

Preparation of Aristas is an important aspect of Ayurveda. Proper preparation and standardization of Aristas ensure safety and efficacy of the final product. The correct selection of ingredients, appropriate processing, and the use of standardization techniques are crucial for the preparation of Aristas. The preparation and standardization of Aristas should be done by qualified Ayurvedic practitioners or under their guidance. Proper storage techniques should be used to ensure the stability and shelf-life of Aristas.

Proper storage techniques are essential to ensure the stability and shelf-life of Aristas. The following are some of the recommended storage techniques for Aristas:

Keep Aristas in airtight containers: Aristas should be stored in airtight containers to prevent moisture and air from entering. This will help to preserve the potency of the Aristas.

Keep Aristas in cool and dry place: Aristas should be stored in a cool and dry place, away from direct sunlight and heat. High temperatures and humidity can affect the stability and shelf-life of Aristas.

Keep Aristas away from strong odors: Aristas should be stored away from strong odors such as strong spices or perfumes. The smell from these items can affect the potency of Aristas.

Avoid frequent opening of containers: Aristas should be stored in containers that are opened as little as possible to prevent exposure to air and moisture.

Labelling and date of manufacturing: Aristas should be labelled with the date of manufacturing, expiry date and the name of the manufacturer.

By following these storage techniques, the shelf-life and potency of Aristas can be preserved, and the Aristas will remain effective for a longer time. It's important to consult a qualified Ayurvedic practitioner or pharmacist for further guidance on storing Aristas.

Additionally, it is important to be aware of the parameters that affect the preparation of Aristas such as temperature, fermentation time, type of containers and preparation conditions to ensure that the active principles are extracted efficiently and the final product is of high quality.

It is also important to note that, Aristas are available in the market, but it's crucial to check the authenticity and quality of the marketed products. Therefore, it's important to be cautious and to buy Aristas from trusted sources.

In conclusion, Aristas are an important aspect of Ayurveda and their proper preparation and standardization are crucial for safety and efficacy. It's important to ensure that the preparation and standardization of Aristas is done by qualified Ayurvedic practitioners or under their guidance and to be aware of the parameters that affect the preparation of Aristas.

Asawas

Aswas

Preparation of Asawas:

Introduction: Asawas are traditional Ayurvedic preparations that are made by boiling the ingredients in ghee or oil. They are used to treat various illnesses and are available in various forms like tablets, pills, and pastes. The preparation of Asawas involves the correct selection of ingredients, appropriate processing, and the use of standardization techniques.

Principle of preparation: The principle of preparation of Asawas is based on the concept of extracting the active principles from the ingredients by boiling them in ghee or oil. The boiling process causes the ingredients to release their active principles, which are then dissolved in ghee or oil to form the final solid preparation.

Method of preparation: The method of preparation of Asawas involves the following steps:

Selection of ingredients: The correct selection of ingredients is crucial for the preparation of Asawas. The ingredients should be fresh, clean, and free from contaminants.

Cleaning and washing of ingredients: The ingredients should be cleaned and washed thoroughly to remove any dirt or dust.

Soaking and grinding of ingredients: Some ingredients may require soaking before boiling to soften them and make them easier to grind. The ingredients are then ground to a fine powder to increase the surface area and facilitate extraction of active principles.

Boiling of ingredients: The ingredients are then boiled in ghee or oil for a specified period. The boiling process causes the ingredients to release their active principles, which are then dissolved in ghee or oil to form the final solid preparation.

Addition of jaggery: Jaggery is added to the mixture after boiling to sweeten it and to increase its shelf life.

Solidification and shaping: After boiling, the mixture is then solidified and shaped into the desired form like tablets, pills, or pastes.

Parameters affecting preparation:

Temperature: The temperature at which the ingredients are boiled plays an important role in the preparation of Asawas. The boiling temperature should be between 80-90 degree Celsius, to ensure that the active principles are extracted efficiently.

Fermentation time: The fermentation time also plays an important role in the preparation of Asawas. If the ingredients are fermented for an appropriate period, it will increase the bioavailability of active ingredients. The fermentation time depends on the type of ingredients used, but it can range from 1-7 days.

Type of containers: The type of containers used for boiling the ingredients also affects the preparation of Asawas. The containers should be made of appropriate materials such as glass or stainless steel to prevent contamination of the final product.

Preparation conditions: The preparation conditions such as lighting, ventilation, and cleanliness of the area should be appropriate to prevent contamination of the final product. The area should be well ventilated, well-lit and clean.

The proportion of ghee or oil to the ingredients should be appropriate, as using more oil or ghee may affect the shelf-life and potency of the product. The proportion can vary depending on the ingredients used, but it is commonly 1:4 (ghee/oil: ingredients).It's important to note that, these values can vary slightly, depending on the ingredients and recipe used, and that the final product should be evaluated by a qualified Ayurvedic practitioner to ensure safety and efficacy.

Standardization of Aristas and Asawas:

Introduction: Standardization is the process of evaluating and controlling the quality of Aristas and Asawas by determining their physical, chemical and biological properties. The standardization of Aristas and Asawas is important to ensure the safety and efficacy of these traditional Ayurvedic preparations.

Description: The description of Aristas and Asawas includes the physical appearance, color, odor, taste, and texture of the preparation. This information can be used to identify any variations in the preparation, which can affect the safety and efficacy of the product.

pH: The pH of Aristas and Asawas is an important parameter to measure. The pH value should be within the range of 6.5-7.5. A pH value outside this range can indicate the presence of impurities or degradation of the active ingredients.

Specific gravity: The specific gravity of Aristas and Asawas is another important parameter to measure. The specific gravity of Aristas and Asawas is typically between 1.2-1.5. A specific gravity value outside this range can indicate the presence of impurities or degradation of the active ingredients.

Alcohol content: The alcohol content of Aristas and Asawas is an important parameter to measure. The alcohol content should be less than 10%. A higher alcohol content can indicate the presence of impurities or degradation of the active ingredients.

Total sugar: The total sugar content of Aristas and Asawas is an important parameter to measure. The total sugar content should be between 10-15%. A higher sugar content can indicate the presence of impurities or degradation of the active ingredients.

Phytochemical analysis: Phytochemical analysis is the process of analyzing the phytochemical compounds present in Aristas and Asawas. This analysis can be used to identify the presence of active ingredients and to determine the purity and potency of the preparation.

Spectroscopic analysis: Spectroscopic analysis is the process of analyzing the preparation using spectroscopic techniques such as UV-visible spectrophotometry, infrared spectrophotometry, and NMR spectroscopy. This analysis can be used to identify the presence of active ingredients and to determine the purity and potency of the preparation.

It's important to note that, these values can vary slightly, depending on the ingredients and recipe used, and that the final product should be evaluated by a qualified Ayurvedic practitioner to ensure safety and efficacy.

Ghutika

Overview of Ghutika in Ayurveda: Ghutika is a type of Ayurvedic formulation that is used for various therapeutic purposes. It is a solid form of medicine that is prepared by mixing powdered herbs or minerals with ghee or oil. Ghutika is easy to administer and can be used for both internal and external use. It is used in the treatment of various ailments such as fever, skin diseases, respiratory disorders and digestive disorders.

Methods of preparation and standardization of Ghutika: The methods of preparation and standardization of Ghutika are important to ensure the safety and efficacy of this traditional Ayurvedic preparation. The following are some of the recommended methods of preparation and standardization of Ghutika:

Selection of ingredients: The ingredients used for the preparation of Ghutika should be of good quality and should be free from contaminants. The ingredients should be obtained from reputable suppliers and should be checked for quality before use.

Proportion of ingredients: The proportion of ingredients used in the preparation of Ghutika is important. The proportion of ghee or oil to the powdered herbs should be appropriate, as using more oil or ghee may affect the shelf-life and potency of the product. The proportion can vary depending on the ingredients used, but it is commonly 1:4 (ghee/oil: ingredients).

Temperature and time of preparation: The temperature and time of preparation should be appropriate. The ingredients should be heated at a temperature of 80-90 degree Celsius for a period of 1-2 hours.

Standardization: Ghutika should be standardized by determining the physical, chemical and biological properties. The pH should be between 6.5-7.5, and the specific gravity should be between 1.2-1.5.

Microbial analysis: Ghutika should be tested for the presence of microorganisms before and after preparation. The total viable count of microorganisms should be less than 10^3 cfu/g.

Heavy metal analysis: Ghutika should be tested for the presence of heavy metals before and after preparation. The heavy metal content should be within the permissible limits as per WHO guidelines.

It's important to note that, these values can vary slightly, depending on the ingredients and recipe used, and that the final product should be evaluated by a qualified Ayurvedic practitioner to ensure safety and efficacy.

Churna

Churna

Overview of Churna in Ayurveda: Churna is a type of Ayurvedic formulation that is used for various therapeutic purposes. It is a powder form of medicine that is prepared by grinding dried herbs or minerals. Churna is easy to administer and can be used for both internal and external use. It is used in the treatment of various ailments such as fever, skin diseases, respiratory disorders and digestive disorders.

Methods of preparation and standardization of Churna: The methods of preparation and standardization of Churna are important to ensure the safety and efficacy of this traditional Ayurvedic preparation. The following are some of the recommended methods of preparation and standardization of Churna:

Selection of ingredients: The ingredients used for the preparation of Churna should be of good quality and should be free from contaminants. The ingredients should be obtained from reputable suppliers and should be checked for quality before use.

Temperature and time of preparation: The temperature and time of preparation should be appropriate. The ingredients should be dried at a temperature of 60-70 degree Celsius for a period of 4-12 hours.

Standardization: Churna should be standardized by determining the physical, chemical and biological properties. The pH should be between 6.5-7.5, and the specific gravity should be between 1.2-1.5.

Microbial analysis: Churna should be tested for the presence of microorganisms before and after preparation. The total viable count of microorganisms should be less than 10^3 cfu/g.

Heavy metal analysis: Churna should be tested for the presence of heavy metals before and after preparation. The heavy metal content should be within the permissible limits as per WHO guidelines.

Ash value: Churna should be tested for the ash value which is an indication of the purity of the product. The ash value should be between 5-10%.

Extractive value: Churna should be tested for the extractive value which is an indication of the active principles present in the product. The extractive value should be between 5-10%.

Lehya

Lehya

Overview of Lehya in Ayurveda: Lehya is a type of Ayurvedic formulation that is used for various therapeutic purposes. It is a semi-solid form of medicine that is prepared by mixing powdered herbs or minerals with sugar. Lehya is easy to administer and can be used for both internal and external use. It is used in the treatment of various ailments such as fever, skin diseases, respiratory disorders and digestive disorders.

Methods of preparation and standardization of Lehya: The methods of preparation and standardization of Lehya are important to ensure the safety and efficacy of this traditional Ayurvedic preparation. The following are some of the recommended methods of preparation and standardization of Lehya:

Selection of ingredients: The ingredients used for the preparation of Lehya should be of good quality and should be free from contaminants. The ingredients should be obtained from reputable suppliers and should be checked for quality before use.

Proportion of ingredients: The proportion of ingredients used in the preparation of Lehya is important. The proportion of sugar to the powdered herbs should be appropriate, as using more sugar may affect the shelf-life and potency of the product. The proportion can vary depending on the ingredients used, but it is commonly 1:4 (sugar: ingredients).

Temperature and time of preparation: The temperature and time of preparation should be appropriate. The ingredients should be heated at a temperature of 80-90 degree Celsius for a period of 1-2 hours.

Standardization: Lehya should be standardized by determining the physical, chemical and biological properties. The pH should be between 6.5-7.5, and the specific gravity should be between 1.2-1.5.

Microbial analysis: Lehya should be tested for the presence of microorganisms before and after preparation. The total viable count of microorganisms should be less than 10^3 cfu/g.

Heavy metal analysis: Lehya should be tested for the presence of heavy metals before and after preparation. The heavy metal content should be within the permissible limits as per WHO guidelines.

Total sugar: Lehya should be tested for the total sugar content which is an indication of the

sweetness of the product. The total sugar content should be between 50-60%.

Moisture content: Lehya should be tested for the moisture content which is an indication of the stability of the product. The moisture content should be less than 10%.

It's important to note that, these values can vary slightly, depending on the ingredients and recipe used, and that the final product should be evaluated by a qualified Ayurvedic practitioner to ensure safety and efficacy.

It's also important to note that, proper storage techniques should be used to ensure the stability and shelf-life of Lehya. The product should be stored in airtight containers and kept in a cool, dry place.

It's recommended to pay attention to the expiry date, the product should be consumed before the expiry date.

Bhasma

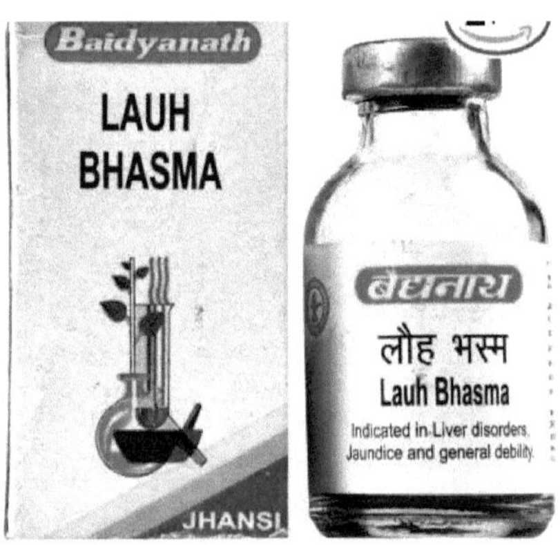

Bhasma

Overview of Bhasma in Ayurveda: Bhasma is a type of Ayurvedic formulation that is used for various therapeutic purposes. It is a fine powder form of medicine that is prepared by calcining herbs or minerals. Bhasma is easy to administer and can be used for both internal and external use.

Methods of preparation and standardization of Bhasma:

The methods of preparation and standardization of Bhasma are important to ensure the safety and efficacy of this traditional Ayurvedic preparation. The following are some of the recommended methods of preparation and standardization of Bhasma:

Selection of ingredients: The ingredients used for the preparation of Bhasma should be of good quality and should be free from contaminants. The ingredients should be obtained from reputable suppliers and should be checked for quality before use.

Temperature and time of preparation: The temperature and time of preparation should be appropriate. The ingredients should be calcined at a temperature of 600-800 degree Celsius for a period of 24-72 hours.

Standardization: Bhasma should be standardized by determining the physical, chemical and biological properties. The pH should be between 6.5-7.5, and the specific gravity should be between 1.2-1.5.

Microbial analysis: Bhasma should be tested for the presence of microorganisms before and after preparation. The total viable count of microorganisms should be less than 10^3 cfu/g.

Heavy metal analysis: Bhasma should be tested for the presence of heavy metals before and after preparation. The heavy metal content should be within the permissible limits as per WHO guidelines.

Loss on ignition: Bhasma should be tested for the loss on ignition which is an indication of the purity of the product. The loss on ignition should be less than 10%.

Fineness: Bhasma should be tested for the fineness which is an indication of the particle size of the product. The fineness should be more than 90%.

It's important to note that, these values can vary slightly, depending on the ingredients and recipe used, and that the final product should be evaluated by a qualified Ayurvedic practitioner to ensure safety and efficacy.

It's also important to note that, proper storage techniques should be used to ensure the stability and shelf-life of Bhasma. The product should be stored in airtight containers and kept in a cool, dry place.

It's recommended to pay attention to the expiry date, the product should be consumed before the expiry date

IV

Neutraceuticals

Definition of Neutraceuticals: Neutraceuticals are non-toxic food or food product that provides medical or health benefits, including the prevention and treatment of disease. The term "neutraceutical" was first coined by Dr. Stephen L. DeFelice in 1989, who defined it as "a food or part of a food that provides medical or health benefits, including the prevention and treatment of disease."

History of Neutraceuticals: The concept of using food as medicine dates back to ancient civilizations, where various plants and herbs were used to treat various ailments. However, the modern concept of neutraceuticals as a distinct category of food and supplements began to take shape in the late 20th century with the increasing awareness of the role of diet and nutrition in preventing and treating chronic diseases.

Definition given by different organizations: The World Health Organization (WHO) defines neutraceuticals as "foods that provide health benefits beyond basic nutrition." The United States Food and Drug Administration (FDA) defines them as "foods or dietary supplements that provide a health benefit." The European Union (EU) defines them as "foods that have a potentially positive effect on health when consumed as part of a varied diet."

Classification of Neutraceuticals

Functional Foods: These are foods that have been modified or fortified with specific ingredients to provide health benefits. Examples of functional foods include fortified breakfast cereals, yogurt with added probiotics, and orange juice with added calcium.

Herbal Supplements: These are supplements made from natural plant extracts or herbs that are believed to have medicinal properties. Examples of herbal supplements include ginseng, echinacea, and ginkgo biloba.

Probiotics and Prebiotics: These are supplements that contain live microorganisms or non-digestible food ingredients that promote the growth of beneficial bacteria in the gut. Probiotics supplements are those supplements that contain live microorganisms like bacteria, yeast, or viruses. Prebiotics are non-digestible food ingredients that promote the growth of beneficial bacteria in the gut.

Nutraceuticals: These are supplements that contain a combination of ingredients, such as vitamins, minerals, and herbs, that are believed to have health benefits. Examples of nutraceuticals include multivitamin and mineral supplements, omega-3 fatty acid supplements, and glucosamine supplements.

Medical foods: These are foods that are specifically formulated to be consumed or administered enterally under the supervision of a physician and are intended for the specific dietary management of a disease or condition for which distinctive nutritional requirements, based on recognized scientific principles, are established by medical evaluation.

Phytochemicals: These are naturally occurring compounds found in plants that are believed to have health benefits. Examples of phytochemicals include lycopene in tomatoes, flavonoids in berries, and resveratrol in red wine.

Whole food supplements: These are supplements that are made from whole foods, such as fruits, vegetables, and grains, and are intended to provide a concentrated source of essential nutrients.

Organic Supplements: These supplements are produced using organic farming methods and are free from synthetic pesticides and fertilizers.

Ayurvedic supplements: These are supplements that are traditionally used in Ayurvedic medicine and are made from natural ingredients such as herbs and minerals.

Homeopathic supplements: These are supplements that are based on the principles of homeopathy and are made from highly diluted natural substances.

General Aspects of Neutraceuticals

Health benefits: Neutraceuticals are believed to provide a range of health benefits, such as reducing the risk of chronic diseases, improving digestion, and boosting the immune system. For example, consuming probiotics can help improve gut health, reducing the risk of inflammatory bowel diseases. Omega-3 fatty acids found in fish oil supplements are believed to help lower the risk of heart disease.

Safety and regulation: Neutraceuticals are considered to be generally safe, but they are not without potential risks. Some neutraceuticals can interact with prescription medications, and some may have side effects or be harmful in high doses. The regulation of neutraceuticals varies by country, but in general, they are considered to be less strictly regulated than pharmaceutical drugs.

Research and Development: The field of neutraceuticals is rapidly advancing, with new products and formulations being developed all the time. However, there is a need for more research to fully understand the safety and effectiveness of many neutraceuticals, as well as to identify new potential health benefits.

Market growth: The global market for neutraceuticals is expected to grow in the coming years, driven by increasing consumer awareness of the link between diet and health, as well as the growing demand for natural and holistic approaches to health and wellness.

Popularity: In recent years, there has been a growing interest in natural and holistic approaches to health, which has led to an increase in the popularity of neutraceuticals. Many people are turning to neutraceuticals as an alternative to traditional pharmaceuticals, and they are often seen as a way to prevent or treat chronic diseases without the side effects associated with drugs.

Role in prevention and treatment: Neutraceuticals play an important role in the prevention and treatment of several diseases. They offer a natural way to improve overall health, boost the immune system, and reduce the risk of chronic diseases. They are also used in the treatment of several ailments like blood pressure, diabetes, cancer, and heart diseases.

Availability: Neutraceuticals are widely available in the form of supplements, functional foods, and fortified foods. They are sold in health food stores, supermarkets, and online retailers.

Personalization: Neutraceuticals are now getting personalized for specific population groups, for example, women's health, children's health, elderly health and sports nutrition.

Cost: The cost of neutraceuticals can vary depending on the type of product, the brand, and the retailer. In general, they tend to be less expensive than pharmaceutical drugs, but they can still be expensive.

Sustainability: Many neutraceuticals are produced using sustainable methods and are sourced from natural ingredients. This makes them a more environmentally friendly option compared to synthetic drugs.

India as a leader in the field of neutraceuticals

India is well-positioned as a leader in the field of neutraceuticals due to a combination of factors such as its rich tradition of Ayurveda and traditional medicine, large population, and growing awareness of the link between diet and health. This has led to a large market for neutraceuticals in India, with a projected growth rate of around 15% during the period 2019-2024.

One of the key strengths of India as a leader in neutraceuticals is its strong research and development infrastructure. There are several research institutions and universities in India that are focused on the development of new products and formulations. This has helped to establish India as a major player in the global neutraceuticals market.

India is also known for its large number of medicinal plants, which are used to make a variety of neutraceuticals such as herbal supplements and Ayurvedic medicines. This natural resources of medicinal plants has helped to establish India as a leader in the field of neutraceuticals.

Another important factor that has helped to establish India as a leader in neutraceuticals is its strong export market. India exports neutraceuticals to countries all over the world, which has helped to establish the country as a major player in the global market.

The Indian government has also been supportive of the development of the neutraceuticals industry in the country, with several policies and initiatives aimed at promoting the growth of the sector. This has led to an increase in the number of domestic manufacturers of neutraceuticals, which has helped to keep costs low and increase availability of these products.

In addition, Ayurvedic and herbal supplements are very popular in India, and this has helped to drive the growth of the neutraceuticals market in the country. Quality control measures are also in place in India to ensure the safety and effectiveness of neutraceuticals. Companies in India are constantly innovating and developing new products, which has helped to keep the market dynamic and competitive.

Legal aspects of neutraceuticals in India

Regulation: In India, neutraceuticals fall under the purview of the Food Safety and Standards Authority of India (FSSAI), which is responsible for regulating the manufacture, distribution, and sale of food products, including neutraceuticals. However, there are some concerns about the regulatory framework for neutraceuticals in India, as it is not as strict as for pharmaceutical drugs.

Product registration: All neutraceuticals sold in India must be registered with the FSSAI. This involves submitting detailed information about the product, including its composition, manufacturing process, and intended use.

Labeling: Neutraceuticals must be labeled with information about the product, including its composition, intended use, and any potential health claims.

Advertisements: The FSSAI has strict guidelines regarding the advertising of neutraceuticals, and all advertisements must be cleared by the authority before they can be aired or published.

Some examples of recent cases involving the sale of food products as neutraceuticals without proper registration and clearance from FSSAI are:

In 2020, a company based in Gujarat, India was found to be selling a product claiming to cure cancer, which was later found to have no scientific basis and was not registered with FSSAI. The company and its directors were charged with fraud and other violations of the Food Safety and Standards Act, and the product was banned from being sold in the country.

In 2019, FSSAI banned the sale of a product marketed as a "herbal supplement" that claimed to help in weight loss and improve digestion. The product was not registered with FSSAI and had no scientific basis for its claims. The company and its directors were charged with violating food safety laws.

In 2018, a company was found to be selling a product claiming to boost the immune system, which was later found to contain undeclared ingredients and was not registered with FSSAI. The company and its directors were charged with violating food safety laws and the product was banned from being sold in the country.

In 2017, a company based in Mumbai, India was found to be selling a product claiming to cure diabetes, which was later found to have no scientific basis and was not registered with FSSAI. The company and its directors were charged with fraud and other violations of the Food Safety and Standards Act, and the product was banned from being sold in the country.

These cases demonstrate the importance of proper regulation and oversight of the neutraceuticals industry to ensure the safety and effectiveness of products and protect consumers from false or misleading claims. It also highlights the importance of FSSAI in monitoring and enforcing the regulations and taking action against violatorsCase studies: In recent times, there have been several cases of food products being sold as neutraceuticals without proper registration and clearance from FSSAI. In one such case, a company was selling a product claiming to cure cancer, which was later found to be fake and had no scientific basis. The company and its directors were charged with fraud and other violations of the Food Safety and Standards Act.

Quality control: There have been some concerns about the quality of some neutraceuticals sold in India, as some products have been found to be contaminated or to contain ingredients that are not listed on the label.

Misleading Claims: Some companies make false or misleading claims about the health benefits of their products, which can be harmful to consumers.

Intellectual property: There have been some concerns about the protection of intellectual property rights for neutraceuticals in India, as some companies have been accused of copying or stealing the formulas of other products.

Lack of standardization: There is a lack of standardization in the field of neutraceuticals in India, and this can lead to confusion and mistrust among consumers.

Import regulations: The import regulations for neutraceuticals in India are not as strict as for pharmaceutical drugs, which has led to some concerns about the quality of imported products.

Market growth and scope of neutraceuticals

Market size: The global market for neutraceuticals is expected to grow in the coming years, driven by increasing consumer awareness of the link between diet and health, as well as the growing demand for natural and holistic approaches to health and wellness. The global market size for neutraceuticals was valued at USD $250 billion in 2020 and is projected to grow at a CAGR of around 7% during the forecast period 2021-2028.

Regional growth: The market for neutraceuticals is growing at different rates in different regions of the world. North America and Europe are currently the largest markets for neutraceuticals, but the Asia-Pacific region is expected to experience the fastest growth due to increasing awareness of the link between diet and health and a growing population.

Product categories: The neutraceuticals market can be segmented into several product categories, such as functional foods, herbal supplements, probiotics and prebiotics, nutraceuticals, and medical foods. The functional foods segment is expected to be the fastest-growing segment during the forecast period.

Consumer demand: Consumer demand for neutraceuticals is driven by a desire to improve overall health, boost the immune system, and reduce the risk of chronic diseases. The increasing awareness of the link between diet and health, as well as the growing demand for natural and holistic approaches to health and wellness, is driving the growth of the market.

Distribution channels: Neutraceuticals are sold through a variety of distribution channels, including supermarkets,health food stores, online retailers, and pharmacies. The internet and e-commerce platforms have also become an important distribution channel for neutraceuticals, as more and more consumers are turning to online platforms to purchase these products.

Research and development: Companies in the neutraceuticals market are investing heavily in research and development to develop new products and formulations, as well as to improve the effectiveness and safety of existing products. This is expected to drive the growth of the market in the coming years.

Personalization: The market for personalized neutraceuticals is expected to grow in the coming years, as more and more consumers are looking for products that are tailored to their specific health needs and concerns. This includes products for specific population groups, such as women's health, children's health, elderly health, and sports nutrition.

Cost: The cost of neutraceuticals can vary depending on the type of product, the brand, and the retailer. In general, they tend to be less expensive than pharmaceutical drugs, but they can still be expensive. The cost-effectiveness of neutraceuticals compared to traditional drugs is one of the factors driving the market growth.

Sustainability: Many neutraceuticals are produced using sustainable methods and are sourced from natural ingredients. This makes them a more environmentally friendly option compared to synthetic drugs, and consumers are becoming more conscious about the environmental impact of the products they purchase.

Government support: Many governments around the world are providing support for the development of the neutraceuticals industry, which is expected to drive the growth of the market in the coming years. This includes funding for research and development, as well as tax incentives for companies operating in the sector.

Types of products available in the market:

Functional foods: These are foods that have been specifically formulated to provide health benefits beyond basic nutrition. Examples of functional foods include fortified cereals, yogurt with added probiotics, and fortified orange juice.

Herbal supplements: These are supplements made from natural ingredients such as herbs, roots, and botanicals. They are often used to support specific health conditions such as joint pain, digestive issues, and mood disorders. Examples of herbal supplements include turmeric, ashwagandha, and ginseng.

Probiotics and prebiotics: Probiotics are live microorganisms that are intended to provide health benefits, while prebiotics are non-digestible carbohydrates that stimulate the growth of beneficial microorganisms in the gut. Examples of probiotics include Lactobacillus and Bifidobacterium strains, while examples of prebiotics include inulin and fructooligosaccharides.

Nutraceuticals: These are products that are derived from food sources and intended to provide health benefits. Examples of nutraceuticals include omega-3 fatty acids, glucosamine, and chondroitin.

Medical foods: These are foods that are formulated to be used in the dietary management of specific medical conditions. Examples of medical foods include low-protein foods for people with kidney disease, and special formulas for people with diabetes.

Sports nutrition: These are products that are specifically formulated to support the dietary needs of athletes and active individuals. Examples include protein powders, energy bars, and sports drinks.

Personalized nutrition: These are products that are tailored to meet the specific health needs and concerns of individual consumers. Examples include products for specific population groups such as women's health, children's health, elderly health and sports nutrition.

Organic products: These are products that are produced using sustainable methods and are sourced from natural ingredients. Examples include organic supplements and organic functional foods.

Ayurvedic products: These are products that are based on Ayurvedic principles, and are made from natural ingredients such as herbs, roots, and botanicals. Examples include Ayurvedic supplements and Ayurvedic functional foods.

Others: Some other types of products that are available in the market include weight management products, beauty supplements, and functional beverages.

Health benefits of neutraceuticals

Improved overall health: Many neutraceuticals are formulated to provide a wide range of health benefits, such as improved immune function, reduced inflammation, and improved digestion.

Reduced risk of chronic diseases: Some neutraceuticals, such as omega-3 fatty acids and probiotics, may help to reduce the risk of chronic diseases such as heart disease, cancer, and diabetes.

Weight management: Some neutraceuticals, such as green tea extract and conjugated linoleic acid (CLA), may help with weight management by reducing body fat and increasing muscle mass.

Mental health: Some neutraceuticals such as omega-3 fatty acids, probiotics, and certain herbal supplements, have been found to have a positive effect on mental health conditions such as depression and anxiety.

Bone health: Some neutraceuticals, such as calcium and vitamin D, may help to improve bone health and reduce the risk of osteoporosis.

Cognitive function: Some neutraceuticals, such as omega-3 fatty acids and ginkgo biloba, may help to improve cognitive function and reduce the risk of age-related cognitive decline.

Eye health: Some neutraceuticals, such as lutein and zeaxanthin, may help to improve eye health and reduce the risk of age-related macular degeneration.

Skin health: Some neutraceuticals, such as vitamin C and collagen, may help to improve skin health by reducing the appearance of wrinkles and fine lines.

Sports performance: Some neutraceuticals, such as creatine and beta-alanine, may help to improve sports performance by increasing muscle strength and endurance.

Personalized benefits: Some neutraceuticals are formulated to meet the specific health needs and concerns of individual consumers, such as women's health, children's health, elderly health, and sports nutrition.

It is important to note that while neutraceuticals may provide health benefits, they are not intended to be used as a substitute for a healthy diet and lifestyle, and should not be used to treat or prevent serious health conditions. Before using any neutraceuticals, it is important to consult with a healthcare professional to determine the appropriate use and any potential risks or interactions with other medications.

Cardiovascular diseases

Cardiovascular diseases (CVDs) are a leading cause of death and disability worldwide, and there is increasing interest in the role of neutraceuticals in preventing and controlling these conditions.

Omega-3 fatty acids: These are a type of polyunsaturated fatty acids found in fish, such as salmon and mackerel, and in certain types of algae. Studies have shown that consuming omega-3 fatty acids can help to lower the risk of heart disease by reducing inflammation, blood pressure, and triglyceride levels.

Fiber: Soluble fibers, such as beta-glucans found in oats, psyllium found in plantago ovata and pectin found in fruits like apples, citrus fruits, may help to lower cholesterol levels and reduce the risk of heart disease.

Coenzyme Q10: This is a nutrient that is found in small amounts in foods such as fatty fish, organ meats, and whole grains. Studies have shown that taking CoQ10 supplements may help to lower blood pressure and improve heart function in people with CVD.

Garlic: Garlic supplements have been found to lower blood pressure, decrease the formation of blood clots, and improve cholesterol levels in people with CVD.

Vitamin D: Vitamin D can play a crucial role in the management of hypertension and the prevention of cardiovascular diseases, as it has been shown to improve endothelial function and reduce inflammation.

Probiotics: Some studies have suggested that certain probiotic strains may have beneficial effects on cardiovascular health by improving lipid metabolism, reducing inflammation and blood pressure.

Flavonoids: Flavonoids are a group of naturally occurring compounds found in fruits, vegetables, and tea. They have antioxidant properties that can help to reduce inflammation and improve the health of blood vessels, which may help to lower the risk of heart disease.

Red yeast rice: It is a traditional Chinese medicine that contains a substance called monacolin K which is structurally identical to the cholesterol-lowering drug lovastatin. Studies have shown that red yeast rice supplements can lower cholesterol levels and improve heart health.

It's important to note that a healthy diet, regular physical activity, and maintaining a healthy weight, not smoking, and controlling blood pressure, cholesterol, and blood sugar levels are key lifestyle changes that can help to prevent and control CVDs, and should be prioritized over taking supplements.

Diabetes

Diabetes is a chronic condition that affects the way the body processes blood sugar (glucose). There is increasing interest in the role of neutraceuticals in treating diabetes.

Magnesium: Magnesium plays a crucial role in glucose metabolism and insulin sensitivity. Studies have shown that low levels of magnesium in the body are associated with an increased risk of diabetes. Magnesium supplements may help to improve insulin sensitivity and lower the risk of diabetes.

Chromium: Chromium is an essential trace mineral that is important for glucose metabolism. Studies have suggested that chromium supplements may help to improve insulin sensitivity and lower blood sugar levels in people with diabetes.

Alpha-lipoic acid: Alpha-lipoic acid is an antioxidant that is found in certain foods and supplements. Studies have suggested that alpha-lipoic acid may help to improve insulin sensitivity and lower blood sugar levels in people with diabetes.

Fiber: Fiber is important for blood sugar control as it slows down the absorption of sugar. Soluble fibers, such as beta-glucans found in oats, psyllium found in plantago ovata and pectin found in fruits like apples, citrus fruits, may help to lower blood sugar levels and improve glucose metabolism in people with diabetes.

Bitter melon: Bitter melon is a vegetable that is commonly used in traditional medicine to treat diabetes. Studies have suggested that bitter melon may help to lower blood sugar levels by increasing insulin sensitivity and decreasing glucose absorption.

Gymnema sylvestre: Gymnema sylvestre is a tropical plant that has traditionally been used to treat diabetes. Studies have shown that gymnema sylvestre may help to lower blood sugar levels by increasing insulin production and decreasing glucose absorption.

Fenugreek: Fenugreek is a herb that has traditionally been used to treat diabetes. Studies have suggested that fenugreek may help to lower blood sugar levels by slowing down the absorption of carbohydrates and increasing insulin sensitivity.

Cancer

Cancer is a complex disease that is characterized by abnormal cell growth and division. There is increasing interest in the role of neutraceuticals in the prevention and treatment of cancer.

Curcumin: Curcumin is a compound that is found in turmeric. Studies have suggested that curcumin may have anti-inflammatory and antioxidant properties, which may help to prevent the development and progression of cancer.

Green tea: Green tea contains compounds called catechins, which have been found to have antioxidant and anti-inflammatory properties. Studies have suggested that green tea may help to reduce the risk of certain types of cancer, including breast cancer and prostate cancer.

Omega-3 fatty acids: Omega-3 fatty acids may help to reduce inflammation and improve immune function, which may help to prevent the development and progression of cancer.

Vitamin D: Vitamin D plays a crucial role in regulating cell growth and division, and may help to reduce the risk of certain types of cancer, including breast cancer and colon cancer.

Resveratrol: Resveratrol is a compound that is found in red grapes, berries and peanuts. Studies have suggested that resveratrol may help to prevent the development and progression of cancer by inhibiting the growth and spread of cancer cells.

Lycopene: Lycopene is a carotenoid found in tomatoes and other red fruits and vegetables. Studies have suggested that lycopene may help to reduce the risk of certain types of cancer, including prostate cancer.

Garlic: Garlic supplements have been found to lower the risk of certain types of cancer, such as stomach cancer, colon cancer and lung cancer.

Irritable bowel syndrome

Irritable Bowel Syndrome (IBS) is a common disorder of the digestive system that is characterized by symptoms such as abdominal pain, bloating, constipation, and diarrhea. There is increasing interest in the role of neutraceuticals in the treatment of IBS.

Fiber: Soluble fibers, such as beta-glucans found in oats, psyllium found in plantago ovata and pectin found in fruits like apples, citrus fruits, may help to relieve symptoms of IBS by improving bowel regularity and reducing constipation and diarrhea.

Probiotics: Probiotics are live microorganisms that are similar to the beneficial microorganisms found in the human gut. Studies have suggested that certain probiotic strains may help to relieve symptoms of IBS by improving gut function and reducing inflammation.

Peppermint oil: Peppermint oil has been found to be effective in relieving symptoms of IBS such as abdominal pain, bloating and gas.

Fennel: Fennel seeds have traditionally been used to treat digestive disorders. Studies have suggested that fennel may help to relieve symptoms of IBS by improving bowel function and reducing bloating and gas.

Turmeric: Turmeric has anti-inflammatory properties and may help to reduce symptoms of IBS such as abdominal pain and diarrhea.

Ginger: Ginger has anti-inflammatory properties and may help to reduce symptoms of IBS such as abdominal pain and bloating.

Various gastrointestinal diseases

There are various gastrointestinal diseases, and there is increasing interest in the role of neutraceuticals in the treatment of these conditions.

Inflammatory Bowel Disease (IBD) such as Crohn's disease and Ulcerative colitis:

Omega-3 fatty acids have anti-inflammatory properties and may help to reduce inflammation in the gut and relieve symptoms of IBD.

Probiotics have been found to improve gut function and reduce inflammation, which may help to relieve symptoms of IBD.

Gastroesophageal reflux disease (GERD):

Fiber supplements such as beta-glucans, psyllium and pectin may help to reduce symptoms of GERD by improving gut function and reducing acid reflux.

Vitamin D supplements may help to reduce the risk of developing GERD by improving muscle function in the esophagus and reducing inflammation.

Peptic ulcer disease:

Probiotics have been found to improve gut function and reduce inflammation, which may help to relieve symptoms of peptic ulcer disease.

Vitamin C supplements may help to reduce the risk of developing peptic ulcers by improving gut function and reducing inflammation.

Diverticulitis:

Fiber supplements such as beta-glucans, psyllium and pectin may help to reduce symptoms of diverticulitis by improving bowel regularity and reducing constipation and diarrhea.

Probiotics have been found to improve gut function and reduce inflammation, which may help to relieve symptoms of diverticulitis.

Vitamin A: High doses of vitamin A can be toxic and cause symptoms such as nausea, headaches, and skin irritation. In severe cases, vitamin A toxicity can lead to liver damage and birth defects.

Vitamin E: High doses of vitamin E can increase the risk of bleeding, especially when taken with blood-thinning medications such as warfarin.

Iron: High doses of iron can lead to toxicity, causing symptoms such as nausea, vomiting, and diarrhea. In severe cases, iron toxicity can lead to organ damage and even death.

Calcium: High doses of calcium can lead to toxicity, causing symptoms such as constipation and kidney stones. In severe cases, calcium toxicity can lead to organ damage and heart problems.

Herbs: Some herbs can be toxic when taken in large doses. For example, too much of ephedra can cause high blood pressure, heart palpitations, and even heart attack or stroke. Similarly, excessive use of kava can cause liver damage.

Probiotics: The safety of probiotics is generally considered to be good, but in rare cases, probiotic supplements have been found to cause infections, especially in people with weakened immune systems.

St. John's Wort: High doses of St. John's Wort can increase the risk of side effects such as dry mouth, dizziness, and gastrointestinal disturbances, and can also interact with certain medications like birth control pills, antidepressants, and blood thinners.

Echinacea: High doses of echinacea can cause side effects such as allergic reactions, nausea, and stomach upset.

Saw palmetto: High doses of saw palmetto can cause side effects such as gastrointestinal disturbance, headache, and allergic reactions.

Ginkgo Biloba: High doses of Ginkgo Biloba can increase the risk of side effects such as headache, allergic reactions, and gastrointestinal disturbances, and can also interact with blood thinning medications.

Milk thistle: High doses of Milk thistle can cause side effects such as allergic reactions, nausea, and gastrointestinal disturbance.

Valerian: High doses of valerian can cause side effects such as dizziness, headache, and gastrointestinal disturbance.

Black cohosh: High doses of black cohosh can cause side effects such as headache, nausea, and gastrointestinal disturbance.

Kava: High doses of kava can cause liver damage.

Selenium: High doses of selenium can cause side effects such as hair loss, brittle nails, and a garlic-like breath odor.

Zinc: High doses of zinc can cause side effects such as nausea, vomiting, and diarrhea.

Medicinal plants as sourse of neutaceutcals

Medicinal plants have been used for centuries to treat a wide range of health conditions. Many of these plants contain compounds that have medicinal properties and can be used as sources of neutraceuticals.

Turmeric: Turmeric contains a compound called curcumin, which has anti-inflammatory and antioxidant properties. Curcumin is believed to have potential health benefits for a wide range of conditions, including cancer, diabetes, and heart disease.

Ginger: Ginger contains compounds called gingerols and shogaols, which have anti-inflammatory properties. These compounds are believed to have potential health benefits for conditions such as osteoarthritis, cancer, and heart disease.

Garlic: Garlic contains compounds called allicin and diallyl sulfide, which have antimicrobial and antioxidant properties. These compounds are believed to have potential health benefits for conditions such as high blood pressure, high cholesterol, and heart disease.

Ginkgo: Ginkgo biloba is a medicinal plant that contains compounds called flavonoids and terpenoids, which are believed to have potential health benefits for conditions such as Alzheimer's disease, age-related memory loss, and anxiety.

Saw palmetto: Saw palmetto is a medicinal plant that contains compounds called phytosterols, which are believed to have potential health benefits for conditions such as benign prostatic hyperplasia (BPH) and hair loss.

Milk thistle: Milk thistle is a medicinal plant that contains a compound called silymarin, which is believed to have potential health benefits for conditions such as liver disease and diabetes.

Echinacea: Echinacea is a medicinal plant that contains compounds called echinacosides and alkylamides, which are believed to have potential health benefits for conditions such as colds, flu, and certain types of infections.

St. John's wort: St. John's wort is a medicinal plant that contains compounds called hypericin and hyperforin, which are believed to have potential health benefits for conditions such as depression, anxiety, and sleep disorders.

Nano formulations of neutraceuticals

Nanoformulations of neutraceuticals are a relatively new field of research that involves the use of nanoparticles to deliver nutraceuticals and other bioactive compounds to the body.

Liposomes: Liposomes are spherical, phospholipid-based nanoparticles that can encapsulate a wide range of nutraceuticals and other bioactive compounds. Liposomes have been found to be effective in delivering nutraceuticals such as curcumin, vitamin C, and omega-3 fatty acids to the body.

Polymeric nanoparticles: Polymeric nanoparticles are made from polymers such as polylactic acid (PLA) and polyethylene glycol (PEG) and can encapsulate a wide range of nutraceuticals and other bioactive compounds. Polymeric nanoparticles have been found to be effective in delivering nutraceuticals such as curcumin, vitamin C, and omega-3 fatty acids to the body.

Dendrimers: Dendrimers are highly branched, nanoscale polymers that can encapsulate a wide range of nutraceuticals and other bioactive compounds. Dendrimers have been found to be effective in delivering nutraceuticals such as curcumin, vitamin C, and omega-3 fatty acids to the body.

Solid lipid nanoparticles (SLNs): SLNs are made from lipids and have a solid, rather than a liquid, core. SLNs can encapsulate a wide range of nutraceuticals and other bioactive compounds. SLNs have been found to be effective in delivering nutraceuticals such as curcumin, vitamin C, and omega-3 fatty acids to the body.

Cyclodextrin-based nanoparticles: Cyclodextrin-based nanoparticles are made from cyclodextrins, which are cyclic molecules made from glucose units. Cyclodextrin-based nanoparticles can encapsulate a wide range of nutraceuticals and other bioactive compounds.

These nanoformulations of nutraceuticals have several advantages over traditional nutraceuticals, including improved bioavailability, targeted delivery, and reduced side effects. However, more research is needed to fully understand the safety and efficacy of these nanoformulations of nutraceuticals. Additionally, it's important to note that the manufacturing process of these nanoformulations is highly regulated and need to comply with the regulations.

Prebiotics and probiotics

Prebiotics and probiotics are two types of dietary supplements that are gaining increasing attention for their potential health benefits.

Prebiotics: Prebiotics are non-digestible carbohydrates that serve as food for the beneficial bacteria in the gut. Examples of prebiotics include inulin, fructooligosaccharides (FOS), and galactooligosaccharides (GOS). Prebiotics are believed to have potential health benefits such as improving gut health, boosting the immune system, and reducing the risk of certain diseases.

Probiotics: Probiotics are live microorganisms that are similar to the beneficial microorganisms found in the human gut. Examples of probiotics include Lactobacillus acidophilus and Bifidobacterium bifidum. Probiotics are believed to have potential health benefits such as improving gut health, boosting the immune system, and reducing the risk of certain diseases.

Probiotics and prebiotics are often used together in what is called synbiotics. A synbiotic is a combination of probiotics and prebiotics that are designed to work together to improve gut health.

V

Herbs as Health Food

Herbs have long been used as natural remedies for various ailments, but they are now gaining popularity as health foods. Herbs are packed with nutrients and antioxidants that can promote overall health and well-being. They are also low in calories and fat, making them a great addition to a healthy diet.

One of the main reasons why herbs are considered health foods is their high nutrient content. Herbs such as parsley, cilantro, and basil are rich in vitamins and minerals such as Vitamin C, Vitamin K, and Iron. These nutrients are essential for maintaining a healthy immune system, promoting healthy bones and teeth, and preventing chronic diseases such as cancer and heart disease.

Herbs are also known for their antioxidant properties. Antioxidants are compounds that protect the body against damage caused by free radicals, which are unstable molecules that can damage cells and lead to chronic diseases. Herbs such as rosemary, thyme, and oregano are rich in antioxidants that can help protect the body against free radical damage.

Another benefit of herbs is their ability to promote healthy digestion. Herbs such as ginger, turmeric, and fennel have anti-inflammatory properties that can help alleviate digestive problems such as bloating, gas, and constipation. They can also help to improve gut health by promoting the growth of good bacteria in the gut.

Herbs are also a great way to add flavor and variety to your diet without adding extra calories and fat. They can be used to add flavor to dishes without the need for high-calorie sauces and dressings. This can help to reduce the risk of weight gain and obesity.

In addition to their nutritional benefits, herbs are also environmentally friendly. Herbs are often grown without the use of pesticides and chemical fertilizers, making them a sustainable choice. They also require less water than other crops, making them a more water-efficient choice.Herbs can be consumed in various forms, including fresh, dried, or as supplements. Herbs like ginger, garlic and turmeric can be used as spices in food preparation. They can also be consumed as teas or extracts. Additionally, many herbs are available in supplement form, making it easy to take them in the right dosage.

Alfalfa

Alfalfa

Alfalfa, also known as Medicago sativa, is a perennial herb that is native to Asia and the Mediterranean region. It is a member of the pea family and is known for its deep roots, which can reach up to 30 feet deep. The plant is commonly used for hay, pasture, and as a green manure crop. However, it is also used as a dietary supplement due to its potential health benefits.

Chemical Constituents: Alfa alfa contains a wide range of bioactive compounds, including phytosterols, flavonoids, isoflavonoids, and phytoestrogens. The plant also contains a variety of vitamins and minerals such as vitamin K, vitamin C, calcium, potassium, and iron. Additionally, alfalfa contains important enzymes and antioxidants that can help to protect the body against damage caused by free radicals.

Market and Formulation: Alfa alfa is available in a variety of forms such as capsules, tablets, powders, and teas. It is also commonly found in multivitamins and other dietary supplements. The market for alfalfa supplements is growing and is expected to continue to grow in the future due to increasing consumer interest in natural health products.

Side Effects and Dosage: Alfalfa is generally considered safe for most people when consumed in moderate amounts. However, high doses of alfalfa supplements may cause side effects such as upset stomach, diarrhea, and bloating. Additionally, people with autoimmune diseases, such as lupus, should avoid alfalfa supplements as it may worsen their condition.

Lower cholesterol levels: Alfalfa contains phytosterols, which can reduce the absorption of cholesterol in the gut.

Prevent cancer: Alfalfa contains compounds such as phytoestrogens and isoflavonoids, which have anti-cancer properties.

Reduce inflammation: Alfalfa contains compounds such as flavonoids and phytosterols, which have anti-inflammatory properties.

Improve bone health: Alfalfa is a good source of calcium and its phytoestrogens may protect against osteoporosis.

Improve digestion: Alfalfa is a good source of fiber and enzymes that can aid in digestion and prevent constipation.

Regulate blood sugar levels: Alfalfa may help to regulate blood sugar levels and improve insulin sensitivity.

Protect and improve kidney function.

Improve skin health: Alfalfa's antioxidants may protect the skin and improve appearance.

Improve hair and nail health: Alfalfa is a good source of silicon, which is essential for healthy hair and nails.

Improve cardiovascular health: Alfalfa may reduce inflammation, improve blood sugar levels, and reduce cholesterol levels.

Improve respiratory health: Alfalfa may reduce inflammation and improve lung function.

Protect and improve liver function.

Improve immune function: Alfalfa may reduce inflammation and provide antioxidants.

Improve nerve function: Alfalfa may provide essential nutrients such as vitamin K and calcium.

Improve fertility: Alfalfa may regulate hormones and improve overall health.

Improve vision: Alfalfa is a good source of carotenoids, which are essential for healthy vision.

Improve sleep: Alfalfa may reduce inflammation and provide essential nutrients such as vitamin K.

Improve energy levels: Alfalfa provides essential nutrients such as iron.

Improve mental health: Alfalfa may reduce inflammation and provide essential nutrients such as vitamin K.

Improve overall health: Alfalfa provides essential nutrients, reduces inflammation and improves the function of various systems in the body.

May help to improve overall health: Alfalfa may help to improve overall health by providing essential nutrients, reducing inflammation, and improving the function of various systems in the body.

Chicory

Chicory

Chicory, also known as Cichorium intybus, is a perennial herb that is native to Europe and Asia. It is a member of the Asteraceae family and is known for its deep roots, which can reach up to 15 feet deep. The plant is commonly used as a coffee substitute and as a dietary supplement due to its potential health benefits.

Chemical Constituents: Chicory contains a wide range of bioactive compounds such as inulin, polyphenols, flavonoids and sesquiterpene lactones. The plant also contains a variety of vitamins and minerals such as vitamin K, vitamin E, and manganese. Additionally, Chicory contains important enzymes, antioxidants and minerals like potassium, calcium and zinc that can help to protect the body against damage caused by free radicals.

Market and Formulation: Chicory is available in a variety of forms such as capsules, tablets, powders, and teas. It is also commonly found in coffee blends, herbal teas and other dietary supplements. The market for chicory supplements is growing and is expected to continue to grow in the future due to increasing consumer interest in natural health products.

Health Benefits

Improve digestion: Chicory is a good source of inulin, a type of soluble fiber that can aid digestion and prevent constipation.

Lower blood sugar levels: Chicory root extract may lower blood sugar levels by slowing down the absorption of carbohydrates in the gut.

Reduce inflammation: Chicory contains polyphenols and flavonoids that have anti-inflammatory properties.

Improve liver function: Chicory may protect the liver from damage and improve function by reducing inflammation and providing antioxidants.

Improve skin health: Chicory's antioxidants may protect the skin from damage and improve appearance.

Improve hair and nail health: Chicory is a good source of minerals like zinc, which is essential for healthy hair and nails.

Improve cardiovascular health: Chicory may reduce inflammation, improve blood sugar levels, and provide antioxidants.

Protect and improve kidney function: Chicory provides important minerals like potassium.

Improve bone health: Chicory is a good source of minerals like calcium and manganese, which are essential for healthy bones.

Improve immune function: Chicory may improve the function of the immune system by providing antioxidants and reducing inflammation.

Improve nerve function: Chicory may provide essential minerals like potassium and calcium.

Improve fertility: Chicory may regulate hormones and improve overall health.

Improve vision: Chicory is a good source of antioxidants, which are essential for healthy vision.

Improve sleep: Chicory may provide antioxidants and reduce inflammation.

Improve energy levels: Chicory may provide essential minerals like potassium and manganese.

Improve mental health: Chicory may reduce inflammation and provide antioxidants.

Improve respiratory health: Chicory may reduce inflammation and provide antioxidants.

Improve blood sugar control: Chicory root extract may lower blood sugar levels by slowing down the absorption of carbohydrates in the gut.

Improveoverall health: Chicory may improve overall health by providing essential minerals and antioxidants, reducing inflammation and improving the function of various systems in the body.

Ginger

Ginger

Ginger, also known as Zingiber officinale, is a perennial herb that is native to Asia. It is a member of the Zingiberaceae family and is known for its underground stem, called rhizome, which is used as a spice and a medicinal herb. The rhizome of ginger contains a wide range of bioactive compounds, such as gingerol, shogaol, and paradol, which are responsible for its health benefits.

Chemical Constituents: Ginger contains a wide range of bioactive compounds such as gingerol, shogaol, and paradol, which are responsible for its anti-inflammatory and antioxidant properties. The rhizome of ginger also contains a variety of vitamins and minerals such as vitamin B6, magnesium, and manganese. Additionally, ginger contains important enzymes and antioxidants that can help to protect the body against damage caused by free radicals.

Market and Formulation: Ginger is available in a variety of forms such as fresh ginger, dried ginger powder, ginger oil, ginger supplements, ginger tea, and ginger cand. The market for ginger supplements is growing and is expected to continue to grow in the future due to increasing consumer interest in natural health products.

Health Benefits

Reduce nausea and vomiting: Ginger has been traditionally used to reduce nausea and vomiting, particularly morning sickness during pregnancy.

Reduce muscle pain and soreness: Ginger has anti-inflammatory properties that can reduce muscle pain and soreness caused by exercise.

Lower blood sugar levels: Ginger may lower blood sugar levels in people with diabetes.

Lower cholesterol levels: Ginger may lower cholesterol levels by reducing the absorption of cholesterol in the gut.

Reduce menstrual pain: Ginger may reduce menstrual pain by reducing inflammation.

Improve brain function: Ginger may improve brain function by reducing inflammation and providing antioxidants.

Improve respiratory health: Ginger may reduce inflammation and provide antioxidants.

Improve heart health: Ginger may reduce inflammation and improve blood circulation.

Improve digestion: Ginger may reduce inflammation and provide antioxidants.

Improve skin health: Ginger's antioxidants may protect the skin from damage and improve appearance.

Improve hair and nail health: Ginger is a good source of minerals like zinc and magnesium, which are essential for healthy hair and nails.

Improve immune function: Ginger may improve the function of the immune system by reducing inflammation and providing antioxidants.

Improve bone health: Ginger is a good source of minerals like manganese and magnesium, which are essential for healthy bones.

Improve nerve function: Ginger may reduce inflammation and provide antioxidants.

Improve fertility: Ginger may regulate hormones and improve overall health.

Improve vision: Ginger is a good source of antioxidants, which are essential for healthy vision.

Improve sleep: Ginger may reduce inflammation and provide antioxidants.

Improve energy levels: Ginger may provide essential minerals like magnesium and manganese.

Improve mental health: Ginger may reduce inflammation and provide antioxidants.

Improve overall health: Ginger may improve overall health by providing essential minerals and antioxidants, reducing inflammation and improving the function of various systems in the body.

Fenugreek

Fenugreek

Fenugreek, also known as Trigonella foenum-graecum, is an annual herb that is native to the Mediterranean region and parts of Asia. It is a member of the Fabaceae family and is known for its seeds, which are used as a spice and a medicinal herb. Fenugreek seeds contain a wide range of bioactive compounds, such as saponins, trigonelline, and diosgenin, which are responsible for its health benefits.

Chemical Constituents: Fenugreek seeds contain a wide range of bioactive compounds such as saponins, trigonelline, and diosgenin, which are responsible for its anti-inflammatory and antioxidant properties. The seeds also contain a variety of vitamins and minerals such as vitamin K, vitamin C, and iron. Additionally, Fenugreek contains important enzymes, antioxidants, and minerals like potassium, calcium, and zinc that can help to protect the body against damage caused by free radicals.

Market and Formulation: Fenugreek is available in a variety of forms such as fenugreek supplements, fenugreek tea, fenugreek oil, and fenugreek powder. The market for Fenugreek supplements is growing and is expected to continue to grow in the future due to increasing consumer interest in natural health products.

Side Effects and Dosage: Fenugreek is generally considered safe for most people when consumed in moderate amounts. However, high doses of Fenugreek supplements may cause side effects such as upset stomach, diarrhea, and bloating. It is recommended to consult with a healthcare professional before taking any supplement, including Fenugreek supplement, to determine the appropriate dosage.

Health Benefits

Lower blood sugar levels: Fenugreek may lower blood sugar levels by slowing down the absorption of carbohydrates in the gut.

Lower cholesterol levels: Fenugreek may lower cholesterol levels by reducing the absorption of cholesterol in the gut.

Increase milk production in lactating women: Fenugreek may increase milk production in lactating women by regulating hormones.

Improve digestion: Fenugreek may improve digestion by reducing inflammation and providing antioxidants.

Improve skin health: Fenugreek's antioxidants may protect the skin from damage and improve appearance.

Improve hair and nail health: Fenugreek is a good source of minerals like iron and zinc, which are essential for healthy hair and nails.

Improve cardiovascular health: Fenugreek may reduce inflammation, improve blood sugar levels, and provide antioxidants.

Protect and improve kidney function: Fenugreek provides important minerals like potassium.

Improve bone health: Fenugreek is a good source of minerals like calcium and zinc, which are essential for healthy bones.

Improve immune function: Fenugreek may improve the function of the immune system by reducing inflammation and providing antioxidants.

Improve nerve function: Fenugreek may provide essential minerals like potassium and calcium.

Improve fertility: Fenugreek may regulate hormones and improve overall health.

Improve vision: Fenugreek is a good source of antioxidants, which are essential for healthy vision.

Improve sleep: Fenugreek may reduce inflammation and provide antioxidants.

Improve energy levels: Fenugreek may provide essential minerals like potassium and zinc.

Improve mental health: Fenugreek may reduce inflammation and provide antioxidants.

Improve respiratory health: Fenugreek may reduce inflammation and provide antioxidants.

Improve digestion: Fenugreek may improve digestion by reducing inflammation and providing antioxidants.

Lower blood sugar levels: Fenugreek may lower blood sugar levels by slowing down the absorption of carbohydrates in the gut.

Improve overall health: Fenugreek may improve overall health by providing essential minerals and antioxidants, reducing inflammation and improving the function of various systems in the body.

Garlic

Garlic

Garlic, also known as Allium sativum, is a perennial herb that is native to Central Asia. It is a member of the Alliaceae family and is known for its bulb, which is used as a spice and a medicinal herb. Garlic bulbs contain a wide range of bioactive compounds, such as allicin, diallyl disulfide, and diallyl trisulfide, which are responsible for its health benefits.

Chemical Constituents: Garlic bulbs contain a wide range of bioactive compounds such as allicin, diallyl disulfide, and diallyl trisulfide, which are responsible for its anti-inflammatory and antioxidant properties. The bulbs also contain a variety of vitamins and minerals such as vitamin C, vitamin B6, and manganese. Additionally, Garlic contains important enzymes and antioxidants that can help to protect the body against damage caused by free radicals.

Market and Formulation: Garlic is available in a variety of forms such as fresh garlic, dried garlic powder, garlic oil, garlic supplements, garlic tea, and garlic cand. The market for garlic supplements is growing and is expected to continue to grow in the future due to increasing consumer interest in natural health products.

Side Effects and Dosage: Garlic is generally considered safe for most people when consumed in moderate amounts. However, high doses of garlic supplements may cause side effects such as upset stomach, diarrhea, and bloating. It is recommended to consult with a healthcare professional before taking any supplement, including garlic supplement, to determine the appropriate dosage.

Health Benefits

Lower blood pressure: Garlic can lower blood pressure by dilating blood vessels and reducing inflammation.

Lower cholesterol levels: Garlic may lower cholesterol levels by reducing the absorption of cholesterol in the gut.

Reduce risk of heart disease: Garlic may reduce the risk of heart disease by improving blood flow, reducing inflammation, and lowering cholesterol levels.

Improve brain function: Garlic may improve brain function by reducing inflammation and providing antioxidants.

Improve respiratory health: Garlic may reduce inflammation and provide antioxidants.

Improve immune function: Garlic may improve the function of the immune system by reducing inflammation and providing antioxidants.

Improve bone health: Garlic is a good source of minerals like manganese and vitamin C, which are essential for healthy bones.

Improve nerve function: Garlic may provide essential minerals like manganese and vitamin C.

Improve digestion: Garlic may reduce inflammation and provide antioxidants.

Improve skin health: Garlic's antioxidants may protect the skin from damage and improve appearance.

Improve hair and nail health: Garlic is a good source of minerals like manganese and vitamin C, which are essential for healthy hair and nails.

Improve cardiovascular health: Garlic may reduce inflammation and provide antioxidants.

Protect and improve kidney function: Garlic provides important minerals like manganese.

Improve sexual function: Garlic may improve sexual function by increasing blood flow.

Improve energy levels: Garlic may provide essential minerals like manganese and vitamin C.

Improve mental health: Garlic may reduce inflammation and provide antioxidants.

Improve blood flow: Garlic may improve blood flow by dilating blood vessels and reducing inflammation.

Improve athletic performance:Garlic may improve athletic performance by increasing blood flow and reducing inflammation.

Reduce risk of certain types of cancer: Garlic may reduce the risk of certain types of cancer by reducing inflammation and providing antioxidants.

Honey

Honey

Honey is a sweet, viscous food substance produced by bees from the nectar of flowers. It is rich in enzymes, antioxidants, and minerals that can provide a wide range of health benefits. The composition of honey can vary depending on the types of flowers that the bees collect nectar from.

Chemical Constituents: Honey contains a variety of bioactive compounds such as enzymes, antioxidants, and minerals, which are responsible for its health benefits. These include enzymes such as glucose oxidase, diastase, and invertase, antioxidants such as flavonoids and phenolic acids, and minerals such as potassium, calcium, and magnesium. Additionally, honey contains important vitamins such as vitamin C and vitamin B6.

Market and Formulation: Honey is a widely used food product and is available in a variety of forms such as raw honey, pasteurized honey, and honey supplements. The market for honey supplements is growing and is expected to continue to grow in the future due to increasing consumer interest in natural health products.

Side Effects and Dosage: Honey is generally considered safe for most people when consumed in moderate amounts. However, high doses of honey supplements may cause side effects such as upset stomach, diarrhea, and bloating. It is recommended to consult with a healthcare professional before taking any supplement, including honey supplement, to determine the appropriate dosage.

Health Benefits

May help to improve digestion: Honey may help to improve digestion by providing enzymes and antioxidants.

May help to improve immune function: Honey may help to improve the function of the immune system by providing antioxidants and reducing inflammation.

May help to improve respiratory health: Honey may help to improve respiratory health by reducing inflammation and providing antioxidants.

May help to improve wound healing: Honey may help to improve wound healing by reducing inflammation and providing antioxidants.

May help to improve skin health: Honey's antioxidants may help to protect the skin from damage and improve its appearance.

May help to improve hair and nail health: Honey is a good source of minerals like potassium and calcium, which are essential for healthy hair and nails.

May help to improve cardiovascular health: Honey may help to improve cardiovascular health by reducing inflammation and providing antioxidants.

May help to improve kidney function: Honey may help to protect the kidneys from damage and improve their function by providing important minerals like potassium.

May help to improve bone health: Honey is a good source of minerals like potassium and calcium, which are essential for healthy bones.

May help to improve sexual function: Honey may help to improve sexual function by increasing blood flow.

May help to improve energy levels: Honey may help to improve energy levels by providing important enzymes and antioxidants.

May help to improve mental health: Honey may help to improve mental health by reducing inflammation and providing antioxidants.

May help to improve blood flow: Honey may help to improve blood flow by providing antioxidants and reducing inflammation.

May help to reduce the risk of certain types of cancer: Honey may help to reduce the risk of certain types of cancer by reducing inflammation and providing antioxidants.

May help to improve overall health: Honey may help to improve overall health by providing essential enzymes, antioxidants, and minerals, reducing inflammation, and improving the function of various systems in the body.

It's important to note that while honey has many potential health benefits, more research is needed to fully understand its effects on human health. Some people may be allergic to honey and should avoid consuming it. Infants under 12 months should not be given honey as it can contain a type of bacteria that can cause botulism in their immature gut.

May help to improve oral health: Honey may help to improve oral health by reducing plaque buildup and promoting healthy teeth and gums.

May help to improve wound healing: Honey has been traditionally used as a wound healing agent. Its antibacterial and anti-inflammatory properties can help to reduce pain and inflammation, promote cell growth and repair, and prevent infection.

May help to improve sleep: Honey may help to improve sleep by providing antioxidants and reducing inflammation.

May help to reduce symptoms of allergies: Some studies suggest that consuming local honey may help to reduce symptoms of allergies by exposing the body to small amounts of pollen.

May help to improve athletic performance: Honey may help to improve athletic performance by providing energy and reducing inflammation.

It's also worth noting that not all honey is created equal. The quality and purity of honey can vary greatly depending on the source and processing methods. It is important to purchase honey from a reputable source and to look for honey that is raw, unprocessed and unpasteurized to gain maximum health benefits.

AMLA

Amla

Amla, also known as Indian Gooseberry, is a small, deciduous tree that is native to India and parts of Southeast Asia. The fruit of the tree, which is green and spherical in shape, is used as a food and a medicinal herb. Amla is rich in antioxidants, vitamins, and minerals, and has been used in Ayurvedic medicine for centuries.

Chemical Constituents: Amla is rich in antioxidants, vitamins, and minerals. The fruit is high in Vitamin C, tannins, flavonoids, and other antioxidants. It also contains minerals such as calcium, iron, and phosphorus. Additionally, Amla contains important amino acids and polyphenols.

Market and Formulation: Amla is available in a variety of forms such as fresh fruit, dried fruit powder, Amla oil, Amla supplements, Amla juice and Amla cand. The market for Amla supplements is growing and is expected to continue to grow in the future due to increasing consumer interest in natural health products.

Side Effects and Dosage: Amla is generally considered safe for most people when consumed in moderate amounts. However, high doses of Amla supplements may cause side effects such as upset stomach, diarrhea, and bloating. It is recommended to consult with a healthcare professional before taking any supplement, including Amla supplement, to determine the appropriate dosage.

Health Benefits:Amla may help to improve digestion by providing antioxidants and other bioactive compounds. It may also help to improve the function of the immune system by reducing inflammation. Additionally, Amla may help to improve respiratory health, wound healing, and skin health. It is a good source of minerals like calcium and iron, which are essential for healthy hair and nails. In terms of cardiovascular health, Amla may help by reducing inflammation and providing antioxidants. It may also protect the kidneys and improve bone health by providing important minerals like calcium. Amla may also improve sexual function, energy levels, mental health, blood flow, and overall health. It may also reduce the risk of certain types of cancer. Amla may also improve oral health, wound healing, liver function, and reduce symptoms of allergies. It may also improve athletic performance. However, it's important to note that while Amla has many potential health benefits, more research is needed to fully understand its effects on human health.

GINSENG

Enter Caption

Ginseng is a perennial plant that is native to Asia and North America. The root of the plant is used as a medicinal herb and is believed to have a wide range of health benefits. Ginseng is rich in ginsenosides, which are compounds that are responsible for its medicinal properties.

Chemical Constituents: Ginseng is rich in ginsenosides, which are believed to be responsible for its medicinal properties. These compounds are thought to have anti-inflammatory, antioxidant, and immune-modulating effects. Additionally, ginseng contains important vitamins, minerals, and amino acids.

Market and Formulation: Ginseng is available in a variety of forms such as fresh root, dried root powder, tinctures, capsules, and teas. The market for ginseng supplements is growing and is expected to continue to grow in the future due to increasing consumer interest in natural health products.

Side Effects and Dosage: Ginseng is generally considered safe for most people when consumed in moderate amounts. However, high doses of ginseng supplements may cause side effects such as insomnia, headaches, and high blood pressure. It is recommended to consult with a healthcare professional before taking any supplement, including ginseng supplement, to determine the appropriate dosage.

Health Benefits

May help to improve mental health: Ginseng may help to improve mental health by reducing inflammation and providing antioxidants.

May help to improve immune function: Ginseng may help to improve the function of the immune system by providing antioxidants and reducing inflammation.

May help to improve cardiovascular health: Ginseng may help to improve cardiovascular health by reducing inflammation and providing antioxidants.

May help to improve sexual function: Ginseng may help to improve sexual function by increasing blood flow.

May help to improve energy levels: Ginseng may help to improve energy levels by providing important antioxidants and other bioactive compounds.

May help to improve athletic performance: Ginseng may help to improve athletic performance by providing energy and reducing inflammation.

May help to reduce symptoms of stress and anxiety: Ginseng may help to reduce symptoms of stress and anxiety by providing antioxidants and reducing inflammation.

May help to improve cognitive function: Ginseng may help to improve cognitive function by providing antioxidants and reducing inflammation.

May help to improve blood sugar control: Ginseng may help to improve blood sugar control by regulating insulin sensitivity and glucose metabolism.

May help to improve lung function: Ginseng may help to improve lung function by reducing inflammation and providing antioxidants.

May help to improve skin health: Ginseng may help to improve skin health by providing antioxidants and reducing inflammation.

May help to improve hair and nail health: Ginseng is a good source of important vitamins and minerals, which are essential for healthy hair and nails.

May help to improve bone health: Ginseng may help to improve bone health by providing antioxidants and reducing inflammation.

May help to reduce the risk of certain types of cancer: Ginseng may help to reduce the risk of certain types of cancer by reducing inflammation and providing antioxidants.

May help to improve overall health: Ginseng may help to improve overall health by providing essential antioxidants, reducing inflammation, and improving the function of various systems in the body.

It's important to note that while ginseng has many potential health benefits, more research is needed to fully understand its effects on human health. Additionally, it's important to consult a healthcare professional before taking any supplement, including ginseng supplement, to determine the appropriate dosage and to make sure it doesn't interact with any medication you are taking. Also, it's important to purchase ginseng supplements from a reputable source to ensure its purity and safety.

Aswagandha

Aswagandha

Ashwagandha, also known as Indian ginseng or winter cherry, is a popular herb in Ayurvedic medicine. It has been used for centuries to promote overall health and well-being.

The plant is a small shrub with yellow or green flowers and red berries. The active compounds in ashwagandha are believed to be alkaloids, steroidal lactones, and saponins. These compounds are thought to be responsible for the herb's medicinal properties.

Ashwagandha is available in various forms including powders, capsules, extracts, and liquid formulations. It is often combined with other herbs in Ayurvedic formulations.

There are no known major side effects associated with ashwagandha, but high doses may cause stomach upset. It is important to consult a healthcare practitioner before taking any new supplement, especially if you are pregnant, nursing, or taking any medications.

The recommended dosage of ashwagandha varies depending on the product and indication. It is generally recommended to take

300-500mg of a standardized extract twice daily.

Ashwagandha is believed to have a variety of health benefits

Reducing stress and anxiety

Improving brain function

Lowering cholesterol levels

Reducing inflammation

Improving fertility in men

Improving heart health

Lowering blood sugar levels

Reducing symptoms of depression

Improving sleep quality

Improving muscle strength and endurance

Improving thyroid function

Improving joint health

Reducing symptoms of menopause

Improving skin health

Reducing symptoms of cancer treatment

Improving respiratory function

Improving liver function

Improving kidney function

Improving immunity

Improving cognitive function in older adults.

It is important to note that while ashwagandha has been used for centuries in traditional medicine, more research is needed to confirm its effectiveness and safety. It is important to consult with a healthcare practitioner before taking ashwagandha or any other supplement.

SPIRULINA

Spirulina powder

Spirulina is a type of blue-green algae that is often consumed as a dietary supplement. It is a rich source of nutrients, including protein, vitamins, and minerals.

The active compounds in spirulina are thought to be phycocyanin, carotenoids, and sulfolipids. These compounds are believed to be responsible for the herb's medicinal properties.

Spirulina is available in various forms including powders, tablets, and capsules. It is often added to smoothies, energy bars, and other foods as a dietary supplement.

There are no known major side effects associated with spirulina, but high doses may cause stomach upset. It is important to consult a healthcare practitioner before taking any new supplement, especially if you are pregnant, nursing, or taking any medications.

The recommended dosage of spirulina varies depending on the product and indication. It is generally recommended to take 1-3 grams per day.

Spirulina is believed to have a variety of health benefits, including:

Boosting energy and endurance

Improving immune function

Lowering cholesterol levels

Reducing inflammation

Improving heart health

Lowering blood pressure

Improving symptoms of allergies

Improving symptoms of premenstrual syndrome (PMS)

Improving symptoms of attention-deficit hyperactivity disorder (ADHD)

Improving symptoms of age-related macular degeneration

Improving symptoms of diabetic neuropathy

Improving symptoms of fatigue

Improving symptoms of muscle weakness

Improving symptoms of hay fever

Improving symptoms of high blood pressure

Improving symptoms of fibromyalgia

Improving symptoms of anxiety

Improving symptoms of depression

Improving symptoms of stress

Improving symptoms of cancer treatment

VI

Herbal Drug and Herb-Food Interactions

Many people believe that herbal medicines are safe because they are natural, but this is not always the case. Herbs can have side effects, just like any other type of medicine. Additionally, when herbs are mixed with other medications, there is a greater chance of interactions occurring. This is because herbs often contain multiple active ingredients, whereas synthetic drugs typically only have one.

Herb-drug-food interactions refer to the impact of herbal supplements, prescription drugs and foods on each other's effectiveness and safety. These interactions can occur at various stages of the pharmacokinetic process, including absorption, distribution, metabolism, and excretion. These interactions can lead to a variety of effects, including increased or decreased drug effectiveness, altered drug metabolism, and potential toxicity.

Herbal supplements, also known as phytomedicines, are derived from plants and are used for medicinal purposes. They are commonly used to treat a variety of conditions, such as anxiety, pain, and sleep disorders. However, many herbs contain active compounds that can interact with prescription drugs in ways that may be harmful to the patient.

Foods can also interact with drugs. For example, some drugs need to be taken with food to prevent stomach irritation, while others should be taken on an empty stomach. Certain foods can also interfere with the absorption of drugs, altering their effectiveness.

It is important to note that these interactions can occur in various combinations, such as herb-drug interactions, herb-food interactions, drug-food interactions, and even herb-herb interactions, making it crucial to be aware of all the supplements and medications an individual is taking and the foods they consume.

The use of herbal supplements and other non-vitamin, non-mineral dietary supplements is prevalent in many countries around the world. In the United States, for example, it is estimated that over 50% of adults use some form of dietary supplement, with herbs and botanicals being among the most commonly used products. According to the National Center for Complementary and Integrative Health, the use of herbal supplements in the U.S. has been steadily increasing over the past decade, with more than one-third of adults reporting use in the past year.A similar trend has been observed in other countries, such as Canada, the United Kingdom, and Australia, where the use of herbal supplements is also common.

Herbs and supplements are used for a variety of reasons, including to improve overall health and well-being, to treat specific health conditions, and as a complementary or alternative therapy to conventional medicine. Some of the most commonly used herbs and supplements include echinacea, ginseng, garlic, fish oil, and saw palmetto.The use of herbs and supplements is particularly prevalent among certain groups of people, such as the elderly, women, and individuals with chronic conditions. Many people take herbs and supplements in addition to prescription medications, which can increase the risk of herb-drug interactions.

It is important to note that while many herbs and supplements are considered safe when used appropriately, some may have potential risks, especially when taken in combination with other medications. Therefore, it is crucial to consult with a healthcare professional before taking any herbs or supplements, especially if you are already taking prescription medication.

Importance of understanding interactions

Understanding herb-drug-food interactions is important for several reasons:

Adverse effects: Herb-drug interactions can lead to a variety of adverse effects, such as increased or decreased drug effectiveness, altered drug metabolism, and potential toxicity. For example, certain herbs can inhibit or induce the enzymes responsible for metabolizing certain drugs, leading to increased or decreased drug levels in the body. This can result in decreased efficacy of the drug or increased risk of side effects.

Interference with prescription medications: Some herbs and supplements can interfere with the effectiveness of prescription medications, potentially making the condition for which the medication was prescribed worse. This can lead to the need for additional treatments or even hospitalization.

Lack of regulation and standardization: Herbs and supplements are not as strictly regulated as prescription drugs. This means that the purity, quality, and potency of these products can vary greatly. This lack of regulation can make it difficult to predict how a particular herb or supplement will interact with other medications.

Need for communication: Understanding interactions is important for communication between patients, healthcare professionals, and other relevant parties. Patients should always inform their healthcare providers of any herbs or supplements they are taking, and healthcare providers should be aware of any potential interactions that may occur.

Personalized treatment: Understanding interactions is crucial to provide personalized treatment plans. It can help healthcare professionals to adjust treatment plans and make recommendations to optimize patient outcomes and avoid potential adverse effects.

Research: Understanding interactions is important for the ongoing research and development of new drugs and therapies. It can help to identify potential interactions early in the development process and help to optimize the design of clinical trials.

Biochemical mechanisms of interactions

The biochemical mechanisms of herb-drug-food interactions are complex and can involve multiple pathways. Some of the main mechanisms include:

Enzyme inhibition and induction: Herbs and supplements can interact with drugs by inhibiting or inducing the enzymes responsible for metabolizing the drugs. For example, some herbs can inhibit the cytochrome P450 enzymes, which are responsible for metabolizing many drugs. This can lead to increased drug levels in the body and an increased risk of side effects. Other herbs can induce these enzymes, leading to decreased drug levels and decreased effectiveness.

Interference with absorption: Some herbs and supplements can interfere with the absorption of drugs in the gastrointestinal tract, leading to decreased drug levels in the body. For example, St. John's wort, a commonly used herb for depression, can decrease the absorption of certain antidepressants.

Interactions with receptors: Some herbs and supplements can interact with drugs by binding to the same receptors in the body. For example, some herbs that bind to the same receptors as blood-thinning drugs, such as warfarin, can increase the risk of bleeding.

Interference with the transport of drugs across biological membranes: Some herbs and supplements can interact with drugs by inhibiting or enhancing the transport of drugs across biological membranes, such as the blood-brain barrier.

Interference with the excretion of drugs: Some herbs and supplements can interact with drugs by inhibiting or enhancing the excretion of drugs through the kidneys or liver, which can lead to increased or decreased drug levels in the body.

These are some of the main mechanisms of herb-drug-food interactions, however, it is important to note that more research is needed to fully understand the complex interactions between herbs, supplements, drugs and food.

Classification of Interactions

Types of interactions:Herb-drug-food interactions

Herb-drug-food interactions can be classified into two main categories: pharmacokinetic interactions and pharmacodynamic interactions.

Pharmacokinetic interactions: These interactions involve changes in the absorption, distribution, metabolism, or excretion of drugs. Examples include:

Interference with the absorption of drugs in the gastrointestinal tract

Inhibition or induction of enzymes responsible for metabolizing drugs

Interference with the transport of drugs across biological membranes

Interference with the excretion of drugs

Pharmacodynamic interactions: These interactions involve changes in the physiological response to drugs. Examples include:

Interactions with receptors, leading to changes in the drug's efficacy or toxicity

Interference with the signaling pathways of drugs

Examples of specific interactions

St. John's Wort can decrease the effectiveness of certain antidepressants by inhibiting the cytochrome P450 enzymes responsible for metabolizing these drugs.

Garlic supplements can increase the risk of bleeding when taken with blood-thinning drugs such as warfarin by inhibiting the activity of clotting factors.

Grapefruit juice can increase the levels of certain drugs, such as statins, in the body by inhibiting the cytochrome P450 enzymes responsible for metabolizing these drugs.

Ginkgo biloba can increase the risk of bleeding when taken with blood-thinning drugs such as aspirin by inhibiting platelet function.

Black Cohosh can interact with estrogen replacement therapy and birth control pills, altering their effectiveness.

It's important to note that this list is not exhaustive and new interactions are being discovered as research continues. It is crucial to consult with a healthcare professional before taking any herbs or supplements, especially if you are already taking prescription medication, as they can help to advise on possible herb-drug-food interactions and help to ensure the safe use of these products.

Mechanisms of Interaction

Enzyme inhibition and induction: One of the main mechanisms of herb-drug-food interactions is the inhibition or induction of enzymes responsible for metabolizing drugs. This can lead to changes in the levels of drugs in the body, which can affect the safety and efficacy of the drugs.

Enzyme inhibition: Herbs and supplements can inhibit the activity of enzymes responsible for metabolizing drugs. This can lead to increased drug levels in the body, which can increase the risk of side effects. For example, St. John's Wort, a commonly used herb for depression, can inhibit the activity of the cytochrome P450 enzymes, which are responsible for metabolizing many drugs. This can lead to increased drug levels and an increased risk of side effects.

Enzyme induction: Some herbs and supplements can induce the activity of enzymes responsible for metabolizing drugs. This can lead to decreased drug levels in the body, which can decrease the effectiveness of the drugs. For example, rifampin, an antibiotic, is a well-known inducer of cytochrome P450 enzymes and can decrease the levels of drugs metabolized by these enzymes.

It's important to note that different herbs and supplements can have different effects on enzymes, and that different people may have different responses to the same herb or supplement. Some herbs and supplements can also have multiple effects on enzymes. Also, different enzymes can be affected by the same herb or supplement in different ways. Therefore, it is crucial to consult with a healthcare professional before taking any herbs or supplements, especially if you are already taking prescription medication, as they can help to advise on possible herb-drug-food interactions and help to ensure the safe use of these products. Interference with absorption

Interference with absorption

Another mechanism of herb-drug-food interactions is interference with the absorption of drugs in the gastrointestinal tract. This can lead to changes in the levels of drugs in the body, which can affect the safety and efficacy of the drugs.

Interference with drug solubility: Some herbs and supplements can change the solubility of drugs, making them less able to dissolve and be absorbed in the gastrointestinal tract. For example, calcium supplements can interfere with the absorption of certain antibiotics such as tetracycline and fluoroquinolones by binding to them in the stomach and preventing their dissolution and absorption.

Interference with drug transport: Some herbs and supplements can bind to the same transporters as drugs, and can compete with them for transport across the gut wall or blood-brain barrier, which can decrease the uptake of drugs in the body.

Interference with pH: Some herbs and supplements can alter the pH of the gastrointestinal tract, which can affect the stability and solubility of drugs, leading to decreased absorption.

Interference with gut motility: Some herbs and supplements can alter gut motility, which can affect the transit time of drugs in the gut and affect their absorption.

Interference with receptors: Herbs and supplements can also interact with drugs by binding to the same receptors in the body, leading to changes in the drug's efficacy or toxicity.

Agonist and Antagonist effect: Some herbs and supplements can bind to the same receptors as drugs and mimic or block their effects. For example, some herbs such as passionflower can bind to the same receptors as benzodiazepines and mimic their calming effects, while other herbs such as kava can bind to the same receptors as benzodiazepines and block their effects, leading to increased anxiety.

Upregulation or Downregulation of receptors: Some herbs and supplements can alter the expression or function of receptors, leading to changes in the drug's efficacy or toxicity. For example, some herbs such as ginseng can upregulate the expression of receptors, leading to increased sensitivity to drugs, while other herbs such as Echinacea can downregulate the expression of receptors, leading to decreased sensitivity to drugs.

It's important to note that different herbs and supplements can have different effects on receptors, and that different people may have different responses to the same herb or supplement. Therefore, it is crucial to consult with a healthcare professional before taking any herbs or supplements, especially if you are already taking prescription medication, as they can help to advise on possible herb-drug-food interactions and help to ensure the safe use of these products.

Types of drug interaction:Herb-drug interaction

Herb-drug interactions refer to the impact that herbal supplements can have on the effectiveness and safety of prescription drugs. These interactions can occur through several different mechanisms, including:

Enzyme inhibition: Some herbs contain compounds that can inhibit the enzymes responsible for metabolizing certain drugs, leading to increased drug levels in the body and an increased risk of side effects. For example, St. John's wort, a commonly used herb for depression, can inhibit the activity of the cytochrome P450 enzymes, which are responsible for metabolizing many drugs. This can lead to increased drug levels and an increased risk of side effects.

Enzyme induction: Other herbs contain compounds that can induce the enzymes responsible for metabolizing certain drugs, leading to decreased drug levels in the body and decreased effectiveness. For example, rifampin, an antibiotic, is a well-known inducer of cytochrome P450 enzymes and can decrease the levels of drugs metabolized by these enzymes.

Interference with absorption: Some herbs contain compounds that can interfere with the absorption of drugs in the gastrointestinal tract, leading to decreased drug levels in the body. For example, tannins found in certain herbs such as black tea can bind to certain drugs in the gut and prevent their absorption.

Interactions with receptors: Some herbs contain compounds that can bind to the same receptors in the body as drugs, leading to changes in the drug's efficacy or toxicity. For example, some herbs such as passionflower can bind to the same receptors as benzodiazepines and mimic their calming effects.

Interference with transport: Some herbs contain compounds that can interfere with the transport of drugs across biological membranes, leading to changes in drug levels in the body. For example, certain flavonoids found in grapefruit juice can inhibit the transport of drugs across the gut wall and blood-brain barrier, leading to changes in drug levels in the body.

Interference with excretion: Some herbs contain compounds that can interfere with the excretion of drugs through the kidneys or liver, leading to changes in drug levels in the body. For example, certain diuretic herbs can affect the function of the kidneys and alter the excretion of drugs that are eliminated through urine.

It's important to note that the interaction between herbs and drugs can be complex and may depend on various factors such as the dose and timing of herb and drug administration, the individual's metabolic status and genetics, and the interactions between multiple herbs and drugs. Also, it's important to note that not all herb-drug interactions have been identified and new interactions are being discovered as research continues. Therefore, it is crucial to consult with a healthcare professional before taking any herbs or supplements, especially if you are already taking prescription medication, as they can help to advise on possible herb-drug interactions and help to ensure the safe use of these products.

Herb-Herb interactions

Herb-Herb interactions refer to the impact that different herbal supplements can have on each other's effectiveness and safety. These interactions can occur through several different mechanisms, including:

Enzyme inhibition or induction: Some herbs contain compounds that can inhibit or induce the enzymes responsible for metabolizing other herbs, leading to changes in their levels in the body and affecting their effectiveness or safety.

Interference with absorption: Some herbs contain compounds that can interfere with the absorption of other herbs in the gastrointestinal tract, leading to decreased herb levels in the body and affecting their effectiveness.

Interactions with receptors: Some herbs contain compounds that can bind to the same receptors in the body as other herbs, leading to changes in their efficacy or toxicity.

Additive or synergistic effects: Some herbs when combined can enhance or reduce each other's effects, leading to changes in their efficacy or toxicity.

Altering the gut microbiome: Some herbs contain compounds that can alter the balance of microorganisms in the gut, leading to changes in the efficacy or toxicity of other herbs.

Herb-drug-food interactions can have serious consequences, including increased risk of side effects, decreased effectiveness of drugs, and increased risk of toxicity. Some examples of adverse effects that can occur as a result of herb-drug-food interactions include:

Increased risk of bleeding: Some herbs and supplements can increase the risk of bleeding when taken with blood-thinning drugs such as warfarin or aspirin by inhibiting the activity of clotting factors. For example, garlic supplements can increase the risk of bleeding when taken with warfarin.

Increased risk of toxicity: Some herbs and supplements can increase the risk of toxicity when taken with certain drugs by increasing drug levels in the body. For example, grapefruit juice can increase the levels of certain drugs such as statins in the body, leading to an increased risk of muscle damage.

Decreased effectiveness of drugs: Some herbs and supplements can decrease the effectiveness of certain drugs by decreasing drug levels in the body or by binding to the same receptors as drugs. For example, St. John's Wort can decrease the effectiveness of certain antidepressants by inhibiting the cytochrome P450 enzymes responsible for metabolizing these drugs.

Interference with treatment: Some herbs and supplements can interfere with the treatment of certain medical conditions by decreasing the effectiveness of drugs or by altering the symptoms of the condition. For example, some herbs such as kava can interfere with the treatment of anxiety disorders by binding to the same receptors as benzodiazepines and blocking their effects.

Allergic reactions: Some herbs and supplements can cause allergic reactions, especially to people who are sensitive to certain plants. For example, some people may develop an allergic reaction to feverfew, which is used to treat headaches and migraines.

Interference with prescription medicines

Interference with prescription medicines is one of the main concerns with herb-drug-food interactions. Herbs and supplements can interact with prescription drugs in several ways, including:

Inhibiting the metabolism of drugs: Some herbs and supplements can inhibit the activity of enzymes responsible for metabolizing drugs, leading to increased drug levels in the body and an increased risk of side effects.

Inducing the metabolism of drugs: Other herbs and supplements can induce the activity of enzymes responsible for metabolizing drugs, leading to decreased drug levels in the body and decreased effectiveness.

Interfering with the absorption of drugs: Some herbs and supplements can interfere with the absorption of drugs in the gastrointestinal tract, leading to decreased drug levels in the body.

Interacting with receptors: Some herbs and supplements can bind to the same receptors in the body as drugs, leading to changes in the drug's efficacy or toxicity.

Interfering with transport: Some herbs and supplements can interfere with the transport of drugs across biological membranes, leading to changes in drug levels in the body.

Interfering with excretion: Some herbs and supplements can interfere with the excretion of drugs through the kidneys or liver, leading to changes in drug levels in the body.

It's important to note that herb-drug-food interactions can also vary depending on the individual's metabolic status, genetics, and underlying health conditions. Therefore, it is crucial to consult with a healthcare professional before taking any herbs or supplements, especially if you are already taking prescription medication, as they can help to advise on possible herb-drug-food interactions and help to ensure the safe use of these products.

Hypercium

Hypericum (St. John's Wort)

St. John's Wort, also known as Hypercium, is a widely used herbal remedy for mild to moderate forms of depression. It contains several active compounds, such as hypericin and hyperforin, which have been shown to affect brain neurotransmitters like serotonin. When taken together with drugs that enhance 5-HT signaling, such as 5-HT re-uptake inhibitors, St. John's Wort may have pharmacodynamic interactions. This herb has been shown to interact clinically with various conventional drugs like immunosuppressants, hormones, cardiovascular drugs and calcium blockers via pharmacokinetic and/or pharmacodynamic mechanisms. Examples of drugs that interact with St. John's Wort include cyclosporine, tacrolimus, prednisone, oral contraceptives, warfarin, phenprocoumon, digoxin, statins, nifedipine, and verapamil.

Hypericum is a perennial herb that is commonly used as a dietary supplement for mood disorders such as depression and anxiety.It has also been used for centuries in traditional medicine for a wide range of ailments, including wounds, burns, and menstrual cramps.

Active compounds

Hypericum contains several active compounds, including hyperforin, hypericin, and flavonoids, which are believed to be responsible for its medicinal properties.

Health benefits

Hypericum has been shown to have anti-inflammatory and antioxidant properties.

It may help to improve mood and reduce symptoms of depression and anxiety.

It may also have potential benefits for symptoms of PMS, seasonal affective disorder, and nerve pain.

Interactions with drugs

Hypericum may interact with a wide range of medications, including antidepressants, birth control pills, and blood thinners.

It can increase the risk of side effects and reduce the effectiveness of these medications.

It can also increase the risk of sun sensitivity when taken with photosensitizing drugs.

Dosage and safety

Hypericum is generally considered safe when consumed in moderate amounts.

High doses of Hypericum may cause side effects such as dry mouth, dizziness, and gastrointestinal discomfort.

It may also interact with certain medications, such as antidepressants, so it's important to consult with a healthcare professional before taking it.

Hypericum is a commonly used dietary supplement for mood disorders such as depression and anxiety.

It may also have potential benefits for symptoms of PMS, seasonal affective disorder, and nerve pain.

However, it may interact with a wide range of medications, including antidepressants, birth control pills, and blood thinners, so it's important to consult with a healthcare professional before taking it.

Kava- Kava

Kava-kava

Kava, also known as Kava-kava, is a herbal remedy made from the roots and rhizome of Piper methysticum plant. It is used for the treatment of anxiety and has been found to be more effective than placebo in treating patients with anxiety disorders. However, the sale of kava is currently prohibited in the UK and some other European countries due to concerns about its potential liver toxicity. In vitro studies have shown that kavalactones, the active compounds in kava, are potent inhibitors of several enzymes in the CYP450 system. However, clinical trials have shown that at therapeutic doses, kava only inhibits the CYP2E1 enzyme and not other enzymes such as CYP3A4, CYP2D6, or CYP1A2. Some possible pharmacodynamic interactions have been reported when combining kava with benzodiazepines, anti-Parkinson or antidepressant drugs.

Kava-Kava is a tropical evergreen shrub that is native to the South Pacific.

The roots and stem of the kava plant are used to make a beverage that has been used for centuries in traditional Pacific Islander cultures for ceremonial, religious, and medicinal purposes.

Active compounds

Kava-Kava contains a group of compounds called kavalactones, which are believed to be responsible for its medicinal properties.

Health benefits

Kava-Kava has been traditionally used to promote relaxation, reduce stress and anxiety, and improve sleep.

It may also have potential benefits for symptoms of ADHD, menopause, and urinary tract infections.

Interactions with drugs

Kava-Kava may interact with a wide range of medications, including sedatives, antidepressants, and blood pressure medication.

It can increase the risk of side effects and reduce the effectiveness of these medications.

It can also increase the risk of liver damage when taken with drugs that are toxic to the liver.

Dosage and safety

Kava-Kava is generally considered safe when consumed in moderate amounts.

High doses of kava-kava may cause side effects such as drowsiness, dizziness, and gastrointestinal discomfort.

It may also interact with certain medications, such as antidepressants, so it's important to consult with a healthcare professional before taking it.

Kava-Kava is a traditional herb from the South Pacific that has been used for centuries for its medicinal properties.It may have potential benefits for symptoms of anxiety, ADHD, menopause, and urinary tract infections.However, it may interact with a wide range of medications, including sedatives, antidepressants, and blood pressure medication, so it's important to consult with a healthcare professional before taking it.

Ginkobiloba

Ginkobiloba

Ginkgo biloba, also known as Ginkobiloba, is an extract from the leaves of the ginkgo tree. It is used to treat cognitive impairments, dementia, intermittent claudication and tinnitus. The effect of ginkgo on various enzymes in the CYP450 system and P-glycoprotein has been investigated in clinical trials using different probe drugs such as alprazolam, midazolam, diazepam, nifedipine, caffeine, chlorzoxazone, debrisoquine, tolbutamide, diclofenac, flurbiprofen, omeprazole, voriconazole, fexofenadine, digoxin, and talinolol. It is commonly believed that ginkgo can interact with anticoagulant drugs, however, clinical trials have shown that it has no additive effect with aspirin on platelet aggregation, and does not change the antiplatelet activity of clopidogrel and cilostazol.

Ginkgo biloba is a tree that is native to China.

The leaves of the ginkgo tree are used to make a dietary supplement that has been used for centuries in traditional Chinese medicine for a wide range of ailments.

Active compounds

Ginkgo biloba contains several active compounds, including flavonoids and terpenoids, which are believed to be responsible for its medicinal properties.

Health benefits

Ginkgo biloba has been traditionally used to improve memory and cognitive function, particularly in older adults.

It may also have potential benefits for symptoms of tinnitus, age-related macular degeneration, and anxiety.

Interactions with drugs

Ginkgo biloba may interact with a wide range of medications, including blood thinners and antiplatelet drugs.

It can increase the risk of bleeding when taken with these medications.

It may also interact with some antidepressants, so it's important to consult with a healthcare professional before taking it.

Dosage and safety

Ginkgo biloba is generally considered safe when consumed in moderate amounts.

High doses of ginkgo biloba may cause side effects such as gastrointestinal discomfort, headaches, and allergic reactions.

It may also interact with certain medications, so it's important to consult with a healthcare professional before taking it.

Ginkgo biloba is a traditional herb from China that has been used for centuries for its medicinal properties.

It may have potential benefits for symptoms of memory and cognitive function, tinnitus, age-related macular degeneration, and anxiety.

However, it may interact with a wide range of medications, including blood thinners and antiplatelet drugs, so it's important to consult with a healthcare professional before taking it.

Ginseng

Ginseng

Ginseng is a perennial plant that is native to North America and Asia. The root of the plant is used to make traditional herbal medicine.

Ginseng has been traditionally used to improve energy, stamina, and overall well-being.

It has also been used to improve cognitive function, reduce stress and anxiety, and boost the immune system.

Some studies have also suggested that ginseng may have potential benefits for managing diabetes, high blood pressure, and other health conditions.

Possible side effects

Ginseng is generally considered safe when consumed in moderate amounts, but it can cause some side effects such as insomnia, headaches, and gastrointestinal discomfort.

High doses of ginseng may cause more serious side effects such as high blood pressure, low blood sugar, and allergic reactions.. A clinical study showed that American ginseng reduced the anticoagulant effect of warfarin in healthy volunteers. However, two recent clinical trials found that American ginseng did not affect the pharmacokinetics of the antiretroviral drugs Indinavir and Zidovudine.

Interactions with drugs

Ginseng may interact with a wide range of medications, including blood thinners, insulin, and blood pressure medication.

It may increase the risk of bleeding when taken with blood thinners and may also lower blood sugar levels when taken with insulin.

It may also interact with blood pressure medication and may cause blood pressure to drop too low.

It's important to consult with a healthcare professional before taking ginseng or any other dietary supplement or herb to ensure safety and effectiveness.

It's important to note that while ginseng has been traditionally used for medicinal purposes, more research is needed to fully understand its effectiveness and potential interactions with drugs.

Garlic

Garlic

Garlic is a perennial herb that is native to Central Asia and is widely used as a food flavoring and seasoning agent.Garlic has been traditionally used for thousands of years for its medicinal properties, it has been used for the treatment of various diseases such as hypertension, high cholesterol, and various types of cancer.

Garlic (Allium sativum L.) is commonly used in phytotherapy to treat hypercholesterolemia and prevent arteriosclerosis, although the clinical evidence for its effectiveness is limited.

Garlic preparations include garlic powder standardized to contain 1.3% alliin and 0.6% allicin, garlic aged extract, which is high in water-soluble phytochemicals like diallyl sulphides, and garlic oil, which is obtained from the distillation of cloves.

Several clinical trials have been conducted to evaluate the potential effects of garlic on CYP enzymes. Results suggest that garlic oil may selectively inhibit the CYP2E1 enzyme, but not others such as CYP1A2, CYP3A4, or CYP2D6.

Active compounds

Garlic contains several active compounds, including allicin, which is responsible for its characteristic odor and is believed to be responsible for its medicinal properties.

Health benefits

Garlic has been traditionally used to improve cardiovascular health, lower blood pressure and cholesterol levels, and prevent blood clots.

It may also have potential benefits for symptoms of cancer, osteoarthritis, and diabetes.

Garlic also has antibacterial and antifungal properties.

Interactions with drugs

Garlic may interact with a wide range of medications, including blood thinners and antiplatelet drugs.

It can increase the risk of bleeding when taken with these medications.

Garlic supplements may also interact with certain medications, such as blood pressure medication, so it's important to consult with a healthcare professional before taking it.

Dosage and safety

Garlic is generally considered safe when consumed in moderate amounts.

High doses of garlic may cause side effects such as gastrointestinal discomfort, headaches, and allergic reactions.

It may also interact with certain medications, so it's important to consult with a healthcare professional before taking it.

Garlic is a commonly used herb that has been used for thousands of years for its medicinal properties.

It may have potential benefits for symptoms of cardiovascular disease, hypertension, high cholesterol, and certain types of cancer.

However, it may interact with a wide range of medications, including blood thinners and antiplatelet drugs, so it's important to consult with a healthcare professional before taking it.

Pepper

Pepper

Pepper is a spice that is derived from the berries of the pepper plant. It is one of the most widely used spices in the world.

Pepper has been traditionally used for thousands of years for its medicinal properties, it has been used to improve digestion, alleviate pain, and as a natural remedy for colds and flu.

Active compounds

Pepper contains several active compounds, including piperine, which is responsible for its characteristic pungent taste and is believed to be responsible for its medicinal properties.

Health benefits

Pepper has been traditionally used to improve digestion and alleviate pain.

It may also have potential benefits for symptoms of cancer, osteoarthritis, and diabetes.

Pepper also has antioxidant properties.

Interactions with drugs

Pepper may interact with a wide range of medications, including blood thinners, antiplatelet drugs, and some antidepressants.

It may also interact with certain medications, such as blood pressure medication, so it's important to consult with a healthcare professional before taking it.

Dosage and safety

Pepper is generally considered safe when consumed in moderate amounts.

High doses of pepper may cause side effects such as gastrointestinal discomfort, headaches, and allergic reactions.

It may also interact with certain medications, so it's important to consult with a healthcare professional before taking it.

Pepper is a commonly used spice that has been used for thousands of years for its medicinal properties.

It may have potential benefits for symptoms of digestion and pain.

However, it may interact with a wide range of medications, including blood thinners, antiplatelet drugs, and some antidepressants, so it's important to consult with a healthcare professional before taking it.

Ephedra

Ephedra

Ephedra, also known as ma huang, is a plant that is native to Asia and has been used for thousands of years in traditional Chinese medicine.

The stems of the ephedra plant contain compounds called ephedrine and pseudoephedrine, which have stimulant and decongestant properties. Active compounds

Ephedra contains several active compounds, including ephedrine and pseudoephedrine, which are responsible for its medicinal properties.

Ephedra has been traditionally used to improve respiratory conditions such as asthma and bronchitis, and as a weight loss aid.

Interactions with drugs

Ephedra may interact with a wide range of medications, including antidepressants, blood pressure medication, and stimulants.

It can increase the risk of side effects and reduce the effectiveness of these medications.

It can also increase the risk of heart attack, stroke and death when taken with certain medications, so it's important to consult with a healthcare professional before taking it.

Dosage and safety

Ephedra is generally considered unsafe when consumed in any amount.

It is banned by FDA as a dietary supplement due to safety concerns and potentially dangerous interactions with other drugs and herbs.

Ephedra is a plant that has been used for thousands of years in traditional Chinese medicine.

It has been traditionally used to improve respiratory conditions such as asthma and bronchitis, and as a weight loss aid.

However, it is generally considered unsafe when consumed in any amount, and is banned by FDA as a dietary supplement due to safety concerns and potentially dangerous interactions with other drugs and herbs. It is important to consult with a healthcare professional before taking it.

VII

Herbal Cometics

The herbal cosmetic industry in India has been growing at a steady pace in recent years, driven by the increasing demand for natural and chemical-free beauty products. According to a report by Mordor Intelligence, the Indian herbal cosmetic market was valued at USD 6.3 billion in 2020 and is projected to grow at a CAGR of 9.5% during the forecast period of 2021-2026. The growth of the market can be attributed to the rising awareness of the benefits of using herbal cosmetics, such as their natural and safe ingredients, effectiveness, and minimal side effects.

In India, herbal cosmetics have been traditionally used for centuries, and the use of Ayurveda and other traditional medicine systems in beauty and personal care products has been gaining popularity. The government of India has also been promoting the use of herbal cosmetics through various initiatives, such as the 'Make in India' campaign and the 'Ayush' ministry.

The significance of herbal cosmetics in the market can be seen in their increasing acceptance among consumers, with many people opting for herbal products over chemical-based cosmetics. Consumers are becoming more conscious of the ingredients used in the cosmetics they use and prefer products that are natural and free of harmful chemicals. Herbal cosmetics are also considered to be more effective in treating skin and hair problems, and are considered more suitable for sensitive skin. The herbal cosmetic industry in India offers a wide range of products, from skincare and hair care to makeup, catering to the diverse needs of consumers.

In addition to being popular among consumers, herbal cosmetics are also being increasingly adopted by the cosmetics industry as a whole, with many companies launching herbal cosmetic lines. With the growing demand for herbal cosmetics, the herbal cosmetic industry in India is expected to continue to grow in the coming years.

The use of herbs and plants in beauty and cosmetic products dates back to ancient civilizations. Herbal cosmetics, also known as natural cosmetics, are formulated using various cosmetic ingredients, with one or more herbal ingredients added to address specific skin concerns. Herbs are commonly used in the development of new cosmetic and pharmaceutical products. Herbal cosmetics are made using crude or extracted forms of herbs and are formulated to provide defined cosmetic benefits only. They do not offer instant cures, but rather aim to balance the body with nature. Many cosmetic and toiletry formulations have been developed based on Indian herbs in recent years. Additionally, modern research has explored the use of Indian herbs in personal care products. The increasing popularity of herbal cosmetics is due to their gentleness on the skin and lack of side effects. Herbal cosmetics are made purely from herbs and shrubs, making them free of side effects and providing the body with nutrients and minerals. The term "cosmeceuticals" was first coined by Raymond Reed, a founding member of the U.S Society of Cosmetics Chemist in 1961. He used the term to describe active and science-based cosmetics.

Herbal cosmetics are products that are made from natural plant-based ingredients, such as herbs, fruits, flowers, and seeds. These ingredients are known for their medicinal properties and are used to enhance the health and appearance of the skin, hair, and teeth. Herbal cosmetics have been used for centuries in different cultures and are becoming increasingly popular in the modern world due to their natural and safe nature.

Herbal cosmetics are defined as products that are made from natural plant-based ingredients and have medicinal properties. They can be used for various purposes such as skin care, hair care, oral hygiene, and as makeup. Herbal cosmetics are considered to be safe and gentle on the skin, and are free from harsh chemicals and synthetic ingredients.

Advantage of Herbal cosmetics

They are made from natural ingredients, which reduces the risk of allergic reactions and skin

irritation.

They are gentle on the skin and can be used by people with sensitive skin.

They are free from harsh chemicals and synthetic ingredients, which makes them safe to use.

They have medicinal properties that can improve the health and appearance of the skin, hair,

and teeth.

They are eco-friendly and biodegradable, which makes them better for the environment.

Comparison with Traditional Cosmetics

Traditional cosmetics are products that are made from synthetic ingredients and chemicals. They are often used for the same purposes as herbal cosmetics, such as skin care, hair care, and makeup. However, traditional cosmetics have several disadvantages compared to herbal cosmetics. Traditional cosmetics often contain harsh chemicals and synthetic ingredients, which can be harmful to the skin and the environment. They may cause allergic reactions and skin irritation, especially for people with sensitive skin.They are not eco-friendly and may take a long time to degrade.

On the other hand, herbal cosmetics are made from natural ingredients and are gentle on the skin. They are safe to use, have medicinal properties, and are better for the environment. Many people prefer herbal cosmetics over traditional cosmetics due to these advantages. Thus, herbal cosmetics are a natural and safe alternative to traditional cosmetics. They are made from natural plant-based ingredients and have medicinal properties. Herbal cosmetics are gaining popularity due to their natural and safe nature and their eco-friendly properties. They are suitable for all skin types and have many benefits for the skin, hair, and teeth.

Status of Herbal Cosmetic Industry in India

Market size and growth: As mentioned earlier, the Indian herbal cosmetic market was valued at USD 6.3 billion in 2020 and is projected to grow at a CAGR of 9.5% during the forecast period of 2021-2026. The skincare segment holds the largest share of the market, followed by hair care and makeup. The increasing awareness of the benefits of herbal cosmetics and the rising demand for natural and chemical-free beauty products are the key drivers of market growth.

Key players and trends: The Indian herbal cosmetic market is highly fragmented, with a large number of small and medium-sized enterprises. However, some of the key players in the market include Patanjali Ayurved, Dabur India Ltd, Himalaya Drug Company, and Baidyanath.

In recent years, there has been an increasing trend of companies launching herbal cosmetic lines, as well as incorporating traditional Ayurvedic ingredients in their products. Many companies are also focusing on developing eco-friendly packaging, as well as promoting their products as cruelty-free and vegan.

In addition, the use of digital platforms and e-commerce channels has been on the rise, with many companies leveraging these channels to reach a wider audience and expand their customer base.

Definition as per Drugs and Cosmetic Act

Regulations and guidelines for herbal cosmetics in India: Herbal cosmetics in India are regulated by the Drugs and Cosmetics Act, 1940, and the Drugs and Cosmetics Rules, 1945. The act defines cosmetics as any article intended to be applied to the human body for cleansing, beautifying, promoting attractiveness, or altering the appearance, and includes any article intended for use as a component of a cosmetic.

Under the act, cosmetics are classified into two categories: those that are "not for therapeutic use" and those that are "for therapeutic use." Herbal cosmetics fall under the category of cosmetics "not for therapeutic use." The act also defines the registration and licensing requirements for manufacturers and importers of cosmetics, as well as the labeling and packaging requirements for cosmetics.

Importance of compliance with the act: Compliance with the Drugs and Cosmetics Act is important to ensure the safety and efficacy of herbal cosmetics. The act lays down regulations to ensure that cosmetics are manufactured, imported, and sold in compliance with the standards of quality, purity, and safety. Compliance with the act is also important to protect consumers from the use of harmful or adulterated cosmetics.

Non-compliance with the act can result in penalties and legal action, as well as damage to the reputation of a company. It is therefore important for manufacturers, importers, and distributors of herbal cosmetics to be aware of and comply with the regulations and guidelines laid down by the act.

In addition to compliance with the Drugs and Cosmetics Act, manufacturers of herbal cosmetics should also comply with other regulations such as the Food Safety and Standards Authority of India (FSSAI) regulations for herbal cosmetics. The FSSAI also lays down guidelines for the labeling, packaging, and advertising of cosmetics, including herbal cosmetics.

Herbal Raw Materials Used in Cosmetics

Overview of commonly used herbal ingredients: Some of the commonly used herbal ingredients in cosmetics include:

Aloe vera: known for its soothing and moisturizing properties, it is commonly used in skincare products

Neem: known for its anti-inflammatory and anti-bacterial properties, it is commonly used in skincare and hair care products

Turmeric: known for its anti-inflammatory and antioxidant properties, it is commonly used in skincare products

Sandalwood: known for its soothing and cooling properties, it is commonly used in skincare and hair care products

Rose: known for its soothing and moisturizing properties, it is commonly used in skincare and hair care products

Tulsi: known for its anti-inflammatory and anti-bacterial properties, it is commonly used in skincare and hair care products

Properties and benefits of each ingredient: Each of the herbal ingredients mentioned above has unique properties and benefits that make them useful in cosmetics. Aloe vera, for example, is known for its soothing and moisturizing properties, making it useful in skincare products. Neem, on the other hand, is known for its anti-inflammatory and anti-bacterial properties, making it useful in skincare and hair care products. Turmeric is known for its anti-inflammatory and antioxidant properties and is commonly used in skincare products. Sandalwood is known for its soothing and cooling properties, making it useful in skincare and hair care products. Rose is known for its soothing and moisturizing properties, making it useful in skincare and hair care products. Tulsi is known for its anti-inflammatory and anti-bacterial properties, making it useful in skincare and hair care products.

Sourcing and quality control of raw materials: Sourcing high-quality herbal raw materials is crucial for the production of effective cosmetics. Companies should ensure that the raw materials they use are sourced from reputable suppliers, and that they comply with the quality standards set by the Drugs and Cosmetics Act. To ensure the quality and safety of the raw materials, companies should also conduct regular testing and quality control checks. It is also essential to verify the authenticity of the raw materials, as there have been instances of counterfeit herbal ingredients in the market.

Sourcing and quality control of raw materials is an essential aspect of the formulation and production of herbal cosmetics. The quality of the raw materials used plays a major role in determining the safety and efficacy of the finished product. The following are some of the key practices and certifications related to sourcing and quality control of raw materials for herbal cosmetics:

Bureau of Indian Standards (BIS) certification: BIS is an organization that sets standards for products and services in India. BIS certification is a mark of quality and compliance with the Indian standards. It is mandatory for cosmetics that are manufactured, imported, or sold in India to comply with the standards set by BIS.

Indian Pharmacopoeia (IP), British Pharmacopoeia (BP), and United States Pharmacopoeia (USP) standards: These are standards that set the specifications for the quality, purity, and strength of the raw materials used in cosmetics. These standards are used as reference to ensure that the raw materials used comply with the required quality standards.

CTFA (Cosmetic, Toiletry, and Fragrance Association) certification: CTFA is an international organization that sets standards for cosmetics and personal care products. CTFA certification is a mark of quality and compliance with the international standards.

Normal tests: These tests are used to ensure that the raw materials used comply with the quality standards set by the Drugs and Cosmetics Act, as well as other standards such as IP, BP, and USP. These tests include but not limited to:

Microbial testing
Heavy metal testing
Pesticide residue testing
Chemical analysis
Physical testing

Finished product quality control: This involves testing the finished product to ensure that it complies with the quality standards set by the Drugs and Cosmetics Act, as well as other standards such as IP, BP, and USP. These tests include but not limited to:

Microbial testing

Heavy metal testing

Pesticide residue testing

Chemical analysis

Physical testing

Sensory testing

Various accelerated stability tests: These tests are used to ensure that the finished product maintains its quality and efficacy throughout its shelf life. These tests include but not limited to:

Temperature and humidity testing

Light stability testing

Oxidative stability testing

Microbial stability testing

Packaging compatibility testing

By implementing these practices, companies can ensure that the raw materials used in their herbal cosmetics comply with the relevant quality standards and regulations, and that the finished products are safe and effective for consumers.

In addition, companies should also take into account the environmental impact of sourcing raw materials and consider using sustainable and ethically-sourced raw materials.

Techniques for preparing herbal cosmetics

There are various techniques used for preparing herbal cosmetics, depending on the type of product and the desired properties. Some of the commonly used techniques include:

Infusion: This involves steeping the herbs in hot water or oil to extract the active ingredients. This method is commonly used for preparing herbal teas, and for extracting the active ingredients in herbs for use in skincare products.

Decoction: This involves boiling the herbs in water to extract the active ingredients. This method is commonly used for preparing herbal teas, and for extracting the active ingredients in herbs for use in hair care products.

Maceration: This involves steeping the herbs in a liquid, such as oil or alcohol, for a prolonged period to extract the active ingredients. This method is commonly used for preparing herbal oils and tinctures.

Cold-pressed extraction: This method involves mechanically pressing the herbs to extract the active ingredients, without the use of heat. This method is commonly used for extracting essential oils from herbs.

Quality control measures: During the formulation and production of herbal cosmetics, companies should implement quality control measures to ensure that the products are safe and effective. This includes regular testing of the raw materials, in-process materials, and finished products to ensure that they comply with the quality standards set by the Drugs and Cosmetics Act. This also includes implementing good manufacturing practices (GMP) to ensure that the products are manufactured in a clean and hygienic environment.

In addition, companies should also conduct stability testing of the products to ensure that they have a long shelf life and maintain their effectiveness throughout the shelf life.

It is also important for companies to keep detailed records of the formulation and production process, including the raw materials used, the manufacturing process, and any test results, in order to maintain transparency and ensure compliance with the regulatory requirements.

Raw Materials of Herbal Origin:Fixed Oils

Fixed oils, also known as carrier oils, are plant-based oils that are extracted from seeds, nuts, or fruits. They are an important ingredient in many herbal cosmetics and are used for their moisturizing and nourishing properties. Some examples of fixed oils that are commonly used in herbal cosmetics include:

Coconut oil: Coconut oil is a popular fixed oil that is known for its moisturizing properties. It is rich in fatty acids and can help to soothe dry and irritated skin. It is also known to be beneficial for hair care as it can help to strengthen hair and prevent breakage.

Olive oil: Olive oil is another popular fixed oil that is known for its moisturizing properties. It is rich in antioxidants and can help to protect the skin from environmental damage. Olive oil is also known to be beneficial for hair care as it can help to nourish the hair and scalp.

Jojoba oil: Jojoba oil is a light, non-greasy oil that is similar to the natural oil produced by the skin, making it easily absorbable. It is rich in vitamin E and can help to soothe dry and irritated skin. It is also known to be beneficial for hair care as it can help to moisturize the hair and scalp.

Sweet Almond oil: Sweet Almond oil is a light and easily absorbed oil that is rich in fatty acids, vitamins and minerals. It is known for its moisturizing properties and can help to soothe dry and irritated skin. It is also known to be beneficial for hair care as it can help to strengthen hair and prevent breakage.

Grapeseed oil: Grapeseed oil is lightweight and non-greasy, making it easily absorbable. It is rich in antioxidants and can help to protect the skin from environmental damage. It is also known to be beneficial for hair care as it can help to nourish the hair and scalp.

These are some of the fixed oils that are commonly used in herbal cosmetics. They are all natural and safe ingredients that can help to improve the health and appearance of the skin, hair, and teeth. These oils are used as base in many products such as creams, lotions, balms, hair oils, lip balms, and many others.

Fixed oils, also known as carrier oils, are vegetable oils that are derived from the seeds, nuts, or kernels of plants. They are used as a base for many herbal cosmetic products such as lotions, creams, and massage oils. Some examples of fixed oils that are commonly used in herbal cosmetics include:

Sweet Almond oil: Sweet Almond oil is a light, non-greasy oil that is extracted from the kernels of almonds. It is known for its emollient properties, which means it can help to moisturize and soothe the skin. It is also rich in vitamins and minerals, making it a popular ingredient in cosmetics for dry, sensitive, and mature skin.

Jojoba oil: Jojoba oil is a light, non-greasy oil that is extracted from the jojoba seed. It is similar to the natural oil produced by the skin, making it an excellent ingredient for use in cosmetics for all skin types. It is also known for its moisturizing properties and can help to reduce the appearance of wrinkles and fine lines.

Grapeseed oil: Grapeseed oil is a light, non-greasy oil that is extracted from the seeds of grapes. It is known for its astringent properties, which means it can help to tighten and tone the skin. It is also rich in antioxidants and vitamins, making it a popular ingredient in cosmetics for oily or acne-prone skin.

Olive oil: Olive oil is a heavy oil that is extracted from the fruit of the olive tree. It is known for its emollient properties, which means it can help to moisturize and soothe the skin. It is also rich in antioxidants and vitamins, making it a popular ingredient in cosmetics for dry, mature, and sensitive skin.

Coconut oil: Coconut oil is a heavy oil that is extracted from the meat of the coconut. It is known for its emollient properties, which means it can help to moisturize and soothe the skin. It is also rich in antioxidants and vitamins, making it a popular ingredient in cosmetics for all skin types, particularly dry or damaged skin.

These are a few examples of fixed oils that are commonly used in herbal cosmetics. They are all natural and safe ingredients that can be used as a base for many cosmetics products. They also have other benefits such as moisturizing, soothing, and protecting the skin. The choice of which oil to use will depend on the desired properties and the type of product that is being made. It's also important to use pure, high-quality ingredients.

Raw Materials of Herbal Origin: waxes

Waxes are a type of natural ingredient that is often used in herbal cosmetics to provide a protective barrier on the skin and to help thicken and stabilize the product. Some examples of waxes that are commonly used in herbal cosmetics include:

Beeswax: Beeswax is a natural wax that is extracted from the honeycomb of bees. It is known for its emollient properties, which means it can help to moisturize and soothe the skin. It also helps to thicken and stabilize products and create a barrier on the skin.

Carnauba wax: Carnauba wax is a natural wax that is extracted from the leaves of the carnauba palm tree. It is known for its thickening properties, which makes it an excellent ingredient for use in lip balms, creams, and lotions. It also helps to create a protective barrier on the skin.

Candelilla wax: Candelilla wax is a natural wax that is extracted from the leaves of the candilla plant. It is known for its emollient properties, which means it can help to moisturize and soothe the skin. It also helps to thicken and stabilize products and create a barrier on the skin.

Jojoba wax: Jojoba wax is derived from the jojoba seed, it is a non-greasy and easily absorbed wax that is known for its moisturizing properties. It is similar to the natural oil produced by the skin, making it an excellent ingredient for use in lip balms, creams, and lotions.

These waxes can be used in a variety of herbal cosmetic products such as lip balms, creams, lotions, salves and many others. They are all natural and safe ingredients that can help to improve the health and appearance of the skin. They also help to thicken and stabilize the products, and provide a protective barrier on the skin to lock in moisture.

Raw Materials of Herbal Origin: Gums

Gums are natural substances that are extracted from plants and are used as thickeners, emulsifiers, and stabilizers in cosmetics and other personal care products. Some examples of gums that are commonly used in herbal cosmetics include:

Xanthan gum: Xanthan gum is a natural gum that is extracted from fermented sugar. It is known for its thickening properties and is often used to provide structure and consistency to cosmetics such as lotions and creams. It also helps to create stable emulsions by binding oil and water-based ingredients together.

Guar gum: Guar gum is a natural gum that is extracted from the seeds of the guar plant. It is known for its thickening properties and is often used to provide structure and consistency to cosmetics such as lotions and creams. It also helps to create stable emulsions by binding oil and water-based ingredients together.

Carrageenan: Carrageenan is a natural gum that is extracted from red seaweed. It is known for its thickening properties and is often used to provide structure and consistency to cosmetics such as lotions and creams. It also helps to create stable emulsions by binding oil and water-based ingredients together.

Gum Arabic: Gum Arabic is a natural gum that is extracted from the acacia tree. It is known for its thickening properties and is often used to provide structure and consistency to cosmetics such as lotions and creams. It also helps to create stable emulsions by binding oil and water-based ingredients together.

These gums are all natural and safe ingredients that can be used to thicken and stabilize cosmetics and other personal care products. They also help to create stable emulsions by binding oil and water-based ingredients together. The choice of which gum to use will depend on the desired properties and the type of product that is being made.

Raw Materials of Herbal Origin: Colours

Colours are natural pigments that are extracted from plants and are used to add visual appeal to cosmetics and other personal care products. Some examples of colours that are commonly used in herbal cosmetics include:

Beetroot powder: Beetroot powder is a natural colour that is extracted from the beetroot plant. It is known for its bright red color and is often used as a natural alternative to synthetic red pigments in cosmetics such as lip balms, lipsticks, and blushes.

Turmeric powder: Turmeric powder is a natural colour that is extracted from the turmeric plant. It is known for its bright yellow color and is often used as a natural alternative to synthetic yellow pigments in cosmetics such as face masks, scrubs, and body lotions.

Annatto seed: Annatto seed is a natural colour that is extracted from the Annatto plant. It is known for its bright orange color and is often used as a natural alternative to synthetic orange pigments in cosmetics such as lip balms, lipsticks, and eyeshadows.

Activated Charcoal: Activated Charcoal is a natural colour that is extracted from charcoal. It is known for its deep black color and is often used as a natural alternative to synthetic black pigments in cosmetics such as mascaras, eyeliners, and soaps.

Alkanet root: Alkanet root is a natural color that is extracted from the root of the alkanet plant. It is known for its deep purple color and is often used as a natural alternative to synthetic purple pigments in cosmetics such as lip balms, lipsticks, and eyeshadows.

These colours are all natural and safe ingredients that can be used to add visual appeal to cosmetics and other personal care products. They are a great alternative to synthetic pigments and dyes, and are gaining popularity in the cosmetics industry. They are used in a variety of herbal cosmetic products such as lip balms, lipsticks, mascaras, face masks, scrubs, and many others. They can also be used as natural alternative for food coloring.

Raw Materials of Herbal Origin: Perfumes

Perfumes are fragrant compounds that are used to add a pleasant scent to cosmetics and other personal care products. Some examples of perfumes that are commonly used in herbal cosmetics include:

Essential oils: Essential oils are concentrated plant extracts that are known for their distinct fragrances. Some popular essential oils used in perfumes include lavender, rose, jasmine, lemon, peppermint, and many others. They are commonly used in aromatherapy and perfumes due to their natural and pleasing fragrances.

Absolutes: Absolutes are similar to essential oils, but are extracted using solvents rather than steam distillation. Some popular absolutes used in perfumes include jasmine, rose, and neroli. They have a more potent and longer lasting fragrance than essential oils.

Hydrosols: Hydrosols are a by-product of essential oil distillation, they are aqueous solutions that contain the water-soluble components of the plant. Some popular hydrosols used in perfumes include rosewater, lavender water, and chamomile water. They are less concentrated than essential oils and absolutes, but still have a pleasant fragrance.

CO2 Extracts: CO2 extracts are similar to essential oils, but are extracted using liquid CO2 instead of steam. Some popular CO2 extracts used in perfumes include vanilla, cinnamon, and ginger. They are known for their natural, potent and long lasting fragrance.

These are a few examples of perfumes that are commonly used in herbal cosmetics. They are all natural and safe ingredients that can be used to add a pleasant scent to cosmetics and other personal care products. Essential oils, absolutes, hydrosols, and CO2 extracts are all natural alternatives to synthetic fragrances and are gaining popularity in the cosmetics industry. They can be used in a variety of herbal cosmetic products such as perfumes, body sprays, lotions, creams, and many others. They can also be used in aromatherapy to promote relaxation and well-being.

It's worth noting that when using essential oils, absolutes and CO2 extracts in perfumes, it's important to use them in low concentrations, as they are highly concentrated and can cause skin irritation if used in high concentrations. It's also important to use pure, high-quality ingredients and to patch test the product before using it on a larger area of the skin.

In addition to being used as fragrances, essential oils, absolutes, hydrosols, and CO2 extracts can also provide other benefits such as soothing, moisturizing, and protecting the skin. For example, lavender essential oil is known for its soothing properties, while peppermint essential oil is known for its cooling and refreshing properties.

Raw Materials of Herbal Origin: Herbs

Herbs are the dried or fresh leaves, flowers, roots, or other parts of plants that are used for medicinal or cosmetic purposes. Some examples of herbs that are commonly used in herbal cosmetics include:

Calendula: Calendula is a herb that is known for its soothing and anti-inflammatory properties. It is often used in cosmetics for sensitive, irritated or damaged skin. It is commonly used in lotions, creams, and ointments.

Chamomile: Chamomile is a herb that is known for its soothing and anti-inflammatory properties. It is often used in cosmetics for sensitive, irritated or damaged skin. It is commonly used in lotions, creams, and ointments.

Comfrey: Comfrey is a herb that is known for its soothing and healing properties. It is often used in cosmetics for damaged or irritated skin. It is commonly used in lotions, creams, and ointments.

Elderflower: Elderflower is a herb that is known for its astringent and toning properties. It is often used in cosmetics for oily or acne-prone skin. It is commonly used in toners, cleansers and face masks.

Marshmallow: Marshmallow is a herb that is known for its soothing and moisturizing properties. It is often used in cosmetics for dry or sensitive skin. It is commonly used in lotions, creams, and ointments.

These are a few examples of herbs that are commonly used in herbal cosmetics. They are all natural and safe ingredients that can be used to provide various benefits to the skin such as soothing, moisturizing, and protecting the skin. Herbs can be used in a variety of herbal cosmetic products such as lotions, creams, ointments, face masks, and many others. They can also be used in herbal teas, tinctures and capsules for medicinal purposes.

Raw Materials of Herbal Origin:protective agents

Protective agents are ingredients that are used to protect the skin from damage caused by environmental factors such as UV radiation, pollution, and other environmental toxins. Some examples of protective agents that are commonly used in herbal cosmetics include:

Vitamin E: Vitamin E is an antioxidant that is known for its ability to protect the skin from damage caused by UV radiation and environmental toxins. It is often used in cosmetics to help prevent wrinkles, fine lines, and age spots.

Green tea extract: Green tea extract is a powerful antioxidant that is known for its ability to protect the skin from damage caused by UV radiation and environmental toxins. It is often used in cosmetics to help prevent wrinkles, fine lines, and age spots.

Aloe vera: Aloe vera is a plant that is known for its soothing and moisturizing properties. It is also known for its ability to protect the skin from damage caused by UV radiation and environmental toxins. It is often used in cosmetics to help prevent wrinkles, fine lines, and age spots.

Shea butter: Shea butter is a plant butter that is known for its ability to protect the skin from damage caused by UV radiation and environmental toxins. It is also known for its moisturizing properties. It is often used in cosmetics to help prevent wrinkles, fine lines, and age spots.

Zinc oxide: Zinc oxide is a mineral that is known for its ability to protect the skin from damage caused by UV radiation. It is often used in cosmetics to help prevent sunburn, wrinkles, fine lines, and age spots.

These are a few examples of protective agents that are commonly used in herbal cosmetics. They are all natural and safe ingredients that can be used to protect the skin from damage caused by environmental factors such as UV radiation, pollution, and other environmental toxins. They can be used in a variety of herbal cosmetic products such as sunscreens, moisturizers, and anti-aging creams. They can also be used in other personal care products such as lip balms, hair care products, and makeup.

In addition to providing protection from environmental factors, many of these protective agents also have additional benefits such as moisturizing, soothing and anti-aging properties. For example, Vitamin E is known for its moisturizing properties while Aloe vera is known for its soothing properties.

Raw Materials of Herbal Origin: Bleaching Agents

Bleaching agents are ingredients that are used to lighten the skin or hair. Some examples of bleaching agents that are commonly used in herbal cosmetics include:

Lemon juice: Lemon juice is a natural bleaching agent that is known for its ability to lighten the skin and hair. It is often used in cosmetics to lighten age spots, freckles, and other dark spots on the skin.

Horseradish: Horseradish is a natural bleaching agent that is known for its ability to lighten the hair. It is often used in hair care products to lighten hair and as a natural alternative to synthetic hair dyes.

Chamomile: Chamomile is a herb that is known for its ability to lighten hair and skin. It is often used in cosmetics to lighten age spots, freckles, and other dark spots on the skin.

Turmeric: Turmeric is a herb that is known for its ability to lighten hair and skin. It is often used in cosmetics to lighten age spots, freckles, and other dark spots on the skin.

Kojic acid: Kojic acid is a natural bleaching agent that is derived from mushrooms. It is known for its ability to lighten the skin and is often used in cosmetics to lighten age spots, freckles, and other dark spots on the skin.

It's important to note that bleaching agents can cause skin irritation, sensitivity and allergic reactions. It's also important to use it only after patch testing, and not to use them for a long period of time. It's also important to use pure, high-quality ingredients, and to be aware that these ingredients may not have the same effect on all skin types.

Raw Materials of Herbal Origin: Antioxidants

Antioxidants are ingredients that are used to protect the skin from damage caused by free radicals. Some examples of antioxidants that are commonly used in herbal cosmetics include:

Vitamin C: Vitamin C is a powerful antioxidant that is known for its ability to protect the skin from damage caused by free radicals. It is often used in cosmetics to help prevent wrinkles, fine lines, and age spots.

Vitamin E: Vitamin E is an antioxidant that is known for its ability to protect the skin from damage caused by free radicals. It is often used in cosmetics to help prevent wrinkles, fine lines, and age spots.

Green tea extract: Green tea extract is a powerful antioxidant that is known for its ability to protect the skin from damage caused by free radicals. It is often used in cosmetics to help prevent wrinkles, fine lines, and age spots.

Coenzyme Q10: Coenzyme Q10 is an antioxidant that is known for its ability to protect the skin from damage caused by free radicals. It is often used in cosmetics to help prevent wrinkles, fine lines, and age spots.

Resveratrol: Resveratrol is a powerful antioxidant that is found in grapes and other fruits. It is known for its ability to protect the skin from damage caused by free radicals. It is often used in cosmetics to help prevent wrinkles, fine lines, and age spots.

These are a few examples of antioxidants that are commonly used in herbal cosmetics. They are all natural and safe ingredients that can be used to protect the skin from damage caused by free radicals. Antioxidants can be used

Skin care products:

Coconut oil

Coconut oil is a versatile oil that is extracted from the kernel of the coconut fruit. It is produced by crushing copra, which is the dried kernel, and contains about 60-65% oil. Coconut oil is rich in glycerides of lower chain fatty acids and has a melting point between 24 to 25°C (75-76°F), making it easily used in liquid or solid forms. It is commonly used in cooking and baking. Coconut oil is also highly valued for its skincare benefits, it is an excellent moisturizer and skin softener.

Sunflower oil is a non-volatile oil obtained from sunflower seeds, which is extracted from the Helianthus annuus plant, a member of the Asteraceae family. It contains beneficial compounds such as lecithin, tocopherols, carotenoids, and waxes. Sunflower oil has smoothing properties and is non-comedogenic. It is a simple and cost-effective oil that has been used for generations in a wide variety of face and body care products

Jojoba oil is a mixture of long-chain, linear liquid wax esters that are extracted from the seeds of the desert shrub Simmondsia chinensis, which belongs to the family Simmondsiaceae. This oil is easily refined to remove any odor or color, it is oxidatively stable and is often used in cosmetics as a moisturizer and as a carrier oil for exotic fragrances. Jojoba oil is similar to human sebum and is used to replenish what skin and hair lose. Sebum protects and moisturizes the skin and hair, but it can be stripped away by chemicals, pollutants, sun, and the aging process, resulting in dry skin and hair. Jojoba oil replenishes sebum and restores the skin and hair's natural pH balance.

Olive oil is a fixed oil obtained from the fruits of Olea europaea, a plant that belongs to the Oleaceae family. The major components of olive oil are triolein, tripalmitin, trilinolein, tristearate, monosterate, triarachidin, squalene, β-sitosterol, and tocopherol. It is used as a skin and hair conditioner in cosmetics such as lotions, shampoos, and other products. Olive oil is also a powerful fatty acid penetration enhancer, which means it helps other ingredients penetrate deeper into the skin for better results.

Aloe vera is a herbal plant species that belongs to the liliaceae family. It is found only in cultivation, and not found in nature, although closely related aloes do occur in northern Africa. Aloe vera is often used in cosmetics due to its ability to heal, moisturize, and soften the skin. To use it, simply cut one of the leaves to extract the soothing gel. The gel contains amino acids like leucine, isoleucine, and saponin glycosides that provide cleansing action, as well as vitamins A, C, E, B, choline, B12 and folic acid that provide antioxidant activity.

Hair care Products:

Amla, also known as Indian gooseberry, is the fruit of a small leafy tree (Emblica officinalis) that grows throughout India. It is known for its high vitamin C content and the precious oil that is extracted from its seeds and pulp, which is used as a treatment for hair and scalp problems. Amla is also used in traditional medicine for eye syndromes, hair loss, and children's ailments.

Rose is a plant that has four species that are mainly used for oil production: Rosa damascena Mill., R. gallica L., R. moschata Herrm. and R. centifolia L. Rose oil and rose water have many therapeutic effects. Rose oil is known to soothe the mind and heal depression, grief, nervous stress and tension. It also helps to heal wounds and improve skin health.

Eucalyptus oil is produced by steam distillation from the leaves of various Eucalyptus species such as E. cinerea F. Muell., E. baueriana F. Muell., E. smithii R. T. Baker, E. bridgesiana R. T. Baker, E. microtheca F. Muell., E. foecunda Schau., E. pulverulenta Sims, E. propinqua Deane and Maiden, E. erythrocorys F. Muell. etc. There are around 700 different species of Eucalyptus in the world, of which at least 500 produce a type of essential oil. They are widely used in the preparation of liniments, inhalants, cough syrups, ointments, toothpaste and also as pharmaceutical flavors. The European Pharmacopoeia monograph for Eucalyptus oil sports a chromatographic profile: 1,8-cineole (eucalyptol; not less than 70%), limonene (4-12%), α-pinene (2-8%), α-phellandrene (less than 1.5%), β-pinene (less than 0.5%), camphor (less than 0.1%)

Grape seed is known to promote the proliferation of hair follicle cells in vitro and possess remarkable hair cycle converting activity from the telogen phase to anagen phase in vivo.

Ginkgo biloba leaf extract also promotes hair regrowth through combined effects on proliferation and apoptosis of the cells in the hair follicle, thus suggesting potential as a hair tonic.

Aloe gel is traditionally used for hair loss and for improvement in hair growth following alopecia. Aloenin is the major constituent responsible for promoting hair growth without irritating the skin. Aloe vera gel is rich in vitamins and minerals that can nourish the hair and scalp, helping to promote healthy hair growth.

Oral Hygiene Products

Clove oil has a long history of use in traditional medicine, particularly in oral care. Its main active component eugenol, has anesthetic and antiseptic properties, making it useful for toothaches, sore throats and other types of oral pain.

The essential oil of eucalyptus, has also been shown to have antimicrobial properties against common oral bacteria, making it a useful ingredient in mouthwash and other oral care products.

Moringa oleifera root is also used in traditional medicine for toothache, due to its antibacterial properties against common oral bacteria.

Meswak has been shown to have anti-inflammatory and antimicrobial properties. It is rich in phytochemical compounds such as tannins, flavonoids, and alkaloids that have been found to inhibit the growth of bacteria such as Streptococcus mutans and Porphyromonas gingivalis, which are known to cause plaque and gingivitis. Additionally, the chewing sticks are believed to stimulate the production of saliva, which helps to neutralize acids in the mouth, and also massage the gums, promoting blood flow and reducing inflammation. Overall, Meswak is a traditional, natural, and effective alternative for oral hygiene and can be used as an adjunctive therapy for the treatment of dental caries and periodontal disease.

Green Tea (Camellia sinensis):

Green tea contains polyphenol contents comprising catechin (C), epicatechin (EC), gallocatechin (GC), epigallocatechin (EGC) epicatechingallate (ECG), and epi-gallocatechingallate. It is anti-inflammatory, antibacterial, anti-viral. Used in the treatment of periodontal disease. Marigold (Calendula officinalisL.) It is native to the Mediterranean areas. It is used for the treatment of skin disorders and pain, to facilitate healing after oral surgery and in oral cavity inflammations. It also has anti-edematous activity. Grape Seed Extract: Grape seed extract contains pro-anthocyanidins (PA) which are potent antioxidants and are known to possess anti-inflammatory, antibacterial and immune-stimulating effects. It has been reported to strengthen collagen-based tissues by increasing collagen cross-links. In a study conducted to determine re-mineralizing effects of grape seed extract on artificial root caries, results showed that it is a promising natural agent for noninvasive root caries therapy. Papaine: Papaine is a proteolytic enzyme that comes from the latex of the leaves and fruits of the green adult papaya. It has anti-inflammatory, bacteriostatic, and bactericidal characteristics and is effective against gram-positive and gram-negative organisms. Similar to human pepsin, papaine acts as a chemical debridement anti-inflammatory agent, which does not damage healthy tissues and accelerates cicatrization process. Papaine acts only in infected tissue as it lacks a plasmatic antiprotease called α-1-anti-trypsin.

VIII

Herbal Excipients & Formulations

Herbal excipients are non-active ingredients that are added to herbal formulations to improve their quality, stability and efficacy. They serve various functions such as binding, bulking, lubricating, and preserving the herbal products. They can be derived from natural sources such as plants, minerals, and animal products, or they can be synthetic. Thus.herbal excipients are substances of natural origin that are used in the formulation of herbal medicines to enhance their stability, appearance, and functionality.

Common herbal excipients

Cellulose: Cellulose is a common excipient used in herbal products as a binding agent. It helps to form a cohesive mass and improves the flowability of powders. Microcrystalline cellulose, a refined form of cellulose, is used in tablet formulations.

Lactose: Lactose is a sugar that is used as a filler in herbal products. It is a good excipient for tablet and capsule formulations as it is easily compressible and helps to bind ingredients together.

Starch: Starch is another common excipient used in herbal products. It is a natural polysaccharide that is used as a filler, binder, and disintegrant in tablets and capsules.

Magnesium stearate: Magnesium stearate is a lubricant that is used to prevent ingredients from sticking to manufacturing equipment. It also helps to improve the flowability of powders and enhances the compressibility of tablets.

Silica: Silica is a mineral that is used as an excipient in herbal products. It is used as an anti-caking agent to prevent ingredients from sticking together. It also helps to improve the flowability of powders.

Gelatin: Gelatin is a protein derived from animal collagen. It is used as a binder and gelling agent in capsules and other soft gel formulations.

Glycerin: Glycerin is a sweet-tasting, colorless and odorless liquid that is used as a humectant in herbal products. It helps to maintain moisture content and prevent the product from drying out.

Herbal excipients play an important role in the formulation of herbal products as they can improve the quality, stability, and efficacy of the final product. They are also useful in masking unpleasant tastes and odors of the active ingredients. It is important to note that excipients should be used in appropriate amounts and be safe for human consumption.

Sources of some common herbal excipients

Cellulose: Cellulose is derived from plant cell walls, and can be obtained from various sources such as wood, cotton, and hemp. Microcrystalline cellulose is a refined form of cellulose that is obtained from wood pulp.

Lactose: Lactose is a sugar that is derived from milk. It is obtained from whey, a byproduct of cheese production.

Starch: Starch is derived from various plants such as corn, potato, and rice.

Magnesium stearate: Magnesium stearate is a salt that is derived from stearic acid and magnesium hydroxide. It can be obtained from animal and vegetable fats and oils.

Silica: Silica is a mineral that is derived from various sources such as sand, quartz, and flint.

Gelatin: Gelatin is a protein that is derived from collagen, which is found in the skin, bones, and connective tissues of animals. It is commonly obtained from pork and beef.

Glycerin: Glycerin is a byproduct of soap production, it is also can be derived from vegetable oils and fats by a process of hydrolysis

It's worth noting that, some of the excipients can be obtained from natural sources, while others are synthetically produced. It's also worth noting that some excipients like gelatin from animal source may not be suitable for certain dietary restrictions.

Significance of Herbal Excipients

Herbal excipients are considered to be safer than synthetic excipients, as they are derived from natural sources and are less likely to cause adverse reactions.

Herbal excipients also contribute to the therapeutic properties of the final formulation and can help to enhance the bioavailability of the active ingredients.

They also help to improve the palatability of the formulation and make it more acceptable to the patient.

Types of Herbal Excipients:

Colorants: natural colorants such as turmeric, saffron, and beetroot are used to improve the appearance of the formulation.

Sweeteners: natural sweeteners such as honey, licorice, and stevia are used to improve the taste of the formulation.

Binders: natural binders such as ghee, honey, and mucilage are used to hold the ingredients together and form a stable preparation.

Diluents: natural diluents such as rice powder, wheat flour, and talc are used to increase the bulk of the formulation and make it easier to handle.

Viscosity builders: natural viscosity builders such as guar gum, xanthan gum, and karaya gum are used to increase the thickness of the formulation.

Disintegrants: natural disintegrants such as cellulose, starch, and clay are used to help the formulation break down and release the active ingredients quickly.

Flavors & perfumes: natural flavors and perfumes such as peppermint, fennel, and sandalwood are used to improve the taste and smell of the formulation.

Herbal excipients play an important role in the formulation of herbal medicines. They contribute to the therapeutic properties of the final formulation, enhance the bioavailability of the active ingredients, improve the palatability of the formulation, and make it more acceptable to the patient. They are derived from natural sources and are less likely to cause adverse reactions than synthetic excipients.

Herbal Formulations

Herbal formulations are the combinations of different herbal ingredients that are used to treat various health conditions.

Conventional Herbal Formulations

Syrups: Herbal syrups are liquid preparations that are usually sweetened and used to treat various ailments such as cough and cold. They are easy to administer and are suitable for both children and adults.

Mixtures: Herbal mixtures are a combination of different herbs and are used to treat various ailments. They are usually administered in the form of a powder, which is mixed with water or other liquids before consumption.

Tablets: Herbal tablets are solid preparations that are used to treat various ailments. They are easy to swallow and can be used to deliver a specific dose of the active ingredient.

Novel Dosage Forms

Phytosomes: Phytosomes are a newer type of herbal formulation that involves the complexation of herbal extracts with phosphatidylcholine. This improves the bioavailability of the active ingredients and makes the formulation more effective.

There are many other types of herbal formulations that are available in the market, each with its own unique characteristics and benefits. Some other examples include:

Capsules: Herbal capsules are similar to tablets but are enclosed in a gelatine or vegetable cellulose shell. They are easy to swallow and can be used to deliver a specific dose of the active ingredient.

Ointments and creams: Herbal ointments and creams are used to treat various skin conditions. They are applied topically to the skin and can be used to deliver a specific dose of the active ingredient.

Tinctures: Herbal tinctures are liquid preparations that are made by steeping herbs in alcohol or glycerine. They are easy to administer and can be used to deliver a specific dose of the active ingredient.

Infusions and decoctions: Herbal infusions and decoctions are made by steeping herbs in hot water. They are used to treat various ailments and can be consumed as a tea.

Poultices and compresses: Herbal poultices and compresses are used to treat various ailments and are applied topically to the skin.

Herbal Syrups

Herbal syrups are liquid preparations that are usually sweetened and used to treat various ailments such as cough and cold. They are easy to administer and are suitable for both children and adults.

Preparation of Herbal Syrups

The preparation of herbal syrups involves the extraction of the active ingredients from the herbs using a suitable solvent such as water, ethanol or glycerol.

The extract is then mixed with a sweetening agent such as honey or sugar and other excipients such as thickening agents and preservatives to form the final syrup.

Administration

Herbal syrups are usually administered orally, and the recommended dosage is usually 1-2 teaspoons, 2-3 times a day.

They can be taken directly or mixed with water or other liquids before consumption.

Advantages of Herbal Syrups:

Herbal syrups are easy to administer and are suitable for both children and adults

They are usually sweetened, which makes them more palatable and acceptable to the patient

They can be used to deliver a specific dose of the active ingredient

They can be stored for a long time, which makes them more convenient to use.

Disadvantages of Herbal Syrups:

Herbal syrups often contain high amounts of sugar, which can be harmful to people with diabetes

They also contain preservatives and other excipients, which may cause allergic reactions in some people.

Herbal syrups can be made from a single herb or a combination of herbs, depending on the intended use.

Herbs that are commonly used to make syrups include thyme, elderberry, licorice, and horehound.

Herbal syrups can be used to treat a wide range of conditions, including respiratory issues, sore throat, cough, cold, flu, and even fever.

Herbal syrups can also be used as a preventive measure, as they can boost the immune system and help to protect against infections.

Some herbal syrups also contain expectorant properties, which can help to clear mucus from the lungs and relieve chest congestion.

The sweetening agents and other excipients used in herbal syrups can also play a therapeutic role. For example, honey is known to have antimicrobial properties and can help to soothe a sore throat.

Some herbal syrups can also be used as a natural remedy for sleep disturbances, as they can help to promote relaxation and calm the mind.

Herbal syrups can be made at home or purchased from a reputable health food store or herbalist. When making syrups at home, it is important to use high-quality herbs and to follow proper preservation techniques to ensure the syrup stays fresh for as long as possible.

Some herbal syrups may have side effects and interact with other medications, so it is important to consult with a healthcare practitioner before taking any herbal syrups, especially if you have a health condition or are taking other medications.

Herbal syrups are generally considered safe for most people when taken as directed, but it is important to follow the recommended dosage and not to exceed the recommended amount.

Herbal mixtures

These are a combination of different herbs and are used to treat various ailments. They are usually administered in the form of a powder, which is mixed with water or other liquids before consumption.

Preparation of Herbal Mixtures

The preparation of herbal mixtures involves the combination of different herbs in specific proportions to create a formula that addresses a specific health condition.

The herbs are usually dried and powdered before being mixed together.

The mixture can be further processed by adding excipients such as binders and preservatives to improve the shelf life and stability of the mixture.

Administration:

Herbal mixtures are usually administered orally, and the recommended dosage is usually 2-3 grams, 2-3 times a day.

They are usually mixed with water or other liquids before consumption.

Advantages of Herbal Mixtures:

Herbal mixtures can be tailored to address specific health conditions and can be more effective than single herb preparations.

They are easy to administer and are suitable for both children and adults

They can be used to deliver a specific dose of the active ingredient.

Disadvantages of Herbal Mixtures:

Herbal mixtures can be more complex to prepare than single herb preparations.

They may contain preservatives and other excipients, which may cause allergic reactions in some people.

Some herbs may interact with each other, or may not be appropriate for certain individuals, so it is important to consult with a healthcare practitioner before taking any herbal mixtures, especially if you have a health condition.

Herbal mixtures can be made from a variety of herbs, depending on the intended use and the health condition being treated.

Herbs that are commonly used in herbal mixtures include ginger, turmeric, cinnamon, licorice, and ashwagandha.

Herbal mixtures can be used to treat a wide range of conditions, including digestive issues, respiratory problems, stress, anxiety, and fatigue.

Some herbal mixtures are also used as a natural remedy for skin conditions, such as eczema, psoriasis, and acne.

Herbal mixtures can also be used as a natural remedy for sleep disturbances, as they can help to promote relaxation and calm the mind.

The combination of different herbs in herbal mixtures can have a synergistic effect, which can enhance the overall effectiveness of the mixture.

Herbal mixtures can also be used as a preventive measure, as they can boost the immune system and help to protect against infections.

Some herbal mixtures also contain adaptogenic properties, which can help the body adapt to stress and improve overall health.

Herbal mixtures can be made at home or purchased from a reputable health food store or herbalist. When making mixtures at home, it is important to use high-quality herbs and to follow proper preservation techniques to ensure the mixture stays fresh for as long as possible.

Herbal tablets

Herbal tablets are solid dosage forms that are made from a combination of herbs and other excipients, such as binders, fillers, and disintegrants. They are usually administered orally and are a convenient form of herbal medicine.

Preparation of Herbal Tablets:

The preparation of herbal tablets involves the combination of different herbs in specific proportions to create a formula that addresses a specific health condition.

The herbs are usually dried and powdered before being mixed together with excipients such as binders, fillers, and disintegrants to form a mixture.

The mixture is then compressed into tablets using a tablet press.

Administration:

Herbal tablets are usually administered orally, and the recommended dosage is usually one or two tablets, 2-3 times a day.

Advantages of Herbal Tablets:

Herbal tablets are easy to administer and are suitable for both children and adults.

They are convenient to transport and can be stored for long periods of time.

They can be used to deliver a specific dose of the active ingredient.

Disadvantages of Herbal Tablets:

Herbal tablets may contain excipients, which may cause allergic reactions in some people.

Herbal tablets may not be as effective as other forms of herbal medicine, such as tinctures or decoctions, because the process of compression can damage the active ingredients.

Thus, herbal tablets are solid dosage forms that are made from a combination of herbs and other excipients. They are usually administered orally and are a convenient form of herbal medicine. However, herbal tablets may contain excipients, which may cause allergic reactions in some people and may not be as effective as other forms of herbal medicine. It is important to consult with a healthcare practitioner before taking any herbal tablets, especially if you have a health condition or are taking other medications, and to follow the recommended dosage. It is also important to purchase tablets from a reliable source, to check for any potential contamination or expired products and to store them properly.

Novel dosage forms

Novel dosage forms such as phytosomes, are a newer form of herbal medicine that utilizes advanced technology to improve the bioavailability and effectiveness of herbal compounds.

Phytosomes :

Phytosomes are a type of novel dosage form that involves the complexation of herbal compounds with phospholipids. This allows for better absorption and bioavailability of the herbal compounds in the body. -Phytosomes are known to improve the solubility and stability of herbal compounds, which makes them more effective. Phytosomes are also known to improve the bioavailability of herbal compounds, which can lead to more potent therapeutic effects.

Phytosomes can be made from a variety of herbs, depending on the intended use and the health condition being treated.

Herbs that are commonly used in phytosomes include milk thistle, ginkgo biloba, curcumin, and resveratrol.

Phytosomes can be used to treat a wide range of conditions, including liver disorders, cognitive decline, and inflammation.

Phytosomes have been shown to be more effective than traditional herbal preparations in treating certain conditions, due to their improved bioavailability.

The phospholipid complex in phytosomes can also help to protect the herbal compounds from degradation in the gut, which can further enhance their effectiveness.

Phytosomes can also be used in combination with other herbal or conventional treatments, to enhance their effectiveness.

Phytosomes are considered a more advanced form of herbal medicine, and may be more appropriate for certain patients or health conditions, such as those with poor nutrient absorption.

Phytosomes can be purchased from reputable health food stores or herbalists, but it is important to purchase them from a reliable source and to check for any potential contamination or expired products.

Phytosomes are usually stored in a cool, dry place, away from light and moisture. It is important to follow the storage instructions provided on the product to ensure the phytosomes remain fresh and effective.

Preparation of Phytosomes:

The preparation of phytosomes involves the complexation of herbal compounds with phospholipids, which can be done through a variety of methods, including sonication, micelle formation, and liposomes.

The resulting phytosomes can be formulated into various dosage forms, including capsules, tablets, and liquid formulations.

Administration:

Phytosomes are usually administered orally and the recommended dosage will depend on the specific product and the health condition being treated.

Advantages of Phytosomes:

Phytosomes have been shown to improve the bioavailability and effectiveness of herbal compounds, which can lead to more potent therapeutic effects.

They can also improve the solubility and stability of herbal compounds, which makes them more effective.

Phytosomes are considered safe, and have a good safety profile.

Disadvantages of Phytosomes:

Phytosomes are still a relatively new form of herbal medicine, and more research is needed to fully understand their potential benefits and risks.

Phytosomes are a more complex and expensive form of herbal medicine, and may not be readily available or accessible to everyone.

IX

Evaluation of Herbal Drugs

The World Health Organization (WHO) is a specialized agency of the United Nations that is responsible for international public health. One of the key areas of focus for the WHO is the evaluation and approval of herbal drugs for use. The WHO has established guidelines and processes for evaluating herbal drugs, which are used by countries around the world to ensure that herbal drugs are safe, effective, and of good quality.

The International Council for Harmonisation of Technical Requirements for Pharmaceuticals for Human Use (ICH) is an organization that brings together regulatory authorities and the pharmaceutical industry to develop guidelines and standards for the development, registration, and post-approval of pharmaceuticals. The ICH guidelines are intended to promote the mutual acceptance of data and to reduce the need for redundant testing of drugs. Like WHO, ICH also focuses on the evaluation and approval of herbal drugs for use.

The World Health Organization (WHO) guidelines

The WHO guidelines for the assessment of the quality of herbal drugs are a key component of the organization's overall guidelines for evaluating and approving herbal drugs for use. These guidelines are intended to ensure that herbal drugs are safe, effective, and of good quality before they are made available to the public.

Assessment of the quality of herbal drugs

Guidelines mentions the use of monographs. Monographs are detailed, scientifically-based documents that provide information on the quality, safety, and efficacy of a particular herbal drug. The WHO has developed monographs for a wide range of herbal drugs, and these monographs serve as a reference for regulatory authorities and manufacturers when assessing the quality of a particular herbal drug.

Assessment of crude plant materials and plant preparations

The WHO guidelines require that crude plant materials and plant preparations be tested for purity, potency, and safety before they can be used to manufacture finished products. This includes testing for contaminants such as heavy metals, pesticides, and microorganisms.

Specific requirements for the assessment of finished herbal products

These requirements include testing for purity, potency, and safety, as well as assessing the product's stability over time. Stability testing is important to ensure that the finished product will remain safe and effective throughout its shelf life.

Documentation of safety data

This includes data from laboratory and animal studies, as well as data from clinical trials. The WHO guidelines require that safety data be collected over a long period of use and at different doses to ensure that the herbal drug is safe for both short-term and long-term use.

Another important component of the WHO guidelines for the assessment of the safety of herbal drugs is the implementation of pharmacovigilance practices. This includes monitoring for adverse events and side effects, both during clinical trials and after the herbal drug has been approved for use. The WHO guidelines require that manufacturers and regulatory authorities report any adverse events or side effects to the WHO, so that the safety of the herbal drug can be continuously monitored.

The WHO guidelines also include specific requirements for the assessment of dose-related efficacy. This includes determining the optimal dose of the herbal drug for its intended use, as well as assessing the safety and efficacy of the herbal drug at different doses.

The WHO guidelines also require that there is evidence for the indications of the herbal drugs, this includes traditional use, scientific literature, and information from experts in traditional medicine.

The WHO guidelines also take into account the safety of combination products and the intended use, which are the conditions and population that the herbal drug is intended to treat.

The WHO guidelines also require that consumer package information and promotion materials accurately reflect the safety and efficacy of the herbal drug.

SOPs

The World Health Organization (WHO) has developed a set of standard operating procedures (SOPs) for the evaluation and approval of herbal drugs. These SOPs provide clear guidance on the steps and criteria required for the assessment of the safety, efficacy, and quality of herbal drugs. The WHO SOPs are intended to ensure that herbal drugs are safe, effective, and of good quality before they are made available to the public, and that they are based on scientific principles and data.

The WHO SOPs include guidelines for:

The preclinical evaluation of herbal drugs, which includes laboratory and animal testing to determine the safety and efficacy of the herbal drug.

The clinical evaluation of herbal drugs, which includes testing the drug in human subjects to assess its safety and efficacy. The WHO SOPs provide guidance on the design, conduct, and reporting of clinical trials.

The review and evaluation of herbal drugs, which includes a review of the data by the WHO Expert Review Panel (ERP) and a recommendation to the WHO on whether the herbal drug should be approved for use.

The approval of herbal drugs, which includes the final decision about whether a herbal drug should be approved for use by the WHO.

The post-approval surveillance of herbal drugs, which includes monitoring the safety and efficacy of the drug after it has been approved for use.

The registration and regulation of herbal drugs, which includes guidance on the steps and criteria required for the registration and regulation of herbal drugs by national regulatory authorities.

The assessment of quality of herbal drugs, which includes guidelines for the use of monographs, the assessment of crude plant materials and plant preparations, and the assessment of finished products, including stability testing.

The assessment of safety of herbal drugs, which includes documentation of safety data, implementation of pharmacovigilance practices, assessment of dose-related efficacy, evidence for indications, safety of combination products, intended use, consumer package information, and promotion materials.

The WHO SOPs are continuously updated and revised to reflect the latest scientific and medical knowledge, and to ensure that they are in line with international standards and best practices. WHO SOPs are also followed by regulatory authorities and manufacturers worldwide, which helps in promoting the mutual acceptance of data and reducing the need for redundant testing of drugs.

Assessment of the quality of herbal drugs

The World Health Organization (WHO) provides guidelines for the assessment of the quality of herbal drugs, which includes a list of quality control parameters that should be considered. These parameters include:

Identification: Herbal drugs should be correctly identified based on botanical, chemical, and/or biological criteria.

Purity: Herbal drugs should be free from contaminants, such as heavy metals, pesticides, and microorganisms.

Potency: Herbal drugs should contain the appropriate levels of active ingredients.

Microbial and chemical contamination: Herbal drugs should be free from microbial and chemical contamination.

Residual solvents: Herbal drugs should not contain residual solvents that are harmful to human health.

Heavy metals: Herbal drugs should not contain heavy metals that are harmful to human health.

Pesticides: Herbal drugs should not contain pesticides that are harmful to human health.

Residue on ignition: Herbal drugs should not contain a significant amount of inorganic residue.

Loss on drying: Herbal drugs should not contain a significant amount of water or solvent residue.

Foreign matter: Herbal drugs should not contain significant amounts of foreign matter.

Assay: Herbal drugs should contain the appropriate levels of active ingredients as specified in the monograph.

Extract ratio: Herbal drugs should have the appropriate ratio of extract to drug material.

pH value: Herbal drugs should have the appropriate pH value.

Ash value: Herbal drugs should not contain a significant amount of ash.

Water-soluble extractive value: Herbal drugs should have the appropriate water-soluble extractive value.

Ethanol-soluble extractive value: Herbal drugs should have the appropriate ethanol-soluble extractive value.

Total ash value: Herbal drugs should not contain a significant amount of total ash.

Loss on drying at 105°C: Herbal drugs should not contain a significant amount of water or solvent residue.

Sulphated ash value: Herbal drugs should not contain a significant amount of sulfated ash.

Identification test: Herbal drugs should be correctly identified based on botanical, chemical, and/or biological criteria.

Foreign organic matter: Herbal drugs should not contain significant amounts of foreign organic matter.

Stability: Herbal drugs should be stable over time and maintain their safety and efficacy throughout the shelf life.

It is worth noting that the above list is not exhaustive, and the WHO guidelines may include other parameters based on the specific characteristics of the herbal drug being evaluated.

ICH Guidelines for herbal Drug Evaluation

The International Council for Harmonisation of Technical Requirements for Pharmaceuticals for Human Use (ICH) has developed guidelines for the evaluation of herbal drugs, which are known as the ICH Guidelines for Herbal Drug Evaluation. The guidelines are intended to provide a harmonized approach to the evaluation and registration of herbal drugs, and to support the mutual acceptance of data among regulatory authorities worldwide.

Introduction: The ICH guidelines for herbal drug evaluation provide a framework for the evaluation of the safety, efficacy, and quality of herbal drugs. The guidelines are intended to ensure that herbal drugs are safe, effective, and of good quality before they are made available to the public.

Objectives The objectives of the ICH guidelines for herbal drug evaluation are: -

To provide a harmonized approach to the evaluation and registration of herbal drugs.

To support the mutual acceptance of data among regulatory authorities worldwide.

To ensure that herbal drugs are safe, effective, and of good quality before they are made available to the public.

Four Broad Categories of ICH Q, S, E and M The ICH guidelines for herbal drug evaluation are divided into four broad categories: Quality (Q), Safety (S), Efficacy (E), and Manufacturing (M). Each of these categories includes specific guidelines and requirements that must be met before a herbal drug can be approved for use.

Quality (Q) guidelines focus on the assessment of the purity, potency, and safety of herbal drugs.

Safety (S) guidelines focus on the assessment of the safety of herbal drugs, including the documentation of safety data, implementation of pharmacovigilance practices, and assessment of dose-related efficacy.

Efficacy (E) guidelines focus on the assessment of the efficacy of herbal drugs, including the evidence for indications, safety of combination products, intended use, consumer package information, and promotion materials.

Manufacturing (M) guidelines focus on the assessment of the quality of herbal drugs, including the use of monographs, the assessment of crude plant materials and plant preparations, and the assessment of finished products, including stability testing. These guidelines cover the good manufacturing practices (GMP) for the production of herbal drugs, and ensure that the herbal drugs are manufactured to a consistent and high-quality standard.

Steps in the ICH drug evaluation process:

The ICH guidelines for herbal drug evaluation include several steps in the evaluation process, which include:

Preclinical evaluation: This includes laboratory and animal testing to determine the safety and efficacy of the herbal drug.

Clinical evaluation: This includes testing the drug in human subjects to assess its safety and efficacy.

Review and evaluation: This includes a review of the data by the ICH Expert Review Panel (ERP) and a recommendation to the ICH on whether the herbal drug should be approved for use.

Approval: This includes the final decision about whether a herbal drug should be approved for use by the ICH.

Post-approval surveillance: This includes monitoring the safety and efficacy of the drug after it has been approved for use.

Criteria for approving a drug for use:

The ICH guidelines for herbal drug evaluation include specific criteria that must be met before a herbal drug can be approved for use. These criteria include the demonstration of safety and efficacy in laboratory and animal studies, as well as in human clinical trials. The ICH also requires that the herbal drug is manufactured to a consistent and high-quality standard, and that it is free from contaminants and meets the appropriate purity, potency, and safety standards.

Examples of drugs that have gone through the ICH evaluation process: It is worth noting that as the ICH guidelines are mainly followed by pharmaceutical companies and regulatory authorities, it is not possible to provide examples of drugs that have gone through the ICH evaluation process.

Quality (Q) guidelines

Quality (Q) guidelines are an important component of the ICH guidelines for herbal drug evaluation. These guidelines focus on the assessment of the purity, potency, and safety of herbal drugs to ensure that they meet the appropriate standards before they are made available to the public. The quality guidelines are intended to ensure that herbal drugs are free from contaminants, such as heavy metals, pesticides, and microorganisms, and that they contain the appropriate levels of active ingredients.

Identification: Herbal drugs should be correctly identified based on botanical, chemical, and/or biological criteria. This helps to ensure that the correct plant species is used for the preparation of the herbal drug and that it does not contain any contaminants or substitutions that could be harmful to human health.

Purity: Herbal drugs should be free from contaminants, such as heavy metals, pesticides, and microorganisms. This helps to ensure that the herbal drug is safe for human consumption and does not contain any harmful substances that could cause adverse effects.

Potency: Herbal drugs should contain the appropriate levels of active ingredients. This helps to ensure that the herbal drug is effective for its intended use and that it contains the appropriate amount of active ingredients to produce the desired therapeutic effect.

Microbial and chemical contamination: Herbal drugs should be free from microbial and chemical contamination. This helps to ensure that the herbal drug is safe for human consumption and does not contain any harmful microorganisms or chemicals that could cause adverse effects.

Residual solvents: Herbal drugs should not contain residual solvents that are harmful to human health. This helps to ensure that the herbal drug is safe for human consumption and does not contain any harmful solvents that could cause adverse effects.

Heavy metals: Herbal drugs should not contain heavy metals that are harmful to human health. This helps to ensure that the herbal drug is safe for human consumption and does not contain any harmful heavy metals that could cause adverse effects.

Pesticides: Herbal drugs should not contain pesticides that are harmful to human health. This helps to ensure that the herbal drug is safe for human consumption and does not contain any harmful pesticides that could cause adverse effects.

Residue on ignition: Herbal drugs should not contain a significant amount of inorganic residue. This helps to ensure that the herbal drug is safe for human consumption and does not contain any harmful inorganic substances that could cause adverse effects.

Loss on drying: Herbal drugs should not contain a significant amount of water or solvent residue. This helps to ensure that the herbal drug is safe for human consumption and does not contain any harmful water or solvent residues that could cause adverse effects.

Foreign matter: Herbal drugs should not contain significant amounts of foreign matter. This helps to ensure that the herbal drug is safe for human consumption and does not contain any harmful foreign materials that could cause adverse effects.

Assay: Herbal drugs should contain the appropriate levels of active ingredients as specified in the monograph. This helps to ensure that the herbal drug is effective for its intended use and contains the appropriate amount of active ingredients to produce the desired therapeutic effect.

Extract ratio: Herbal drugs should have the appropriate ratio of extract to drug material. This helps to ensure that the herbal drug is effective for its intended use and contains the appropriate amount of active ingredients to produce the desired therapeutic effect.

pH value: Herbal drugs should have the appropriate pH value. This helps to ensure that the herbal drug is safe for human consumption and does not contain any harmful pH levels that could cause adverse effects.

Ash value: Herbal drugs should not contain a significant amount of ash. This helps to ensure that the herbal drug is safe for human consumption and does not contain any harmful ash that could cause adverse effects.

Water-soluble extractive value: Herbal drugs should have the appropriate water-soluble extractive value. This helps to ensure that the herbal drug is effective for its intended use and contains the appropriate amount of active ingredients to produce the desired therapeutic effect.

Ethanol-soluble extractive value: Herbal drugs should have the appropriate ethanol-soluble extractive value. This helps to ensure that the herbal drug is effective for its intended use and contains the appropriate amount of active ingredients to produce the desired therapeutic effect.

Total ash value: Herbal drugs should not contain a significant amount of total ash. This helps to ensure that the herbal drug is safe for human consumption and does not contain any harmful ash that could cause adverse effects.

Loss on drying at 105°C: Herbal drugs should not contain a significant amount of water or solvent residue. This helps to ensure that the herbal drug is safe for human consumption and does not contain any harmful water or solvent residues that could cause adverse effects.

Sulphated ash value: Herbal drugs should not contain a significant amount of sulfated ash. This helps to ensure that the herbal drug is safe for human consumption and does not contain any harmful sulfated ash that could cause adverse effects.

Identification test: Herbal drugs should be correctly identified based on botanical, chemical, and/or biological criteria. This helps to ensure that the correct plant species is used for the preparation of the herbal drug and that it does not contain any contaminants or substitutions that could be harmful to human health.

Foreign organic matter: Herbal drugs should not contain significant amounts of foreign organic matter. This helps to ensure that the herbal drug is safe for human consumption

Safety (S) guidelines

Safety (S) guidelines are an important component of the ICH guidelines for herbal drug evaluation. These guidelines focus on the assessment of the safety of herbal drugs, including the documentation of safety data, implementation of pharmacovigilance practices, and assessment of dose-related efficacy. The safety guidelines are intended to ensure that herbal drugs are safe for human consumption, and that any potential adverse effects are identified and mitigated before the drug is made available to the public.

Documentation of safety data: Herbal drugs should have sufficient safety data to demonstrate their safety for human consumption. This includes data from preclinical studies, clinical trials, and post-market surveillance.

Implementation of pharmacovigilance practices: Herbal drugs should have a pharmacovigilance plan in place to monitor their safety post-market. This includes the collection and reporting of adverse event data, and the implementation of risk management measures to mitigate any potential safety risks.

Assessment of dose-related efficacy: Herbal drugs should be tested at various doses to determine the appropriate dose for human consumption and to assess any potential dose-related adverse effects.

Long-term use: Herbal drugs should be evaluated for safety in long-term use. This is important as some adverse effects may not be immediately apparent, but could occur with prolonged use.

Combination products: Herbal drugs that are combined with other herbal or chemical products should be evaluated for safety and efficacy of the combination.

Consumer package information: Herbal drugs should have clear and accurate information on the package to inform the consumer about the intended use, dosage, and potential side effects.

Promotion materials: Herbal drugs should not be promoted in a way that misleads the consumer, exaggerates the benefits or hides the risks associated with the herbal drug.

Efficacy (E) guidelines

Efficacy guidelines focus on the assessment of the efficacy of herbal drugs, including the evidence for indications, safety of combination products, intended use, consumer package information, and promotion materials.

Efficacy (E) guidelines are an important component of the ICH guidelines for herbal drug evaluation. These guidelines focus on the assessment of the efficacy of herbal drugs, including the evidence for indications, safety of combination products, intended use, consumer package information, and promotion materials. The efficacy guidelines are intended to ensure that herbal drugs are effective for their intended use, and that any potential benefits and risks are accurately communicated to the public.

Evidence for indications: Herbal drugs should have sufficient evidence to demonstrate their effectiveness for the indications for which they are intended to be used. This includes data from preclinical studies, clinical trials, and post-market surveillance.

Safety of combination products: Herbal drugs that are combined with other herbal or chemical products should be evaluated for safety and efficacy of the combination.

Intended use: Herbal drugs should be clearly labeled and marketed for their intended use, and not for any unproven or misleading indications.

Consumer package information: Herbal drugs should have clear and accurate information on the package to inform the consumer about the intended use, dosage, and potential benefits.

Promotion materials: Herbal drugs should not be promoted in a way that misleads the consumer, exaggerates the benefits or hides the risks associated with the herbal drug.

Clinical studies: Herbal drugs should have appropriate clinical studies conducted to determine their safety and efficacy in humans.

Evidence of efficacy: Herbal drugs should have appropriate evidence of efficacy from clinical studies, observational studies or traditional use.

Manufacturing (M) guidelines

Manufacturing guidelines focus on the assessment of the quality of herbal drugs, including the use of monographs, the assessment of crude plant materials and plant preparations, and the assessment of finished products, including stability testing. These guidelines cover the good manufacturing practices (GMP) for the production of herbal drugs, and ensure that the herbal drugs are manufactured to a consistent and high-quality standard

Use of monographs: Herbal drugs should be manufactured in accordance with established monographs, which provide detailed information on the appropriate standards for the preparation, composition, and quality of the herbal drug.

Assessment of crude plant materials and plant preparations: Herbal drugs should be made from appropriate and high-quality crude plant materials and plant preparations. This includes assessment of the botanical identity, purity, and potency of the raw materials used in the production of the herbal drug.

Good manufacturing practices (GMP): Herbal drugs should be manufactured in accordance with GMP, which includes guidelines for facility design, equipment and utensils, production and process controls, laboratory controls, packaging, labeling, storage and distribution, and complaint handling.

Stability testing: Herbal drugs should be tested for stability to ensure that they maintain their purity, potency and safety over time. This includes testing the herbal drugs under different storage conditions and at different intervals to ensure that they remain stable throughout their shelf life.

Quality control: Herbal drugs should be manufactured under the supervision of a qualified quality control unit to ensure that the product meets the appropriate standards for purity, potency, and safety.

Traceability: Herbal drugs should have a system in place for traceability, which allows for the identification of all raw materials, intermediates, and finished products and their suppliers, manufacturers and distributors.

Comparison of WHO and ICH Guidelines

A. Overview of similarities and differences between the WHO and ICH guidelines

Both WHO and ICH guidelines provide standards for the evaluation of drugs, including herbal drugs.

WHO guidelines focus on the assessment of the quality, safety, and efficacy of herbal drugs, while ICH guidelines also include guidelines for good manufacturing practices (GMP) and stability testing.

WHO guidelines are primarily intended for use in low- and middle-income countries, while ICH guidelines are intended for use in developed countries.

Discussion of the pros and cons of each set of guidelines

WHO guidelines may be more accessible and applicable for countries with limited resources for drug evaluation.

ICH guidelines may provide more comprehensive standards for the evaluation of drugs, including GMP and stability testing.

WHO guidelines may be more flexible and adaptable to different cultural and traditional uses of herbal drugs.

ICH guidelines may provide more stringent standards for the safety and efficacy of herbal drugs.

Analysis of which guidelines may be more appropriate for certain types of drugs or situations

WHO guidelines may be more appropriate for the evaluation of herbal drugs used in traditional medicine in low- and middle-income countries.

ICH guidelines may be more appropriate for the evaluation of herbal drugs intended for use in developed countries.

In situations where strict standards for GMP and stability testing are necessary, ICH guidelines may be more appropriate.

In situations where the cultural and traditional use of herbal drugs is an important consideration, WHO guidelines may be more appropriate.

It is worth noting that the above analysis is general and the appropriate guidelines may depend on specific circumstances and characteristics of the herbal drug being evaluated. It is also important to note that both WHO and ICH guidelines are continuously updated to reflect new scientific and rV. Implications of the WHO and ICH guidelines for the future of drug evaluation A. The WHO and ICH guidelines provide important standards for the evaluation of drugs, including herbal drugs. As more research is conducted on the safety and efficacy of herbal drugs, these guidelines will continue to evolve and provide updated standards for drug evaluation.

The use of herbal drugs is becoming increasingly popular worldwide, and the WHO and ICH guidelines will play an important role in ensuring that these drugs are safe and effective for human consumption.

The WHO guidelines, in particular, may be important for the evaluation of herbal drugs used in traditional medicine in low- and middle-income countries, while the ICH guidelines may be more appropriate for the evaluation of herbal drugs intended for use in developed countries.

In the future, it will be important for the WHO and ICH guidelines to continue to evolve and adapt to new scientific and regulatory developments, and to take into account cultural and traditional uses of herbal drugs.

X

The Indian system of Medicine

The Indian systems of medicine, also known as AYUSH, consist of various traditional healing practices and therapies that have been used in India for centuries. The AYUSH systems include Ayurveda, Unani, Siddha, and Homeopathy, as well as therapies such as Yoga and Naturopathy. These systems have evolved over time and have become an integral part of Indian culture and tradition.

In 1995, the Indian government established a separate department of Indian systems of medicine and homeopathy (ISM&H) to ensure the optimal development and propagation of AYUSH. The main goal of the ISM &H department is to promote and preserve these traditional systems of medicine, and to make the more accessible to the general public. The department also works to improve the quality of AYUSH education and research, and to develop new and innovative forms of AYUSH treatments.

The use of AYUSH systems has grown in popularity in recent years due to the increasing recognition of their effectiveness and safety. These systems are based on natural, holistic approaches to health and wellness, and they have been shown to be effective in treating a wide range of health conditions. The Indian government also encourages the integration of AYUSH with modern medical practices to provide a holistic care to the patients.

Ayurveda

Introduction

Definition of Ayurveda: Ayurveda is an ancient system of medicine that originated in India. It is based on the belief that health and wellness depend on a delicate balance between the mind, body, and spirit. The word "Ayurveda" is derived from the two Sanskrit words "ayus" meaning life and "veda" meaning knowledge, hence Ayurveda means "the knowledge of life." Ayurveda aims to promote good health, prevent illnesses and treat diseases through a combination of natural therapies, including herbal medicine, diet, and lifestyle changes.

Brief history of Ayurveda: Ayurveda is one of the oldest systems of medicine in the world, with roots dating back to ancient India. It is believed to have originated in the Vedic period, around 6000-3000 BCE. The principles and practices of Ayurveda were first written down in the ancient texts known as the Vedas. Over the centuries, Ayurveda has been developed and refined by Indian sages and scholars. Ayurveda spread to Southeast Asia, Central Asia, and parts of China, where it influenced the development of traditional Chinese medicine. Today, Ayurveda is widely practiced in India and other parts of the world as a complementary and alternative medicine.

In recent years, Ayurveda has gained recognition and popularity around the world for its effectiveness and safety. It is also being integrated with modern medical practices, providing a holistic care to the patients. Ayurveda is currently recognized and practiced in India and many other countries around the world.The use of herbal medicines and diet in maintaining health: Ayurveda places a strong emphasis on the use of natural remedies, such as herbs, minerals, and animal products, to treat various ailments. These remedies are believed to work by restoring balance to the doshas. Ayurveda also emphasizes the importance of a healthy diet that is tailored to an individual's unique dosha balance. This includes the use of seasonal and locally available foods, as well as a balance of different tastes and qualities.

Vedas and Ayurveda-Connection between the Vedas and Ayurveda & Basic principles of Ayurveda

Connection between the Vedas and Ayurveda: The Vedas are ancient texts that are considered the foundation of Hinduism, and they contain many references to Ayurveda. The Vedas describe the principles of Ayurveda in detail, including the concept of the three doshas (vata, pitta, and kapha), which are considered the fundamental principles of Ayurvedic physiology. The Vedas also contain information about the use of herbs, minerals, and other natural substances for medicinal purposes. Additionally, the Vedas contain descriptions of surgical procedures, which form the basis of Ayurvedic surgery.

Basic principles of Ayurveda: Ayurveda is based on the belief that health and wellness depend on a delicate balance between the mind, body, and spirit. The three doshas (vata, pitta, and kapha) are considered the fundamental principles of Ayurveda, and each person is believed to have a unique combination of doshas. According to Ayurveda, imbalances in the doshas can lead to illnesses, and restoring balance to the doshas is the key to good health. Ayurveda also emphasizes the importance of maintaining a healthy diet and lifestyle, and using natural therapies such as herbal medicine, massage, and yoga to promote health and prevent illness.

Tridosha and Panchakarma

Explanation of the Tridosha concept: In Ayurveda, the Tridosha concept refers to the three fundamental principles that govern the functioning of the human body, namely vata, pitta, and kapha. These three doshas are believed to be responsible for all physical and mental processes in the body. Vata is related to movement, pitta is related to metabolism and temperature, and kapha is related to structure and lubrication. Each individual has a unique combination of these doshas and the balance of these doshas is considered to be the key to good health. An imbalance in the doshas can lead to various illnesses, and restoring balance is the goal of Ayurvedic treatment.

Panchakarma treatment in Ayurveda: Panchakarma is a purification and detoxification process that is an integral part of Ayurvedic medicine. The word "Panchakarma" means "five actions" and refers to five different procedures that are used to cleanse the body and restore balance to the doshas. The five procedures are: Vamana (therapeutic emesis), Virechana (therapeutic purgation), Basti (therapeutic enema), Nasya (nasal therapy) and Raktamokshana (bloodletting). These treatments are used to eliminate toxins from the body and restore balance to the doshas. They are usually done under the guidance of an Ayurvedic practitioner and are tailored to the individual's needs.

Ayurvedic Dosage Forms

Ayurvedic medicine uses a variety of dosage forms, including herbal decoctions, powders, tablets, capsules, and oils. Herbal decoctions are made by boiling herbs in water to extract the active ingredients. Powders are made by drying and grinding the herbs into a fine powder. Tablets and capsules are made by compacting powders into a solid form. Oils are made by infusing herbs in a base oil. Ayurvedic medicine also uses medicated ghees and honey, which are used as a vehicle to administer drugs.

Standardisation of Ayurvedic preparations: Standardisation of Ayurvedic preparations is a process of ensuring that the Ayurvedic medicine has a consistent quality and potency. It involves the identification and quantification of the active ingredients present in the medicine. The standardisation of Ayurvedic preparations is important for ensuring the safety and efficacy of the medicine. The standardisation process includes the use of quality control methods such as HPTLC, HPLC and other modern analytical techniques. The standardisation of Ayurvedic preparations is essential to ensure the safety and efficacy of the medicine, and it helps to establish the therapeutic properties of Ayurvedic medicines.

Ayurvedic Treatment

Types of Ayurvedic treatment: Ayurvedic treatment includes a wide range of natural therapies, including herbal medicine, diet, and lifestyle changes, as well as physical therapies such as massage, yoga, and meditation. Ayurvedic practitioners may also recommend Panchakarma, a purification and detoxification process, as a treatment. Ayurvedic treatment is tailored to the individual's needs and is based on the principles of the Tridosha. Ayurvedic practitioners use the concept of the Tridosha to diagnose illness and develop an individualized treatment plan.

Common ailments treated with Ayurveda: Ayurveda is used to treat a wide variety of illnesses, including common ailments such as headaches, colds, and flu, as well as chronic conditions such as asthma, diabetes, and heart disease. Ayurveda is also used to treat mental and emotional conditions such as anxiety, depression, and stress. Additionally, Ayurveda is used to support overall wellness and prevent illness. Some of the common ailments treated with Ayurveda include:

Digestive disorders like acidity, constipation, and indigestion

Respiratory disorders like asthma and bronchitis

Musculoskeletal disorders like arthritis and back pain

Skin disorders like eczema, psoriasis, and acne

Stress-related disorders like anxiety and depression

Gynecological disorders like PCOS, infertility, and menstrual irregularities

Metabolic disorders like obesity and diabetes

Chronic diseases like cancer, heart diseases and autoimmune disorders.

It is important to note that Ayurveda should not be used as a substitute for conventional medical treatment, but rather as a complementary therapy. It's always best to consult with a qualified Ayurvedic practitioner before starting any Ayurvedic treatment.

Siddha:

Introduction

Definition of Siddha medicine: Siddha medicine is an ancient system of medicine that originated in South India. It is based on the belief that good health and wellness depend on a balance between the body and mind, and the natural forces of the universe. The word "Siddha" means "perfection" or "accomplishment" and refers to the ultimate goal of achieving good health and longevity. Siddha medicine uses a combination of herbal medicines, minerals, and animal products, and also emphasizes on spiritual healing and yoga practices.

Brief history of Siddha medicine: Siddha medicine has its origins in ancient South India, and is believed to have originated around 2nd century BC. The principles and practices of Siddha were first written down in the ancient texts known as the Siddha literature. Over the centuries, Siddha medicine has been developed and refined by Siddha sages and scholars. Siddha medicine spread to other parts of India and Southeast Asia, where it influenced the development of traditional medicine. Today, Siddha medicine is widely practiced in South India and other parts of the world as a complementary and alternative medicine.

Basic Principles of Siddha

The concept of the five elements: Siddha medicine is based on the belief that the human body and the universe are made up of five elements: earth, water, fire, air, and ether. These elements are believed to interact with each other and to be present in different proportions in the body. Imbalances in the elements are believed to cause illness, and restoring balance to the elements is the key to good health.

The human body and its relationship to the five elements: According to Siddha medicine, the human body is made up of the five elements, each of which is associated with specific organs and functions. Earth is associated with the bones and muscles, water with the blood and lymph, fire with the metabolism and digestion, air with the breath and movement, and ether with the senses and consciousness. The balance of these elements in the body is believed to be essential for good health.

Role of the three doshas (vatha, pitha, kapha) in Siddha medicine: In Siddha medicine, the three doshas (vatha, pitha, kapha) are considered the fundamental principles that govern the functioning of the human body, similar to Ayurveda. These three doshas are believed to be responsible for all physical and mental processes in the body. Vatha is related to movement, pitha is related to metabolism and temperature, and kapha is related to structure and lubrication. Each individual has a unique combination of these doshas and the balance of these doshas is considered to be the key to good health. An imbalance in the doshas can lead to various illnesses, and restoring balance is the goal of Siddha treatment.

Herbs used in Siddha System

Overview of the herbs commonly used in Siddha medicine: Siddha medicine uses a wide variety of herbs, including those that are native to South India, as well as some that are imported from other parts of the world. Some of the commonly used herbs in Siddha medicine include: Guggulu, Shankhapushpi, Vidanga, Guduchi, Licorice, Vidanga, Vidanga, Shankhapushpi, Turmeric, licorice, and many more.

Properties and uses of key herbs in Siddha system: Many of the herbs used in Siddha medicine have medicinal properties that have been studied and documented. For example, Guggulu is used to treat joint pain and inflammation, Shankhapushpi is used to improve cognitive function, Guduchi is used to improve immunity and Vidanga is used to treat skin disorders.

Methods of preparation and administration of herbal remedies: Herbs are used in Siddha medicine in a variety of forms, including decoctions, powders, and oils. Decoctions are made by boiling herbs in water to extract the active ingredients. Powders are made by drying and grinding the herbs into a fine powder. Oils are made by infusing herbs in a base oil. Herbs are also used to make medicated ghees and honey, which are used as a vehicle to administer drugs. The method of preparation and administration of herbal remedies depends on the type of herb and the condition being treated. It's always best to consult with a qualified Siddha practitioner before starting any herbal treatment.

Siddha Treatment

Overview of the different types of treatment used in Siddha medicine: Siddha treatment includes a wide range of natural therapies, including herbal medicine, diet, and lifestyle changes, as well as physical therapies such as massage, yoga, and meditation. Siddha practitioners may also recommend Panchakarma, a purification and detoxification process, as a treatment. Siddha treatment is tailored to the individual's needs and is based on the principles of the Tridosha. Siddha practitioners use the concept of the Tridosha to diagnose illness and develop an individualized treatment plan.

Common ailments treated with Siddha medicine: Siddha medicine is used to treat a wide variety of illnesses, including common ailments such as headaches, colds, and flu, as well as chronic conditions such as asthma, diabetes, and heart disease. Siddha medicine is also used to treat mental and emotional conditions such as anxiety, depression, and stress. Additionally, Siddha medicine is used to support overall wellness and prevent illness.

Some of the common ailments treated with Siddha medicine

Digestive disorders like acidity, constipation, and indigestion

Respiratory disorders like asthma and bronchitis

Musculoskeletal disorders like arthritis and back pain

Skin disorders like eczema, psoriasis, and acne

Stress-related disorders like anxiety and depression

Gynecological disorders like PCOS, infertility, and menstrual irregularities

Metabolic disorders like obesity and diabetes

Chronic diseases like cancer, heart diseases and autoimmune disorders.

It is important to note that Siddha medicine should not be used as a substitute for conventional medical treatment, but rather as a complementary therapy. It's always best to consult with a qualified Siddha practitioner before starting any Siddha treatment.

Importance of diet and lifestyle in Siddha treatment: Diet and lifestyle are considered to be an important aspect of Siddha treatment. Siddha practitioners recommend a diet thatis balanced and tailored to the individual's needs, taking into account their individual body type, dosha balance, and the condition being treated. A healthy diet in Siddha system is one that is rich in fresh fruits and vegetables, whole grains, and lean protein. It's also important to avoid processed foods and foods that are high in sugar, salt, and unhealthy fats. Lifestyle changes, such as regular exercise, yoga and meditation, are also recommended to improve overall health and prevent illness. The goal of Siddha treatment is not only to alleviate symptoms but also to promote overall wellness and prevent future illnesses.

Unani

Definition of Unani medicine: Unani medicine is an ancient system of medicine that originated in Greece and was later developed in the Islamic world. It is based on the belief that good health depends on the balance of the four humors, blood, phlegm, yellow bile, and black bile in the body. Unani medicine uses natural substances, mostly herbs, minerals, and animal products, and it emphasizes on the use of diet and lifestyle changes to maintain a balance of the four humors.

Brief history of Unani medicine: Unani medicine has its origins in ancient Greece and was developed by Greek physicians such as Hippocrates and Galen. The principles and practices of Unani were later adopted and developed by the Islamic scholars and were spread to other parts of the world, especially the Middle East and South Asia. Unani medicine reached its peak in the Islamic Golden Age and was later integrated into the traditional medicine systems of India, Pakistan, and Bangladesh. Today, Unani medicine is widely practiced in South Asia, the Middle East, and other parts of the world as a complementary and alternative medicine.

Basic Principles of Unani

The concept of the four humors: Unani medicine is based on the belief that the human body and the universe are made up of four humors: blood, phlegm, yellow bile, and black bile. These humors are believed to interact with each other and to be present in different proportions in the body. Imbalances in the humors are believed to cause illness, and restoring balance to the humors is the key to good health.

The human body and its relationship to the four humors: According to Unani medicine, the human body is made up of the four humors, each of which is associated with specific organs and functions. Blood is associated with the heart and circulation, phlegm with the brain and lungs, yellow bile with the liver and gallbladder, and black bile with the spleen and stomach. The balance of these humors in the body is believed to be essential for good health.

Role of the three temperaments (sanguine, phlegmatic, and melancholic) in Unani medicine: In Unani medicine, the three temperaments (sanguine, phlegmatic, and melancholic) are considered to be the fundamental principles that govern the functioning of the human body. Each individual is believed to have a unique combination of these temperaments, which determine their physical and mental characteristics. Sanguine is related to a balanced and healthy state, Phlegmatic is related to a cold and moist stateand Melancholic is related to a hot and dry state. An imbalance in the temperaments can lead to various illnesses, and restoring balance is the goal of Unani treatment.

Herbs used in Unani System

Overview of the herbs commonly used in Unani medicine: Unani medicine uses a wide variety of herbs, including those that are native to the Middle East and South Asia, as well as some that are imported from other parts of the world. Some of the commonly used herbs in Unani medicine include:

Senna, Cumin, Fenugreek, Licorice, Ginger, Turmeric, Clove, and many more.

Properties and uses of key herbs in Unani system: Many of the herbs used in Unani medicine have medicinal properties that have been studied and documented. For example, Senna is used as a laxative, Cumin is used to improve digestion, Fenugreek is used to lower cholesterol, and Licorice is used to soothe the throat.

Methods of preparation and administration of herbal remedies: Herbs are used in Unani medicine in a variety of forms, including decoctions, powders, and oils. Decoctions are made by boiling herbs in water to extract the active ingredients. Powders are made by drying and grinding the herbs into a fine powder. Oils are made by infusing herbs in a base oil. Herbs are also used to make medicated syrups and jams, which are used as a vehicle to administer drugs. The method of preparation and administration of herbal remedies depends on the type of herb and the condition being treated. It's always best to consult with a qualified Unani practitioner before starting any herbal treatment.

Unani Treatment

Overview of the different types of treatment used in Unani medicine: Unani treatment includes a wide range of natural therapies, including herbal medicine, diet, and lifestyle changes, as well as physical therapies such as massage, yoga, and meditation. Unani practitioners may also recommend Panchkarma, a purification and detoxification process, as a treatment. Unani treatment is tailored to the individual's needs and is based on the principles of the four humors and three temperaments. Unani practitioners use the concept of the four humors and three temperaments to diagnose illness and develop an individualized treatment plan.

Common ailments treated with Unani medicine: Unani medicine is used to treat a wide variety of illnesses, including common ailments such as headaches, colds, and flu, as well as chronic conditions such as asthma, diabetes, and heart disease. Unani medicine is also used to treat mental and emotional conditions such as anxiety, depression, and stress. Additionally, Unani medicine is used to support overall wellness and prevent illness.

Some of the common ailments treated with Unani medicine

Digestive disorders like acidity, constipation, and indigestion

Respiratory disorders like asthma and bronchitis

Musculoskeletal disorders like arthritis and back pain

Skin disorders like eczema, psoriasis, and acne

Stress-related disorders like anxiety and depression

Gynecological disorders like PCOS, infertility, and menstrual irregularities

Metabolic disorders like obesity and diabetes

Chronic diseases like cancer, heart diseases and autoimmune disorders.

It is important to note that Unani medicine should not be used as a substitute for conventional medical treatment, but rather as a complementary therapy. It's always best to consult with a qualified Unani practitioner before starting any Unani treatment.

Importance of diet and lifestyle in Unani treatment: Diet and lifestyle are considered to be an important aspect of Unani treatment. Unani practitioners recommend a diet that is balanced and tailored to the individual's needs, taking into account their individual body type, humor balance, and the condition being treated. A healthy diet in Unani system is one that is rich in fresh fruits and vegetables, whole grains, and lean protein. It's also important to avoid processed foods

Unani system of diagnosis: Unani practitioners use a combination of physical examination, observation, and patient history to diagnose illness. The practitioner will assess the patient's pulse, tongue, and eyes to determine the balance of the four humors. They will also ask about the patient's symptoms, medical history, and lifestyle habits to gain a complete understanding of the patient's condition.

Unani system of therapeutics: Unani therapeutics is based on the principle of restoring balance to the four humors. Unani practitioners use a variety of natural therapies to achieve this, including herbal medicine, diet, and lifestyle changes. They may also recommend physical therapies such as massage and yoga to promote health and well-being. Unani practitioners may also use Panchkarma, a purification and detoxification process, as a treatment. The goal of Unani treatment is not only to alleviate symptoms but also to promote overall wellness and prevent future illnesses.

It's important to note that Unani medicine is a holistic approach and it's always best to consult with a qualified Unani practitioner before starting any treatment.

Homeopathy

Introduction

Definition of Homeopathy: Homeopathy is a system of medicine that is based on the principle of "like cures like". This principle states that a substance that causes symptoms in a healthy person can be used to treat similar symptoms in a sick person. Homeopathy uses highly diluted substances, which are believed to stimulate the body's own healing response. The goal of homeopathic treatment is to not only alleviate symptoms but also to address the underlying cause of the illness and promote overall wellness.

Brief history of Homeopathy: Homeopathy was developed in the late 18th century by a German physician named Samuel Hahnemann. Hahnemann was dissatisfied with the medical practices of his time, which often relied on treatments that were harsh and caused unpleasant side effects. He began experimenting with using highly diluted substances to treat illness, and he observed that these dilutions were still able to produce a therapeutic effect. Hahnemann's ideas were met with skepticism by many of his contemporaries, but he was able to gain a following and homeopathy soon became popular throughout Europe and America. Today, homeopathy is considered a complementary and alternative medicine and it's widely used in many countries around the world. Homeopathy is based on the "Law of Similars" which is also known as "Like cures Like" and it's used to treat a wide range of illnesses, including chronic and acute conditions. Homeopathy is known for its gentle, non-toxic and non-invasive approach and it's considered safe for people of all ages including infants, children, pregnant women and elderly.

Theory and Principle of Homeopathy

The principle of "like cures like": The fundamental principle of homeopathy is "like cures like," which states that a substance that can cause symptoms in a healthy person can be used to treat similar symptoms in a sick person. This principle is based on the idea that the body has the ability to heal itself and that the symptoms of an illness are the body's attempt to do so. For example, if a person is experiencing symptoms of a cold, such as a runny nose and sneezing, a homeopath may prescribe a homeopathic remedy made from the substance that causes those symptoms in a healthy person, such as coryza (the common cold). The belief is that by giving the patient a small dose of the same substance, it will stimulate the body's own healing response and help to alleviate the symptoms.

The concept of dilution and succussion: Homeopathy uses highly diluted substances, which are believed to stimulate the body's own healing response. This is achieved through the process of dilution and succussion, which involves repeatedly diluting a substance in water or alcohol and then vigorously shaking it (succussing) before each dilution. This process is believed to increase the energy or "potency" of the substance. The dilution of the substance is carried out in such a way that it makes the final remedy safe for consumption and also to make sure that the final remedy is not toxic. The dilution is usually done in a ratio of 1 part of the mother tincture to 9 or 99 parts of water or alcohol. This process is called "potentization" and it's believed to make the remedy more effective.

The importance of individualization in homeopathic treatment: Homeopathy is an individualized medicine, which means that the treatment is tailored to the unique needs of each person. A homeopath will take into account not only a person's physical symptoms but also their mental and emotional state, their overall health, and their lifestyle. Homeopaths believe that each person is unique and that their illness is unique, so they take into account every aspect of a person's life to determine the best course of treatment. The homeopath will ask many questions about the person's symptoms, medical history, and lifestyle habits to gain a complete understanding of the person's condition

List of Remedies

Overview of commonly used homeopathic remedies: There are many different homeopathic remedies available, and the choice of remedy will depend on the individual's symptoms and overall health. Some of the most commonly used remedies include:

Aconitum napellus: used for acute illnesses such as fever, colds, and flu, as well as for anxiety and fear

Arnica montana: used for injuries, bruising, and soreness, as well as for shock and emotional trauma

Belladonna: used for fever, headaches, and inflammation

Calcarea carbonica: used for a wide range of conditions, including anxiety, fatigue, and osteoporosis

Calendula: used for wound healing and skin conditions such as eczema and psoriasis

Chamomilla: used for teething pain and colic in infants, as well as for irritability and insomnia in adults

Hypericum: used for injuries to nerves and nerve pain, such as sciatica and shingles

Ignatia: used for emotional trauma, grief, and stress-related conditions

Nux vomica: used for indigestion, constipation, and other digestive complaints, as well as for headaches and stress

Pulsatilla: used for a wide range of conditions, including respiratory infections, menstrual complaints, and emotional problems

Properties and uses of key remedies: Each homeopathic remedy has its own set of characteristics and uses. For example, Aconitum napellus is considered a remedy for acute illnesses such as fever, colds, and flu, as well as for anxiety and fear. Arnica montana is used for injuries, bruising, and soreness, as well as for shock and emotional trauma. Belladonna is used for fever, headaches, and inflammation. Calcarea carbonica is used for a wide range of conditions, including anxiety, fatigue, and osteoporosis. Calendula is used for wound healing and skin conditions such as eczema and psoriasis. Chamomilla is used for teething pain and colic in infants, as well as for irritability and insomnia in adults. Hypericum is used for injuries to nerves and nerve pain, such as sciatica and shingles. Ignatia is used for emotional trauma, grief, and stress-related conditions.

Homeopathic Treatment

Overview of different types of homeopathic treatment: Homeopathy uses a variety of natural therapies to treat illness, including herbal medicine, diet, and lifestyle changes. Some of the most common types of homeopathic treatment include:

Constitutional treatment: This type of treatment is individualized and takes into account the person's overall health, symptoms, and lifestyle. The homeopath will select the remedy that best matches the person's unique set of symptoms and characteristics.

Acute treatment: This type of treatment is used for acute illnesses such as colds, flu, and injuries. The homeopath will select a remedy that is specific to the person's symptoms and that is most likely to stimulate the person's healing response.

Drainage treatment: This type of treatment is used to remove toxins and waste products from the body. Drainage remedies are used to support the body's own detoxification processes and to help the person feel better.

Common ailments treated with homeopathy: Homeopathy can be used to treat a wide range of illnesses, including chronic and acute conditions.

Some of the most common ailments treated with homeopathy

Respiratory disorders like asthma and bronchitis

Digestive disorders like acidity, constipation, and indigestion

Musculoskeletal disorders like arthritis and back pain

Skin disorders like eczema, psoriasis, and acne

Stress-related disorders like anxiety and depression

Gynecological disorders like PCOS, infertility, and menstrual irregularities

Metabolic disorders like obesity and diabetes

Chronic diseases like cancer, heart diseases and autoimmune disorders

It's important to note that homeopathy should not be used as a substitute for conventional medical treatment, but rather as a complementary therapy. It's always best to consult with a qualified homeopath before starting any homeopathic treatment.

Importance of diet and lifestyle in homeopathic treatment: Diet and lifestyle play an important role in homeopathic treatment. Homeopaths recommend a balanced diet that is tailored to the individual's needs, taking into account their unique health condition and symptoms. A healthy diet in homeopathy is one that is rich in fresh fruits and vegetables, whole grains, and lean protein. It's also important to avoid processed foods and to drink plenty of water to help the body detoxify. Homeopaths also recommend regular exercise and stress management techniques such as yoga and meditation. They may also suggest avoiding certain foods or substances that may aggravate the condition being treated. Additionally, homeopaths consider the emotional and mental well-being of the patient and suggest remedies to address those issues.

Homeopathic diagnosis and prognosis:

Homeopathic diagnosis is a holistic process that involves taking into account not just the physical symptoms of a person but also their mental and emotional state, overall health and lifestyle. A homeopath will ask a patient many questions about their symptoms, medical history, and lifestyle habits to gain a complete understanding of the person's condition.

The homeopath will also observe the patient's physical features, such as their pulse, tongue, and eyes, to determine the balance of the body's vital energy or "vital force." The homeopath will then select the remedy that best matches the person's unique set of symptoms and characteristics. The choice of remedy is based on the homeopathic principle of "like cures like."

The homeopath's role is not only to alleviate symptoms but also to address the underlying cause of the illness and promote overall wellness. The homeopath will also provide dietary and lifestyle recommendations to support the healing process. The homeopath will also monitor the patient's progress and adjust the treatment as needed.

XI

Stability Testing of Herbal Drugs

Stability testing is crucial for ensuring the safety and efficacy of herbal drugs because it helps to determine the shelf life of the product and identify any potential degradation or changes in the active ingredients over time. Herbal drugs are complex mixtures of naturally occurring compounds and their composition can vary depending on the source and processing of the plant material. Without proper stability testing, it may be difficult to know how the active ingredients of a herbal drug may change over time, which could lead to an ineffective or even harmful product.Additionally, stability testing allows manufacturers to ensure that their products meet the required specifications and quality standards, and that they remain within the established shelf life throughout their distribution and storage. This helps to ensure that the consumers receive a safe and consistent product.Furthermore, stability testing also helps to ensure that the herbal drugs are able to maintain their therapeutic properties and remain effective over time. It also helps to identify any potential degradation of the active ingredients and the factors that may contribute to it such as temperature, humidity, light, and exposure to oxygen.

The objectives of stability testing for herbal drugs include determining the shelf life of the product and identifying any potential degradation or changes in the active ingredients over time. This helps to ensure that the product remains safe and effective throughout its shelf life, and that consumers receive a consistent product. Additionally, stability testing also helps manufacturers to ensure that their products meet the required specifications and quality standards, and that they remain within the established shelf life throughout their distribution and storage.

The World Health Organization (WHO) has established guidelines for stability testing of herbal drugs, which are intended to ensure the quality and safety of these products. These guidelines provide recommendations for conducting stability studies, including the types of studies required, the sample sizes, and the storage conditions for the study samples. They also provide guidance on the analytical methods that should be used to test the stability of herbal drugs, and on the data analysis methods that should be used to interpret the results of the stability studies.

The WHO guidelines also provide recommendations for the storage conditions of herbal drugs, including the recommended temperature, humidity, and light exposure. These guidelines are important for ensuring that the herbal drugs are stored in a manner that will preserve their quality and safety.

Mechanisms affecting stability refers to the different ways in which herbal drugs can degrade or change over time. There are three main types of degradation that can occur in herbal drugs: chemical, physical and microbial degradation.Chemical degradation refers to changes in the chemical structure of the active ingredients in the herbal drug, which can occur due to reactions with other compounds or with environmental factors such as light and oxygen. These changes can result in the formation of new compounds or the breakdown of existing compounds, which can affect the safety and efficacy of the product.Physical degradation refers to changes in the physical properties of the herbal drug, such as changes in color, texture, or particle size. These changes can occur due to factors such as temperature, humidity, or mechanical stress.Microbial degradation refers to the growth and activity of microorganisms in the herbal drug, which can lead to changes in the chemical composition of the product and the formation of potentially harmful compounds.

Factors that can contribute to stability issues in herbal drugs

Temperature: High temperatures can accelerate chemical reactions and physical changes in herbal drugs, leading to degradation of the active ingredients.

Humidity: High humidity can promote the growth of microorganisms and can also lead to physical changes in the herbal drug, such as changes in particle size and texture.

Light: Exposure to light can cause chemical changes in herbal drugs, particularly those containing photosensitive compounds.

Oxygen: Exposure to oxygen can cause oxidation of the active ingredients in herbal drugs, leading to chemical degradation.

Challenges in stability testing

Challenges in stability testing refer to the difficulties and obstacles that can arise when testing the stability of herbal drugs.One of the main challenges in stability testing of herbal drugs is the limitations of the analytical methods used to test the stability of these products. Herbal drugs are complex mixtures of naturally occurring compounds and their composition can vary depending on the source and processing of the plant material. This complexity makes it challenging to identify and quantify the active ingredients, and to ensure consistency in the composition of the product. Some of the analytical methods that are commonly used for stability testing of herbal drugs include chromatographic techniques, spectrophotometry, and microscopy, each of them have their own limitations.

Another challenge in stability testing of herbal drugs is determining the shelf life of the product. The shelf life of a herbal drug is dependent on many factors, including the active ingredients, storage conditions, and packaging. Determining the shelf life of a herbal drug is a complex process and requires consideration of all these factors.

Additionally, considering different climatic zones when conducting stability testing is important as different regions have different environmental conditions that can affect the stability of herbal drugs. For example, products intended for use in tropical regions may be more susceptible to degradation due to high temperatures and humidity, while products intended for use in colder regions may be more susceptible to freezing.

Lastly, long-term storage can also have an impact on the quality of herbal drugs, as the active ingredients may degrade over time. It's important to consider the intended storage conditions and the potential impact of long-term storage when conducting stability testing.

Analytical methods are used to test the stability of herbal drugs and determine the concentration of active ingredients over time. There are several analytical methods that are commonly used for stability testing of herbal drugs, including:

Chromatographic techniques: Chromatographic techniques such as High-Performance Liquid Chromatography (HPLC) and Gas Chromatography (GC) are used to separate and identify the different compounds in a sample. These methods are widely used for the analysis of herbal drugs and provide good sensitivity and specificity. However, they can be time-consuming, require highly skilled personnel and can be costly.

Spectrophotometry: Spectrophotometry methods such as UV-vis and IR spectrophotometry are used to measure the absorption or transmission of light by a sample. These methods are relatively simple and fast, and can be used to quantitatively analyze the active ingredients in herbal drugs. However, they may not be able to distinguish between different isomers or provide information on the chemical structure of the compounds.

Microscopy: Microscopy methods such as light and electron microscopy are used to examine the physical characteristics of herbal drugs, such as particle size and shape. These methods are useful for identifying physical changes in the product over time. However, they are not suitable for the quantitative analysis of active ingredients.

It's important to select the appropriate analytical method based on the specific characteristics of the herbal drug being tested, such as the active ingredients, the concentration of the active ingredients, the intended use of the product, and the storage conditions. Each method has its own strengths and limitations and the selection should be made according to the specific needs of the analysis.

Shelf life refers to the period of time during which a product remains safe and effective, assuming it is stored under the recommended conditions. It is important to determine the shelf life of a herbal drug in order to ensure that the product remains safe and effective throughout its distribution and storage.

The shelf life of a herbal drug is dependent on many factors, including the active ingredients, storage conditions, and packaging. The active ingredients in a herbal drug can degrade over time due to chemical reactions or exposure to environmental factors such as light and oxygen. Therefore, the stability of the active ingredients is a key factor in determining the shelf life of a herbal drug.

Storage conditions can also impact the shelf life of a herbal drug. For example, high temperatures and humidity can accelerate the degradation of active ingredients and promote the growth of microorganisms. Similarly, exposure to light and oxygen can also affect the stability of the active ingredients. Therefore, it's important to determine the appropriate storage conditions for a herbal drug in order to ensure its shelf life.

Packaging can also play a role in determining the shelf life of a herbal drug. The type of packaging used can affect the stability of the product by protecting it from environmental factors such as light and oxygen. For example, a product that is packaged in a dark, airtight container will have a longer shelf life than one that is packaged in a clear container that is exposed to light.

Considering different climatic zones when conducting stability testing is important because different regions have different environmental conditions that can affect the stability of herbal drugs. For example, products intended for use in tropical regions may be more susceptible to degradation due to high temperatures and humidity, while products intended for use in colder regions may be more susceptible to freezing.

Temperature is a key environmental factor that can affect the stability of herbal drugs. High temperatures can accelerate chemical reactions and physical changes in herbal drugs, leading to degradation of the active ingredients. Therefore, it's important to consider the typical temperatures in the region where the product will be used when conducting stability testing.

Humidity is another environmental factor that can affect the stability of herbal drugs. High humidity can promote the growth of microorganisms and can also lead to physical changes in the herbal drug, such as changes in particle size and texture. This means that it's important to consider the typical humidity levels in the region where the product will be used when conducting stability testing.

Light is another environmental factor that can affect the stability of herbal drugs. Exposure to light can cause chemical changes in herbal drugs, particularly those containing photosensitive compounds. Therefore, it's important to consider the typical light exposure in the region where the product will be used when conducting stability testing.

Evaluating the long-term stability of herbal drugs is important to ensure that the product remains safe and effective throughout its shelf life. Long-term storage can have an impact on the quality of herbal drugs, as the active ingredients may degrade over time. It's important to consider the intended storage conditions and the potential impact of long-term storage when conducting stability testing.

Active ingredients are one of the most important factors that can impact long-term stability of herbal drugs. Some active ingredients are more stable than others, and may be less susceptible to degradation over time. The stability of the active ingredients can be affected by factors such as exposure to light, oxygen and temperature, thus it's important to consider these factors when evaluating the long-term stability of herbal drugs.

Packaging can also play a role in the long-term stability of herbal drugs. The type of packaging used can affect the stability of the product by protecting it from environmental factors such as light and oxygen. For example, a product that is packaged in a dark, airtight container will have a longer shelf life than one that is packaged in a clear container that is exposed to light.

Storage conditions can also impact the long-term stability of herbal drugs. For example, high temperatures and humidity can accelerate the degradation of active ingredients and promote the growth of microorganisms. Similarly, exposure to light and oxygen can also affect the stability of the active ingredients. Therefore, it's important to determine the appropriate storage conditions for a herbal drug in order to ensure its long-term stability.

ICH guide line for Stability Testing

The International Council for Harmonisation of Technical Requirements for Pharmaceuticals for Human Use (ICH) has established guidelines for stability testing of herbal drugs, which are intended to ensure the quality and safety of these products. These guidelines are internationally recognized and provide recommendations for conducting stability studies, including the types of studies required, the sample sizes, and the storage conditions for the study samples.

The ICH guidelines provide specific requirements for batch selection, testing conditions, and storage conditions for stability testing of herbal drugs. For batch selection, the guidelines recommend that a sufficient number of batches should be tested to establish the stability profile of the product. The testing conditions should be representative of the intended storage conditions of the product.The ICH guidelines also provide recommendations for the storage conditions of herbal drugs, including the recommended temperature, humidity, and light exposure. These guidelines are important for ensuring that the herbal drugs are stored in a manner that will preserve their quality and safety.The ICH guidelines also provide guidance on the analytical methods that should be used to test the stability of herbal drugs, and on the data analysis methods that should be used to interpret the results of the stability studies.

Types of stability study Explanation of the different types of stability studies that can be conducted, including short-term, intermediate-term, and long-term studies. Discussion of the specific objectives and methods used in each type of study and the importance of selecting the appropriate study design based on the specific characteristics of the herbal drug being tested.

Types of stability studies

1. Short-term stability studies: These studies are typically conducted over a period of one to three months and are used to establish the initial stability profile of a product. They are designed to identify any potential issues that may arise during storage and distribution.
2. Intermediate-term stability studies: These studies are typically conducted over a period of three to twelve months and are used to confirm the stability profile of a product. They are designed to identify any changes that may occur over an extended period of time and to provide data on the product's shelf life.
3. Long-term stability studies: These studies are typically conducted over a period of one to three years and are used to establish the long-term stability of a product. They are designed to identify any changes that may occur over an extended period of time and to provide data on the product's shelf life.

4. Accelerated Stability Testing: This method involves exposing the product to extreme storage conditions, such as high temperatures and humidity, to simulate the effects of long-term storage over a shorter period of time.

Methods for stability testing

1. Real-Time Stability Testing: This method involves storing the product under normal storage conditions and monitoring it over an extended period of time. This allows for the determination of the shelf-life of the product under typical storage conditions.
2. Stress Testing: This method involves subjecting the product to various environmental stressors, such as extreme temperatures or UV light, to determine its tolerance to these conditions.
3. Challenge Testing: This method involves exposing the product to specific microorganisms or environmental conditions to determine its susceptibility to degradation or contamination.
4. Physical Testing: This method involves measuring the physical characteristics of the product, such as particle size, color, and texture, to determine if any changes have occurred over time.
5. Analytical Testing: This method involves analyzing the chemical composition of the product, such as the concentration of active ingredients, to determine if any changes have occurred over time.
6. Microbiological Testing: This method involves analyzing the product for the presence of microorganisms, such as bacteria or fungi, to determine if any changes have occurred over time.

The appropriate testing method will depend on the specific characteristics of the herbal drug being tested and the stability information required. It's important to use a combination of testing methods to get a comprehensive understanding of the stability profile of the product.

Each type of stability study has its own specific objectives and methods. Short-term studies are conducted to identify any potential issues that may arise during storage and distribution, intermediate-term studies are used to confirm the stability profile of a product and long-term studies are used to establish the long-term stability of a product.

Protocol for stability study

A protocol for a stability study outlines the steps and procedures that will be followed during the study. The protocol should be well-defined and followed consistently to ensure the accuracy and reliability of the stability data.

The steps involved in conducting a stability study typically include:

Sample preparation: This includes selecting the appropriate number of batches to be tested, and preparing the samples according to the specifications outlined in the protocol.

Analytical methods: This includes selecting the appropriate analytical methods to be used, such as chromatographic techniques, spectrophotometry, or microscopy, and ensuring that they are properly validated.

Data collection: This includes collecting data on the stability of the product, including the concentration of active ingredients, physical characteristics and any other relevant parameters, over the course of the study.

Data analysis: This includes analyzing the data collected during the study, and interpreting the results. This may include statistical analysis to determine if any changes in the product are statistically significant.

Storage conditions: Stability studies are performed under specific storage conditions (i.e. temperature, humidity and light), this conditions must be controlled to ensure the accuracy and reliability of the results.

It's important to ensure that the protocol is followed consistently throughout the study and that the samples are stored and handled according to the specified storage conditions. Any deviations from the protocol should be documented and justified.

Storage Conditions

Considering storage conditions when conducting stability testing of herbal drugs is important as it can have a significant impact on the quality and safety of the product. The International Council for Harmonisation of Technical Requirements for Pharmaceuticals for Human Use (ICH) and the World Health Organization (WHO) have both established guidelines for storage conditions for stability testing of herbal drugs.

According to ICH guidelines, the storage conditions for stability testing should be representative of the intended storage conditions of the product and the conditions should be clearly specified in the stability protocol. The guidelines recommend that the stability samples should be stored at the appropriate temperature, humidity and light conditions, depending on the product characteristics.

The WHO guidelines also recommend that the storage conditions for stability testing should be representative of the intended storage conditions of the product. The guidelines recommend that herbal drug products should be stored under conditions that will preserve their quality and safety, and that the storage conditions should be specified in the product information.

The specific storage requirements for temperature, humidity, and light exposure vary depending on the product and the active ingredients it contains. For example, some herbal drugs may be sensitive to high temperatures and humidity, while others may be sensitive to light exposure. It's important to consider the product-specific characteristics when determining the appropriate storage conditions for stability testing.

XII

Patenting and Regulatory Requirements of Natural products

Patent:

A patent is a legal right granted by a government to an inventor for a certain period of time, typically 20 years from the date of filing, to prevent others from making, using, selling, or importing an invention without the patent holder's permission. Patents are granted for new, useful, and non-obvious inventions, including products and processes. In the context of natural products, patents may be granted for new uses or compositions of natural products, or for processes used to extract or produce them.

Intellectual property rights (IPR)

It refer to a set of legal rights that protect the creators and owners of certain types of creative and innovative works and inventions. IPR includes patents, trademarks, copyrights, and trade secrets. In the context of natural products, IPR can be used to protect traditional knowledge and innovations related to natural products, such as new uses or compositions of natural products, or methods of extraction or production.

The patenting and regulatory requirements for natural products are important because they determine who has the legal right to control and profit from the use of natural products. These requirements also have implications for the conservation and sustainable use of natural resources, as well as for the rights of indigenous and local communities who have traditionally used natural products.The importance and relevance of patenting and regulatory requirements for natural products has become increasingly apparent in recent years, as natural products have gained recognition for their medicinal and other uses, and as the demand for natural products has grown. This has led to a rise in bio-prospecting and bio-piracy, where companies and individuals seek to patent and profit from the use of natural products without proper recognition or compensation of the communities and countries where these products originate. The issue of patenting and regulation of natural products is thus of great importance for fair and sustainable use of these resources.

Farmers' Rights:

Farmers' rights refer to the legal rights and recognition given to farmers for their contributions to the conservation and sustainable use of plant genetic resources. These rights include the right to save, use, exchange, and sell farm-saved seed, and the right to participate in decision-making related to the use and conservation of plant genetic resources.

Farmers have been the custodians of plant genetic resources for thousands of years, and they have developed a wide range of traditional knowledge and practices related to the management, breeding and use of these resources. They have also played a vital role in maintaining the diversity and adaptability of plant genetic resources, which is essential for food security and sustainable agriculture.

The concept of farmers‘ rights is recognized in several international conventions and agreements. The International Treaty on Plant Genetic Resources for Food and Agriculture, adopted in 2001 by the Food and Agriculture Organization of the United Nations, recognizes the crucial role of farmers in the conservation and sustainable use of plant genetic resources and establishes a framework for the fair and equitable sharing of the benefits arising from their use. The treaty also requires the recognition and protection of traditional knowledge and innovations of farmers related to plant genetic resources.

Additionally, national laws and policies can also recognize and protect farmers' rights. For example, some countries have implemented laws and regulations that prohibit the patenting of plant varieties that have been developed or used by farmers. Other countries have established systems for the registration and protection of traditional knowledge and innovations of farmers related to plant genetic resources.

In India, the Protection of Plant Varieties and Farmers‘ Rights (PPV&FR) Act 2001 was enacted to provide for the protection of plant varieties, the rights of farmers and the registration of new plant varieties. The act provides for the establishment of a National Bureau of Plant Genetic Resources and a Plant Varieties Board, which are responsible for registering new plant varieties and protecting the rights of farmers and plant breeders.

Under the PPV&FR Act, farmers are given the rights to save, use, sow, resow, exchange, share or sell their farm-saved seed/ propagating material, subject to the provision of the act and the rules made thereunder. This means that farmers in India have the legal right to use and exchange their own seed without fear of infringement of any intellectual property rights.

The PPV&FR act also recognizes the rights of farmers as "Plant Breeders" and provides for the registration of new plant varieties developed by them. The act also establishes a system of community rights, which recognizes the rights of communities over the plant varieties that are traditionally under their management and use. This is aimed at protecting the traditional knowledge and innovations of the farmers and communities related to plant genetic resources.

In addition, the act also provides for the establishment of a benefit-sharing fund, which is used to provide financial assistance to farmers and rural communities for the conservation, development, and use of plant genetic resources.

Farmers' rights are the legal rights that recognize the contributions of farmers to the conservation and sustainable use of plant genetic resources. These rights include the right to save, use, exchange, and sell farm-saved seed, and the right to participate in decision-making related to the use and conservation of plant genetic resources. The recognition and protection of farmers' rights is an important aspect of ensuring fair and equitable sharing of benefits arising from the use of plant genetic resources and for the conservation of biodiversity.

The PPV&FR Act 2001 in India provides a strong legal framework for the protection of plant varieties, the rights of farmers and the registration of new plant varieties. The act recognizes the rights of farmers to save, use, exchange, and sell their farm-saved seed, and also recognizes the rights of farmers as "Plant Breeders" and established a system of community rights for the traditional knowledge and innovations of the farmers and communities related to plant genetic resources. The act also establishes a benefit-sharing fund for the conservation, development, and use of plant genetic resources, which is intended to provide financial assistance to farmers and rural communities.

The 9 specific rights granted to farmers

Right to save, use, exchange, and sell farm-saved seed or propagating material of the protected varieties.

Right to participate in the decision-making process related to the conservation and use of plant genetic resources.

Right to be recognized and compensated for the contributions made by farmers in the conservation and sustainable use of plant genetic resources.

Right to be informed about the availability and use of protected varieties and their characteristics.

Right to access the information on the registration of protected varieties and the rights of farmers.

Right to participate in the research and development of plant genetic resources.

Right to access the benefits arising from the use of plant genetic resources, including through benefit-sharing agreements.

Right to access technical and financial assistance for the conservation and sustainable use of plant genetic resources.

Right to be protected from bio-piracy and the unauthorized use of their traditional knowledge and innovations related to plant genetic resources.

Please note that the specific rights that are granted to farmers may vary depending on the legislation in different countries or regions. The above rights are based on international conventions and agreements such as the International Treaty on Plant Genetic Resources for Food and Agriculture and the Protection of Plant Varieties and Farmers' Rights (PPV&FR) Act 2001 in India.

Breeder's right :

Breeder's rights, also known as plant breeder's rights, are legal rights granted to the breeder of a new plant variety, giving them exclusive control over the production, sale, and distribution of that variety. These rights are intended to encourage plant breeding by providing breeders with an incentive to invest time and resources in developing new plant varieties. To be eligible for breeder's rights, a plant variety must be new, distinct, uniform, and stable. A new variety is one that has not been sold or otherwise disposed of for purposes of exploitation for more than one year in the country of origin, and for more than four years in other countries. A variety is considered distinct if it is different from any other variety that has been officially published, and uniform and stable if it shows the same characteristics under similar environmental conditions.

The breeder's rights usually last for a certain period of time, typically 20-25 years for most countries, starting from the date of grant. During this period, the breeder has the exclusive right to produce, sell, and distribute the protected variety, as well as to license others to do so. Breeder's rights also include the right to prevent others from producing, selling, or distributing the protected variety without their permission, as well as the right t to prevent others from using the protected variety as a parent for the breeding of another variety.

The international standard for breeder's rights is set by the International Union for the Protection of New Varieties of Plants (UPOV) and is governed by the UPOV Convention. UPOV is an intergovernmental organization based in Geneva, Switzerland and it provides a framework for the protection of new plant varieties through the grant of breeder's rights. Countries that are members of UPOV are required to provide protection for new plant varieties that meet the UPOV criteria for distinctness, uniformity, and stability.

In addition to the UPOV Convention, many countries also have their own national laws and regulations governing breeder's rights. These laws and regulations may have different requirements and standards for obtaining and enforcing breeder's rights, and may also include provisions for the protection of farmers' rights, the use of traditional knowledge, and the sharing of benefits arising from the use of protected plant varieties.

In summary, breeder's rights are legal rights granted to the breeder of a new plant variety, giving them exclusive control over the production, sale and distribution of that variety. These rights are intended to encourage plant breeding by providing breeders with an incentive to invest time and resources in developing new plant varieties. The international standard for breeder's rights is set by the UPOV Convention, and many countries also have their own national laws and regulations governing breeder's rights.

Bioprospecting :

Bioprospecting is the process of searching for and discovering new biological resources, such as microorganisms, plants, and animals, with the potential for medicinal, agricultural, or industrial use. It is a form of biotechnology that involves the exploration, collection, and study of biodiversity to discover new compounds, genes, or other useful resources. Bioprospecting is often conducted in remote or understudied regions, such as tropical rainforests and ocean environments, where the diversity of life is greatest.

The process of bioprospecting typically includes several stages, such as:

Exploration: the identification and characterization of new biological resources.

Collection: the gathering of samples of the identified resources.

Screening: the laboratory testing of samples to identify those with potential medicinal or industrial use.

Development: the further study and development of promising resources, leading to the production of new products or processes.

Bioprospecting has the potential to lead to the discovery of new drugs, agricultural products, industrial enzymes, and other useful compounds. For example, the anti-cancer drug taxol was discovered through bioprospecting of the Pacific yew tree, and the anti-inflammatory drug aspirin was derived from willow bark. Bioprospecting also plays an important role in the discovery of new enzymes and other useful compounds for industrial applications, such as biofuels and bioplastics.

The Convention on Biological Diversity (CBD) and the Nagoya Protocol, adopted in 2010, provide a framework for the fair and equitable sharing of the benefits arising from the use of genetic resources, including those used in bioprospecting.

On the other hand, Bio-piracy is the unauthorized use or misuse of biological resources and traditional knowledge, such as genetic resources, traditional medicinal knowledge, and other forms of intellectual property. Bio-piracy can involve the collection, use, or commercialization of biological resources without the prior informed consent of the local communities or countries where the resources are found, or without fair and equitable benefit sharing agreements. Bio-piracy can also involve the unauthorized use of traditional knowledge, such as traditional medicinal practices, without the consent of the communities or individuals who hold that knowledge.

The impact of bio-piracy on natural products can be significant. It can lead to the loss of control over valuable resources and the potential benefits that they can provide. Bio-piracy can also undermine the rights of local communities and countries to control access to and use of their resources, and to receive a fair share of the benefits from their use. Additionally, Bio-piracy can also lead to the exploitation and commercialization of traditional knowledge without proper recognition or compensation of the communities who hold that knowledge.

Both bioprospecting and bio-piracy are subject to international and national laws and regulations, such as the Convention on Biological Diversity and the Nagoya Protocol, which establish frameworks for access, benefit-sharing, and the responsible use of genetic resources. It is important to conduct bioprospecting activities in a legal and ethical manner, taking into consideration the rights of local communities and countries, and to follow fair and equitable benefit-sharing agreements.However, bioprospecting has also been a source of controversy, as it raises issues of ownership, access, and benefit-sharing related to the use of biological resources.

Patenting aspects of Traditional Knowledge and Natural Products

Traditional knowledge refers to the knowledge, skills, and practices that are passed down through generations within a community or culture. It includes knowledge and practices related to agriculture, medicine, craftsmanship, and other aspects of daily life. Traditional knowledge encompasses a wide range of topics, including medicinal plants, traditional farming practices, and indigenous technologies. It is often unique to a particular culture or community, and can be passed down orally or through practice. Traditional knowledge is often based on long-term observation, experimentation, and adaptation to local conditions, and can be considered as a form of intellectual property.

Traditional knowledge can also include traditional ecological knowledge, which is the knowledge of indigenous and local communities about the relationships between living organisms and their environment, including the management of natural resources. Traditional ecological knowledge can include knowledge of the use of plants and animals for food, medicine, and other purposes, as well as the management of ecosystems, such as forests, wetlands, and fisheries.

Traditional knowledge is an important source of knowledge and innovation, and can be used to develop new products, technologies, and practices. However, traditional knowledge is also vulnerable to being misused, or taken without proper recognition or compensation, which can lead to the loss of control over valuable resources and the potential benefits that they can provide. Therefore, it is important to ensure that traditional knowledge is protected and its use is regulated in a fair and equitable manner, taking into consideration the rights of local communities and countries.

Why they are important?

Patenting and regulatory requirements for traditional knowledge and natural products are important for several reasons:

Protection of Traditional Knowledge: Patenting and regulatory requirements provide a framework for protecting traditional knowledge and ensuring that it is not misused or taken without proper recognition or compensation. This helps to ensure that traditional knowledge is not exploited for commercial gain without the consent of the communities or individuals who hold that knowledge.

Promoting Innovation and Development: Patenting and regulatory requirements can also promote innovation and development by providing an incentive for research and development of new products and technologies based on traditional knowledge and natural products.

Conservation of Biodiversity: Patenting and regulatory requirements can also contribute to the conservation of biodiversity by providing an economic incentive to protect and manage natural resources.

Support of Livelihoods: Patenting and regulatory requirements can also help to support the livelihoods of local communities, particularly those living in or near areas of high biodiversity, through the sharing of benefits arising from the use of their resources.

Ethical Considerations: Patenting and regulatory requirements are also guided by ethical considerations, such as the protection of human rights and the rights of indigenous and local communities, as well as the responsible use of genetic resources.

Compliance with International and National Laws: Patenting and regulatory requirements are subject to international and national laws and regulations, such as the Convention on Biological Diversity and the Nagoya Protocol, which establish frameworks for access, benefit-sharing, and the responsible use of genetic resources.

Recognition of Traditional Knowledge Holders: Patenting and regulatory requirements ensure that traditional knowledge holders are recognized, respected and compensated for their knowledge, skills and innovations.

Ensuring access to traditional and natural products: Patenting and regulatory requirements ensure that traditional and natural products are accessible to the communities and individuals who need them, and prevent monopolies by companies

Traditional Knowledge and Patenting

Traditional knowledge is a valuable resource that has been passed down through generations in various cultures and communities. It includes knowledge and practices related to agriculture, medicine, craftsmanship, and other aspects of daily life. Traditional knowledge encompasses a wide range of topics, including medicinal plants, traditional farming practices, and indigenous technologies. It is often unique to a particular culture or community, and can be passed down orally or through practice.

However, the patenting of traditional knowledge has been a source of controversy and debate. One of the main challenges surrounding the patenting of traditional knowledge is the issue of ownership. Traditional knowledge is often held collectively by a community or culture, and does not have a clear individual or legal owner. This can make it difficult to obtain consent and ensure fair and equitable benefit-sharing agreements.

Another challenge is the issue of access. Patenting traditional knowledge can restrict access to it, particularly for the communities and individuals who traditionally use and rely on it. This can lead to a loss of control over valuable resources and the potential benefits that they can provide.

The benefit-sharing is also a major concern, as many patents have been granted on traditional knowledge and natural products without proper recognition or compensation to the local communities who have traditionally used these resources. This can lead to the exploitation of traditional knowledge and natural resources for commercial gain without the consent of the communities or individuals who hold that knowledge.

To address these challenges, international and national legal frameworks and policies have been developed to protect traditional knowledge and ensure fair and equitable benefit-sharing agreements. Examples include the Convention on Biological Diversity and the Nagoya Protocol, which establish frameworks for access, benefit-sharing, and the responsible use of genetic resources. Additionally, many countries have enacted their own laws and regulations to protect traditional knowledge, such as the Protection of Plant Varieties and Farmers' Rights (PPV&FR) Act 2001 in India.

Natural Products and Patenting

Natural products are resources found in nature, such as plants, animals, and microorganisms, that have various uses in various industries and sectors. These include medicinal plants, agricultural crops, and marine organisms, among others. Natural products have been used for centuries in traditional medicine and are an important source of new drugs and other products.

However, the patenting of natural products has also been a source of controversy and debate. One of the main challenges surrounding the patenting of natural products is the issue of biopiracy. Biopiracy refers to the unauthorized use of traditional knowledge, genetic resources, and other forms of life without the consent of the communities and individuals who hold that knowledge. This can lead to the exploitation of natural resources for commercial gain without proper recognition or compensation to the local communities and countries where these resources are found.

Another challenge is the impact on local communities and biodiversity. Patenting natural products can restrict access to them, particularly for the communities and individuals who traditionally use and rely on them. This can lead to a loss of control over valuable resources and the potential benefits that they can provide, as well as a negative impact on local communities and biodiversity.

To address these challenges, international and national legal frameworks and policies have been developed to protect natural products and ensure fair and equitable benefit-sharing agreements. Examples include the Convention on Biological Diversity and the Nagoya Protocol, which establish frameworks for access, benefit-sharing, and the responsible use of genetic resources. Additionally, many countries have enacted their own laws and regulations to protect natural products and traditional knowledge, such as the Protection of Plant Varieties and Farmers' Rights (PPV&FR) Act 2001 in India.

Case Studies of Traditional Knowledge and Natural Products

Neem Tree

Turmeric

Case Study: Neem and Turmeric Detailed examination of the patenting and regulatory requirements for neem and turmeric as examples of natural products Analysis of the challenges and controversies surrounding the patenting and regulation of these products, including any legal disputes or ongoing debates

Neem and turmeric are examples of natural products that have been traditionally used in various cultures for medicinal and other purposes. Both neem and turmeric have been the subject of significant research and development in recent years, leading to the discovery of their various therapeutic properties and potential uses in various industries.

In the case of neem, several patents have been granted in the past for the use of neem extracts and compounds in various products, such as pesticides, fungicides, and contraceptives. However, many of these patents have been challenged and revoked on the grounds that they covered traditional knowledge and uses of neem that were already well-known in India and other countries where neem is commonly used.

One example is the patent granted by the European Patent Office (EPO) in 1995 to the US Department of Agriculture (USDA) and W.R. Grace & Co., for the use of neem oil as a fungicide. This patent was challenged and revoked by the EPO in 2000, following a successful opposition filed by the Indian government and several non-governmental organizations on the grounds that the use of neem oil as a fungicide was already known in India.

In the case of turmeric, several patents have been granted for the use of turmeric extracts and compounds in various products, such as cosmetics, food supplements, and drugs. However, some of these patents have been challenged on the grounds that they covered traditional knowledge and uses of turmeric that were already known in India and other countries where turmeric is commonly used.

In India, the Protection of Plant Varieties and Farmers' Rights (PPV&FR) Act 2001 provides a framework for the protection of plant varieties and the rights of farmers, including the rights to save, use, exchange, and sell farm-saved seed of protected varieties. The act also provides for the protection of traditional knowledge and innovations related to plant varieties, and for the sharing of benefits arising from the use of protected plant varieties.

The use of Neem as an insecticide and fungicide has been known for centuries in India and other countries where it is native. In many cases, patents have been granted on Neem extracts and compounds, which have been challenged and revoked on the grounds that they covered traditional knowledge and uses of Neem that were already well-known.

Turmeric is a popular spice and medicinal herb in India, and has been used for centuries in traditional medicine. The active ingredient in Turmeric, curcumin, has been the subject of extensive research in recent years, leading to the discovery of its various therapeutic properties and potential uses in various industries.

The patenting of Neem and Turmeric raises concerns about biopiracy, as the knowledge and uses of these natural products have been traditionally passed down through generations in local communities.

The patenting of Neem and Turmeric also raises concerns about the impact on the livelihoods of farmers and local communities who have traditionally grown and used these natural products.

There have been cases where companies have been granted patents on Neem and Turmeric extracts and compounds, without proper recognition or compensation to the local communities who have traditionally used these natural products.

The patenting of Neem and Turmeric also raises concerns about the potential impact on the availability and affordability of these natural products for traditional and medicinal use.

There is a need for fair and equitable benefit-sharing agreements to ensure that local communities and countries where these natural products are found, are properly recognized and compensated for their traditional knowledge and innovations related to these products.

The patenting and regulation of natural products, such as Neem and Turmeric, should also take into consideration the conservation of biodiversity and the sustainable use of these resources for future generations.

The patenting and regulation of natural products should also be guided by ethical considerations, such as the protection of human rights and the rights of indigenous and local communities.

There is a need for a harmonized and balanced approach to the patenting and regulation of natural products, taking into account the interests of all stakeholders, including local communities, countries where these natural products are found, industry and research institutions, and the international community. This includes the development of robust legal frameworks and policies that ensure fair and equitable access to and benefit-sharing of these natural products, while also promoting conservation and sustainable use of these resources.

XIII

Regulatory issues -Herbal drugs

Overview of the pharmaceutical industry in India:

The Indian pharmaceutical industry is one of the fastest-growing industries in the country. It is a diverse and complex industry that includes both domestic and foreign players, and produces a wide range of products, from generic drugs to innovative therapies. The Indian pharmaceutical market is estimated to be worth around $40 billion, and is projected to grow at a compounded annual growth rate (CAGR) of around 8-9%. The industry is characterized by a large number of small and medium-sized enterprises (SMEs) and a few large multinational companies.

The Need for regulations in the pharmaceutical industry: The pharmaceutical industry plays a vital role in ensuring public health and well-being. However, the safety, efficacy, and quality of drugs are of paramount importance and must be ensured through a robust regulatory system. The regulatory system in India is designed to protect consumer rights, ensure the safety and efficacy of drugs, and promote ethical practices in the industry. The regulations also aim to balance the protection of public health with the promotion of innovation and access to new treatments.

Brief history of the development of regulations for Ayurvedic, Siddha, and Unani (ASU) drugs in India: The traditional systems of medicine, Ayurveda, Siddha, and Unani have been practiced in India for centuries. However, the regulation of these systems of medicine was not formalized until the 1940s with the introduction of the Drugs and Cosmetics Act, 1940. Over the years, the regulations for ASU drugs have evolved to include guidelines for registration, manufacturing, and sale of these drugs. In recent years, there has been an increased focus on promoting the use of traditional medicine systems, including ASU, as an alternative to modern medicine.

The legal framework for ASU drugs in India is primarily governed by the Drugs and Cosmetics Act, 1940 and its rules. The Act provides the framework for the regulation of all drugs, including ASU drugs, in the country. The Act and its rules outline the requirements for registration, manufacturing, and sale of drugs, as well as the penalties for non-compliance.

Specific regulations and guidelines related to the registration, manufacturing, and sale of ASU drugs: The Drugs and Cosmetics Act and its rules also include specific provisions for the regulation of ASU drugs. For example, the Act provides for the registration of ASU drugs with the Central Licensing Authority, which is responsible for ensuring that these drugs meet the standards of safety, efficacy, and quality. The Act also includes guidelines for the manufacturing of ASU drugs, which must comply with Good Manufacturing Practices (GMP) as specified by the Ayurvedic, Siddha and Unani Drugs Technical Advisory Board (ASU-DTAB).

Additionally, the sale of ASU drugs is subject to certain restrictions such as the requirement for the drugs to be labeled with specific information, including the name of the ingredients, and the name and address of the manufacturer. The Act also provides for the formation of State Licensing Authority (SLA) which is responsible for the regulation of sale and distribution of drugs within the state.

The Ministry of AYUSH has also formulated guidelines for the promotion, development, and regulation of ASU drugs in the country. These guidelines outline the procedures for registration of ASU drugs, and provide for the formation of a Central Council for Research in Ayurvedic Sciences (CCRAS), Central Council for Research in Siddha (CCRS) and Central Council for Research in Unani Medicine (CCRUM) to conduct research in these traditional medicine systems.

The Drugs and Cosmetics Act also provides for the establishment of a Central Ayurvedic, Siddha, and Unani Drugs Laboratory (CASUDL) for the testing of ASU drugs. The laboratory is responsible for conducting quality control tests on ASU drugs to ensure that they meet the standards of safety, efficacy, and quality.

The Act also provides for the formation of a National Ayurvedic, Siddha, and Unani Drugs Formulary (NAUDF) which contains a list of ASU drugs that have been approved by the Central Licensing Authority. The NAUDF serves as a reference for practitioners, manufacturers, and regulatory authorities and helps to ensure that only safe and efficacious drugs are used.

The Act also includes provisions for the regulation of advertising of ASU drugs. The Act prohibits the advertising of drugs that make false or misleading claims, and also prohibits the advertising of new drugs until they have been approved by the Central Licensing Authority.

Challenges faced by manufacturers and practitioners in complying with the regulations: Compliance with the regulations for ASU drugs can be challenging for manufacturers and practitioners. The registration process for ASU drugs can be time-consuming and costly, which can be a barrier for small and medium-sized enterprises (SMEs) and start-ups. The GMP standards for the manufacturing of ASU drugs can also be difficult to implement, particularly for small-scale manufacturers who may lack the resources and expertise to comply with the regulations. Additionally, the requirement for ASU drugs to be labeled with specific information and the restrictions on advertising can also be challenging for manufacturers and practitioners to comply with.

Impact of the regulations on access to ASU drugs for consumers: The regulations for ASU drugs can also have an impact on access to these drugs for consumers. The registration process for ASU drugs can lead to a delay in the availability of new drugs in the market. The restrictions on advertising of ASU drugs may also make it difficult for consumers to access information about these drugs, which can impact their ability to make informed decisions about their healthcare. Additionally, the cost of compliance with the regulations can be passed on to consumers in the form of higher drug prices.

Potential for future developments in the regulation of ASU drugs: There is potential for future developments in the regulation of ASU drugs that could promote safe and efficacious use of these drugs while addressing the challenges faced by manufacturers and practitioners in complying with the regulations and by consumers in accessing these drugs. The integration of traditional medicine systems with modern medicine could lead to the development of new regulatory mechanisms that take into account the unique characteristics of ASU drugs and the traditional medicine systems from which they originate. Additionally, the development of new technologies such as digital platforms for the registration, manufacturing, and sale of ASU drugs could make the process more efficient and cost-effective.

Manufacturing of ASU Drugs

Regulations for the manufacturing of ASU drugs in India: The manufacturing of ASU drugs in India is regulated by the Drugs and Cosmetics Act, 1940 and its rules, as well as guidelines issued by the Ayurvedic, Siddha and Unani Drugs Technical Advisory Board (ASU-DTAB). These regulations and guidelines outline the standards for Good Manufacturing Practices (GMP) that must be followed by manufacturers of ASU drugs. These standards cover areas such as the quality of raw materials, the production process, the testing of finished products, and the storage and distribution of drugs.

Guidelines for compliance with Good Manufacturing Practices (GMP): The ASU-DTAB has issued guidelines for GMP for ASU drugs, which are based on the principles of GMP as outlined in the World Health Organization (WHO) guidelines. These guidelines cover areas such as the design and construction of manufacturing facilities, the qualification and training of personnel, the control of raw materials and finished products, and the documentation and record-keeping requirements. Manufacturers of ASU drugs are expected to comply with these guidelines in order to ensure the safety and efficacy of their products.

The regulations for the manufacturing of ASU drugs in India are outlined in the Drugs and Cosmetics Act, 1940 and its rules, as well as guidelines issued by the Ayurvedic, Siddha and Unani Drugs Technical Advisory Board (ASU-DTAB). These regulations and guidelines cover various aspects of the manufacturing process, including:

Quality of raw materials: The regulations require that manufacturers use only high-quality raw materials in the production of ASU drugs. The raw materials must be sourced from reputable suppliers, and must be free from contaminants and impurities.

Production process: The regulations require that manufacturers have a detailed and well-documented production process that ensures the consistency and quality of the finished product. This includes guidelines for the preparation of drugs, the methods used, and the controls in place to ensure the safety and efficacy of the finished product.

Testing of finished products: The regulations require that manufacturers test finished products to ensure they meet the standards of safety, efficacy, and quality. This includes testing for the presence of contaminants and impurities, as well as testing for the potency and efficacy of the active ingredients.

Storage and distribution: The regulations require that manufacturers store and distribute drugs in a manner that ensures their safety and efficacy. This includes guidelines for the storage conditions, the handling of drugs, and the transportation of drugs.

Compliance with these regulations is essential to ensure the safety and efficacy of ASU drugs. Non-compliance can result in penalties such as fines, revocation of licenses, and even criminal prosecution.

ASU DTAB

The Drugs & Cosmetics Act, 1940 is the primary legislation governing the regulation of drugs and health in India.In India, the regulation of Ayurvedic, Siddha, and Unani (ASU) drugs is governed by the Drugs and Cosmetics Act, 1940 and the Drugs and Cosmetics Rules, 1945. The regulation of ASU drugs is carried out by the Ayurveda, Siddha, and Unani Drugs Technical Advisory Board (ASU DTAB) and the Ayurveda, Siddha, and Unani Drugs Consultative Committee (ASU DCC).The ASU DTAB is responsible for advising the Central Government on matters related to the manufacture, sale, and distribution of ASU drugs. The ASU DCC is responsible for advising the Central Government on the standards of quality, safety, and efficacy of ASU drugs.The Ayurvedic, Siddha, and Unani (ASU) Drug Technical Advisory Board (DTAB) is a statutory body in India that provides technical advice to the Central Government on matters related to the regulation of ASU drugs. It is established under the Drugs and Cosmetics Act, 1940 and operates under the Ministry of AYUSH.

The main functions of the ASU DTAB

Advising the Central Government on the recognition of new drugs, new indications and new routes of administration of ASU drugs.

Advising on the formulation of standards for the quality and purity of ASU drugs.

Advising on the regulation of the manufacture, sale and distribution of ASU drugs.

Advising on the regulation of the import and export of ASU drugs.

Advising on the regulation of the import and export of raw materials used in the manufacture of ASU drugs.

Advising on the regulation of the research and development of ASU drugs.

Advising on the regulation of the clinical trials of ASU drugs.

The ASU DTAB is composed of experts in the field of Ayurveda, Siddha and Unani medicine, as well as representatives from the Central Government, State Governments, and other relevant organizations. The board meets periodically to discuss and decide on various matters related to the regulation of ASU drugs.

It's worth noting that the ASU DTAB is one of the key regulatory bodies that oversees the manufacture, sale, and distribution of ASU drugs in India, and manufacturers must comply with its guidelines and recommendations in order to be able to manufacture and sell the drugs.

Compostion

The composition of the Ayurvedic, Siddha, and Unani (ASU) Drug Technical Advisory Board (DTAB) is defined in the Drugs and Cosmetics Act, 1940 and is subject to change from time to time. However, traditionally it is composed of the following members:

The Director General of Health Services (DGHS) - Chairman

The Director of the Central Council for Research in Ayurveda and Siddha (CCRAS)

The Director of the Central Council for Research in Unani Medicine (CCRUM)

The Director of the Pharmacopoeia Commission for Indian Medicine and Homoeopathy (PCIM&H)

Four experts nominated by the Central Government on the recommendations of the Central Council of Indian Medicine (CCIM)

Two experts nominated by the Central Government on the recommendations of the Central Council of Homoeopathy (CCH)

One representative each from the Ministry of Health and Family Welfare, Ministry of Law, Ministry of Commerce and Industry, Ministry of Ayush, Indian Medical Association and Indian Drugs Manufacturers Association.

The Joint Secretary (Drugs) in the Ministry of Health and Family Welfare - Member-Secretary

It's worth noting that the above-mentioned composition is not exhaustive and there might be additional members depending on the current regulations and the need of the Central Government.

ASU DCC:

The Ayurvedic, Siddha, and Unani (ASU) Drugs Consultative Committee (DCC) is a statutory body in India that provides technical advice to the Central Licensing Authority (CLA) on matters related to the licensing of ASU drugs. It operates under the Ministry of AYUSH and it is established under the Drugs and Cosmetics Act, 1940.

Description of the functions and working activities of the ASU-DTAB: The ASU-DTAB is responsible for a wide range of functions and working activities related to the regulation of ASU drugs. Some of the key functions and activities of the board include:

Formulating guidelines for the manufacture and sale of ASU drugs: The ASU-DTAB is responsible for issuing guidelines for the manufacture and sale of ASU drugs, including guidelines for Good Manufacturing Practices (GMP), which manufacturers of ASU drugs are expected to comply with. The ASU-DTAB also conducts inspections of manufacturing units to ensure that these guidelines are being followed.

Advising on the registration of ASU drugs: The ASU-DTAB provides advice to the Central Licensing Authority on the registration of ASU drugs. The board reviews the data provided by the manufacturers and assesses the safety and efficacy of the drugs before making a recommendation to the Central Licensing Authority.

Conducting research on ASU drugs: The ASU-DTAB conducts research on ASU drugs to improve the understanding of these traditional medicine systems and to develop new guidelines and standards for the regulation of these drugs.

Providing training and education: The ASU-DTAB provides training and education to manufacturers, practitioners, and other stakeholders on the regulations and guidelines for the manufacture and sale of ASU drugs.

It is important to note that the ASU-DTAB plays a vital role in ensuring the safety, efficacy and quality of ASU drugs.

The ASU-DCC is responsible for providing expert advice on various aspects of the regulation of ASU drugs. Some of the key functions and activities of the committee include:

Providing expert advice on ASU drugs: The ASU-DCC provides expert advice to the Central and State Governments on technical matters related to the regulation of ASU drugs. This includes providing advice on the registration, manufacturing, and sale of these drugs, as well as on the formulation of guidelines and standards for these drugs.

Reviewing and evaluating data related to ASU drugs: The ASU-DCC reviews and evaluates data related to ASU drugs, such as data on their safety, efficacy, and quality. The committee also assesses the data provided by manufacturers for the registration of ASU drugs, and makes recommendations to the Central Licensing Authority.

Providing recommendations on the development of ASU drugs: The ASU-DCC provides recommendations to the Central and State Governments on the development of ASU drugs, including the identification of new areas for research, the development of new technologies, and the promotion of traditional medicine systems.

Monitoring the implementation of regulations: The ASU-DCC monitors the implementation of regulations related to ASU drugs and provides feedback to the Central and State Governments on areas where improvements are needed.

Conducting research on ASU drugs: The ASU-DCC conducts research on ASU drugs to improve the understanding of these traditional medicine systems and to develop new guidelines and standards for the regulation of these drugs.

ASU-DCC plays a vital role in providing expert advice on ASU drugs and it also monitors the compliance of the regulations, conduct research and provide recommendations to the government for the development of ASU drugs.

The main functions of the ASU DCC

Advising the CLA on applications for licenses to manufacture ASU drugs.

Advising on the recognition of new drugs, new indications and new routes of administration of ASU drugs.

Advising on the formulation of standards for the quality and purity of ASU drugs.

Advising on the regulation of the import and export of ASU drugs.

Advising on the regulation of the import and export of raw materials used in the manufacture of ASU drugs.

Advising on the regulation of the research and development of ASU drugs.

Advising on the regulation of the clinical trials of ASU drugs.

Advising on the regulation of the advertising of ASU drugs.

Advising on the regulation of the distribution of ASU drugs.

Advising on the regulation of the sale of ASU drugs.

The ASU DCC is composed of experts in the field of Ayurveda, Siddha and Unani medicine, as well as representatives from the Central Government, State Governments, and other relevant organizations. The board meets periodically to discuss and decide on various matters related to the regulation of ASU drugs.

It's worth noting that the ASU DCC is one of the key regulatory bodies that oversees the licensing and regulation of ASU drugs in India, and manufacturers must comply with its guidelines and recommendations in order to be able to manufacture and sell the drugs.

Compostion of ASU DCC

The composition of the Ayurvedic, Siddha, and Unani (ASU) Drugs Consultative Committee (DCC) is defined in the Drugs and Cosmetics Act, 1940 and is subject to change from time to time. However, traditionally it is composed of the following members:

The Director General of Health Services (DGHS) - Chairman

The Director of the Central Council for Research in Ayurveda and Siddha (CCRAS)

The Director of the Central Council for Research in Unani Medicine (CCRUM)

The Director of the Pharmacopoeia Commission for Indian Medicine and Homoeopathy (PCIM&H)

Two experts nominated by the Central Government on the recommendations of the Central Council of Indian Medicine (CCIM)

Two experts nominated by the Central Government on the recommendations of the Central Council of Homoeopathy (CCH)

One representative each from the Ministry of Health and Family Welfare, Ministry of Law, Ministry of Commerce and Industry, Ministry of Ayush, Indian Medical Association and Indian Drugs Manufacturers Association.

The Joint Secretary (Drugs) in the Ministry of Health and Family Welfare - Member-Secretary

It's worth noting that the above-mentioned composition is not exhaustive and there might be additional members depending on the current regulations and the need of the Central Government. The composition of the DCC may change based on the current regulations, The DCC is responsible for providing technical advice to the Central Licensing Authority (CLA) on applications for licenses to manufacture, import and sale of ASU drugs.

Regulation of Manufacture of ASU drugs - Schedule Z of Drugs & Cosmetics Act for ASU Drugs

The manufacture of ASU drugs is governed by the Schedule Z of the Drugs and Cosmetics Act, 1940, which lays down the requirements for the manufacture, sale, and distribution of ASU drugs. The Schedule Z requires that ASU drugs be manufactured in accordance with the standards of the Ayurvedic, Siddha, and Unani Formulary of India (ASU Formulary). ASU Formulary is a compendium of monographs of ASU drugs that includes information on the botanical identity, botanical description, and chemical composition of the drugs. The manufacturers of ASU drugs are required to comply with the standards laid down in the ASU Formulary in order to ensure the quality, safety, and efficacy of the drugs. The ASU Formulary also provides guidelines for the preparation and manufacturing of ASU drugs. These guidelines include information on the selection of raw materials, the manufacturing process, and the quality control measures that must be in place to ensure that the final product meets the standards of identity, purity, strength, and quality. ASU Formulary includes monographs for various ASU drugs, which provide detailed information on the ingredients, preparation method, quality control, and testing methods for these drugs. This information serves as a reference for manufacturers to ensure that their products meet the appropriate standards. It's worth noting that the standards laid down in the ASU Formulary are subject to change and manufacturers must stay updated with the latest standards and guidelines in order to comply with the regulations.

Additionally, manufacturers must obtain a license from the Central Licensing Authority before they can manufacture and sell the drugs. The Central Licensing Authority is responsible for issuing licenses for the manufacture of ASU drugs and ensuring that the manufacturers comply with the standards laid down in the formularies and the Drugs and Cosmetics Act 1940 and the rules made there under.

Manufacturers must submit an application for a license and meet the requirements including GMP, standards of raw materials, testing protocols, finished products, and compliance with the rules and regulations outlined in the Drugs & Cosmetics Rules, 1945. They must also comply with the guidelines and regulations set by the relevant regulatory bodies such as CDSCO, DTAB, IPC, and NPPA.

The license is granted after the manufacturer has met the necessary requirements and their facility has been inspected and found to be in compliance with the regulations.

CONDITIONS FOR COMMERCIAL MANUFACTURING OF ASU DRUGS

License of the manufacturing unit and intended formulations

GMP Compliance

Adequate infrastructural facility, staff, equipment, reference books, record keeping etc

Compliance to Standards given in the pharmacopoeia.

The raw materials used in the manufacturing process must be of high quality and meet the standards set by the Ayurvedic Pharmacopoeia of India, the Unani Pharmacopoeia of India, or the Siddha Formulary of India, depending on the type of ASU drug being manufactured.

Manufacturing process should be in compliance with the monograph of the drug as per the pharmacopoeia

The finished product must be tested and meet the standards set by the pharmacopoeia, including for heavy metals, microbial contamination, and other impurities.

The manufacturer must keep detailed records of the manufacturing process and raw materials used, and these records must be made available for inspection by the relevant authorities.

The manufacturing unit must be inspected by the relevant authorities before and after the grant of the manufacturing license.

The manufacturer must comply with the guidelines and regulations set by the relevant regulatory bodies such as CDSCO, DTAB, IPC, and NPPA.

It's worth noting that the above-mentioned list is not exhaustive and there might be additional conditions depending on the type of ASU drugs and the specific regulations of the state or central government.

Some of the requirements for licensing of Ayurvedic, Siddha, and Unani (ASU) medicines in India. The manufacturing unit must comply with the Good Manufacturing Practices (GMP) requirements as prescribed in Schedule T of the Drugs & Cosmetics Rules, 1945, and Schedule M1 for Homoeopathic medicines.

The standards of identity, purity, and strength of ASU medicines must meet the standards given in the respective pharmacopeias, such as the Ayurvedic Pharmacopoeia of India, the Unani Pharmacopoeia of India, and the Siddha Formulary of India. In addition, standardized classical formulations prescribed in National Formularies must be followed and in-house standards and testing protocols for proprietary medicines must be established.

Regarding the limit of heavy metals for exports, it's effective from 14th October, 2006 and the limits are:

Lead: 10.0 ppm

Arsenic: 3.0 ppm

Cadmium: 0.3 ppm

Mercury: 1.0 ppm

Manufacturers of ASU medicines must ensure that their products meet these limits before exporting them. It's also worth noting that these regulations are subject to change and manufacturers must stay updated with the latest regulations and guidelines.

Labeling and packing of Ayurvedic, Siddha, and Unani (ASU) medicines must comply with the rules and regulations outlined in Rule 161 of the Drugs & Cosmetics Rules, 1945.

Information must be included on the label:

The name of the drug as given in the Ayurvedic Pharmacopoeia of India (API), the Unani Pharmacopoeia of India (UPI), or an authoritative book included in the First Schedule of the Act.

The quantity of the drug in the metric system (g, ml, etc.).

The name and address of the manufacturer.

The manufacturing license number or "M.L."

The batch number or lot number.

The date of manufacture.

The date of expiry, if applicable.

The words "Ayurvedic medicine," "Siddha medicine," or "Unani medicine" must be mentioned.

If the medicine is for external use only, the words "for external uses only" must be mentioned.

If the medicine is for distribution to the medical profession as a free sample, the words "Physicians sample not to be sold" must be mentioned

Labeling and packing of export products of ASU medicines must comply with the rules and regulations outlined in Rule 161-A of the Drugs & Cosmetics Rules,1945. The following information must be included on the label:

Labeling and packing must meet the requirements of the laws of the country to which the products are exported.

The name of the ASU drug (single or compound formulation).

The name and address of the manufacturer with the manufacturing license number.

The batch number or lot number.

The date of manufacture and the date "best for use before"

The main ingredients with quantity, if required by the importing country.

There are also proposed requirements and guidelines outlined in Schedule Z for permission to manufacture ASU drugs for sale or to undertake clinical trials. It's important to stay updated with the latest regulations and guidelines, including shelf life of the products.

The standards laid down in the Ayurvedic, Siddha and Unani (ASU) Formulary include the standards for identity, purity, strength and quality of the ASU drugs.

Identity standards refer to the name, description and the ingredients of the drug that should be consistent with the standard text.

Purity standards refer to the presence of impurities such as heavy metals, microbial contamination, and other contaminants.

Strength standards refer to the concentration of active ingredients in the drug.

Quality standards refer to the overall quality of the drug, including its physical appearance, taste, odor, and consistency.

XIV

General Introduction to Herbal Industry

The herbal industry is a rapidly growing sector that encompasses the cultivation, harvesting, processing, manufacturing, and distribution of herbal products. Herbal products are made from plants or plant extracts and are used for medicinal, therapeutic, or nutritional purposes. The industry includes a wide variety of products such as herbal supplements, herbal teas, herbal cosmetics, and herbal medicines.Herbal products have been used for centuries in traditional medicine systems, such as Ayurveda and Chinese medicine. In recent years, there has been a resurgence of interest in herbal products due to the growing awareness of the potential health benefits they offer. This has led to an increase in the demand for herbal products and a corresponding growth in the herbal industry.The herbal industry is a complex and diverse field that encompasses many different types of products and production methods. Some herbal products are produced by small, family-run businesses while others are produced by large, multinational corporations. The industry also includes a wide range of different distribution channels, from traditional brick-and-mortar stores to online retailers.

One of the major challenges facing the herbal industry is the lack of standardization and regulation of herbal products. Unlike pharmaceutical drugs, which are heavily regulated by the FDA, herbal products are not subject to the same level of oversight. This can make it difficult for consumers to determine the quality and safety of the products they are buying. To address this issue, many organizations have been established to promote the standardization and regulation of herbal products.

Another challenge facing the herbal industry is the lack of scientific research on the safety and efficacy of herbal products. While many herbal products have been used for centuries in traditional medicine systems, there is still a need for more rigorous scientific study to determine their safety and effectiveness. This is an area where the industry is actively working to improve, with many companies investing in research and development to better understand the potential health benefits of their products.

Despite these challenges, the herbal industry continues to grow and evolve. With the increasing demand for natural and organic products, the herbal industry is well positioned to continue to grow in the coming years. The herbal industry is also becoming more mainstream, with many large retailers now offering a wide range of herbal products.

As the herbal industry continues to grow, it is important for consumers to be informed and make informed decisions about the products they buy. This includes being aware of the potential benefits and risks of herbal products, understanding the different production methods and distribution channels, and knowing where to find reliable information about the quality and safety of herbal products.

Herbal drugs industry: Present scope and future prospects.

The herbal drugs industry is a rapidly growing sector that encompasses the cultivation, harvesting, processing, manufacturing, and distribution of herbal products for medicinal use. Herbal drugs are made from plants or plant extracts and are used for various therapeutic purposes such as treatment of diseases, management of symptoms and as an alternative medicine.

The present scope of the herbal drugs industry is quite vast, as it includes a wide range of products such as herbal supplements, herbal teas, herbal cosmetics, and herbal medicines. The industry is driven by the increasing demand for natural and organic products, as well as a growing awareness of the potential health benefits of herbal drugs.

In recent years, there has been a resurgence of interest in herbal drugs due to the growing awareness of their potential health benefits. This has led to an increase in the demand for herbal drugs and a corresponding growth in the herbal drugs industry. The industry is also becoming more mainstream, with many large retailers now offering a wide range of herbal drugs.

The future prospects of the herbal drugs industry are very promising, as the demand for herbal drugs is expected to continue to grow in the coming years. The increasing popularity of alternative medicine, combined with an aging population and an increasing focus on preventive healthcare, is likely to drive the growth of the herbal drugs industry. Additionally, advances in technology and research are helping to improve the quality and effectiveness of herbal drugs, which is also expected to contribute to the growth of the industry.

However, the industry also faces certain challenges such as lack of standardization, regulation, and scientific research on the safety and efficacy of herbal drugs. This can make it difficult for consumers to determine the quality and safety of the products they are buying. To address this issue, many organizations have been established to promote the standardization and regulation of herbal drugs.

The herbal drugs industry is also increasingly adopting modern technologies and techniques to improve the quality and effectiveness of their products. For example, many companies are now using advanced extraction methods to extract active ingredients from plants in a more efficient and effective way. This is allowing for the production of higher-quality herbal drugs that are more potent and consistent in their effects. Additionally, many companies are now using genetic engineering and biotechnology to produce plants with higher concentrations of active ingredients, which can also improve the effectiveness of herbal drugs.

Another important trend in the herbal drugs industry is the growing use of herbal drugs in combination with conventional drugs. This is known as "integrative medicine" and is becoming increasingly popular as a way to provide more comprehensive and effective treatment for various health conditions. Integrative medicine combines the best of both worlds, utilizing the benefits of both conventional drugs and herbal drugs, to provide a more holistic approach to health and wellness.

Additionally, the herbal drugs industry is also actively working to improve the safety and efficacy of their products. Many companies are now investing in research and development to better understand the potential health benefits of their products and to ensure that their products are safe and effective. This includes conducting clinical trials and conducting research on the mechanisms of action of herbal drugs, which can help to improve the quality and effectiveness of herbal drugs.

Role of Herbal drug Industry in the country's Economy

The herbal drugs industry in India plays a significant role in the country's economy. India is known for its rich tradition of Ayurveda and other traditional medicine systems, which have been using herbs for medicinal purposes for thousands of years. As a result, India has a vast wealth of knowledge and experience in the cultivation, harvesting, and use of herbs for medicinal purposes.

The Indian government is also actively promoting the growth of the herbal drugs industry in the country. This includes initiatives to support the cultivation and harvesting of herbs, as well as efforts to improve the standardization and regulation of herbal drugs. Additionally, the government is also investing in research and development to better understand the potential health benefits of herbal drugs and to ensure that they are safe and effective.

India is one of the largest exporter of herbal drugs and herbal products in the world, with exports valued at over $1 billion. It's also one of the largest producer of medicinal plants, and the industry provides employment to a large number of people in rural areas.

However, the industry also faces certain challenges in India such as lack of standardization, regulation, and scientific research on the safety and efficacy of herbal drugs. This can make it difficult for consumers to determine the quality and safety of the products they are buying. Additionally, there is also a lack of awareness among consumers regarding the correct usage and dosage of herbal drugs which can lead to adverse effects.

One real-time case study of the herbal drugs industry is the use of turmeric as a treatment for inflammation and pain. Turmeric, a spice commonly used in Indian and Southeast Asian cuisine, has been used for medicinal purposes for centuries in Ayurvedic and traditional Chinese medicine.

Recent scientific research has shown that turmeric contains a compound called curcumin, which has anti-inflammatory and antioxidant properties. This has led to an increase in the use of turmeric as a treatment for a wide range of conditions, including arthritis, inflammatory bowel disease, and even cancer.

Many companies in the herbal drugs industry have begun to produce turmeric supplements in the form of capsules, tablets, and liquids. These supplements are becoming increasingly popular as a natural alternative to non-steroidal anti-inflammatory drugs (NSAIDs) such as ibuprofen and aspirin, which can have potentially harmful side effects.

Several clinical studies have been conducted on the efficacy of turmeric supplements, and the results have been promising. A randomized, double-blind, placebo-controlled study published in the Journal of Clinical Rheumatology found that a turmeric supplement was effective in reducing pain and improving function in patients with knee osteoarthritis. Another study published in the Journal of Medicinal Food found that a turmeric supplement reduced pain and improved function in patients with rheumatoid arthritis.

This case study highlights the potential of herbal drugs such as turmeric to be effective in treating various conditions. It also shows how the herbal drugs industry is actively researching and developing herbal products to promote their use as an alternative or complementary medicine to conventional drugs.

It's also worth mentioning that turmeric supplements should always be used under the guidance of a healthcare professional and some people should avoid using turmeric supplements if they are taking blood thinning medications, or have gallbladder issues.

Another real-time case study of the herbal drugs industry is the use of ginseng as a treatment for fatigue and stress. Ginseng, a root commonly used in traditional Chinese and Korean medicine, has been used for medicinal purposes for centuries.

Recent scientific research has shown that ginseng contains compounds called ginsenosides, which have adaptogenic properties. This means that they help the body adapt to stress by regulating the immune and endocrine systems. This has led to an increase in the use of ginseng as a treatment for a wide range of conditions, including fatigue, stress, and even diabetes.

Many companies in the herbal drugs industry have begun to produce ginseng supplements in the form of capsules, tablets, and liquids. These supplements are becoming increasingly popular as a natural alternative to conventional drugs such as antidepressants and anti-anxiety medications, which can have potentially harmful side effects.

It's also worth mentioning that as with any supplement, ginseng should be used under the guidance of a healthcare professional, and it should be avoided by pregnant or breastfeeding women, or people who are taking blood thinning medications.

India has a rich tradition of using medicinal and aromatic plants (MAPs) for various ailments and diseases. These plants have been used in Ayurveda, Unani, and Siddha systems of medicine for centuries. The plant-based industry in India is mainly centered around the cultivation, processing, and export of MAPs.

The government of India has recognized the importance of MAPs and has taken several initiatives to promote their cultivation and use. The Ministry of AYUSH (Ayurveda, Yoga and Naturopathy, Unani, Siddha, and Homeopathy) is the primary government body responsible for the development and promotion of traditional systems of medicine, including the use of MAPs.

The Indian Council of Medical Research (ICMR) also plays a significant role in the research and development of MAPs. They have several research centers dedicated to the study of MAPs and their medicinal properties.

The Central Institute of Medicinal and Aromatic Plants (CIMAP) is a premier research institute in India that conducts research on MAPs and their cultivation. They also provide training and technical assistance to farmers and entrepreneurs involved in the cultivation and processing of MAPs.

The National Medicinal Plant Board (NMPB) is another government body that promotes the cultivation and sustainable use of MAPs in India. They provide financial assistance to farmers and entrepreneurs involved in the MAPs sector.

India has a rich tradition of using medicinal and aromatic plants (MAPs) for various ailments and diseases. These plants have been used in Ayurveda, Unani, and Siddha systems of medicine for centuries. The plant-based industry in India is mainly centered around the cultivation, processing, and export of MAPs.

The government of India has recognized the importance of MAPs and has taken several initiatives to promote their cultivation and use. The Ministry of AYUSH (Ayurveda, Yoga and Naturopathy, Unani, Siddha, and Homeopathy) is the primary government body responsible for the development and promotion of traditional systems of medicine, including the use of MAPs.

The Indian Council of Medical Research (ICMR) also plays a significant role in the research and development of MAPs. They have several research centers dedicated to the study of MAPs and their medicinal properties.

The Central Institute of Medicinal and Aromatic Plants (CIMAP) is a premier research institute in India that conducts research on MAPs and their cultivation. They also provide training and technical assistance to farmers and entrepreneurs involved in the cultivation and processing of MAPs.

The National Medicinal Plant Board (NMPB) is another government body that promotes the cultivation and sustainable use of MAPs in India. They provide financial assistance to farmers and entrepreneurs involved in the MAPs sector.

There are also several private companies and organizations involved in the cultivation, processing, and export of MAPs in India. These include companies such as Dabur, Baidyanath, and Himalaya, which have a strong presence in the herbal medicine market.

List of some of the major plant-based industries in India:

Overview of plant-based industries in India: India has a rich history and tradition of using medicinal and aromatic plants for various purposes. The plant-based industry in India encompasses various sectors such as ayurvedic medicine, herbal supplements, essential oils, and traditional medicine. The industry is a significant contributor to the Indian economy, providing employment opportunities and generating income for farmers and rural communities.

Importance of medicinal and aromatic plants in India: Medicinal and aromatic plants play a crucial role in the Indian healthcare system. They have been used for centuries in traditional medicine to treat a wide range of ailments. They are also used in the cosmetics and fragrance industry. With the increasing demand for natural and organic products, the importance of medicinal and aromatic plants is growing. These plants are also known for their medicinal properties and are used to treat a wide range of ailments such as skin diseases, digestive disorders, and respiratory problems. Additionally, they are also a sustainable source of livelihood for many farmers and rural communities in India

Types of plant-based industries in India

India has a diverse range of plant-based industries, including but not limited to:

Ayurvedic medicine: Ayurveda is an ancient system of medicine that originated in India. It uses a combination of herbs, minerals, and metals to treat various ailments. The Ayurvedic medicine industry in India is valued at over $2 billion and is expected to grow at a CAGR of 8-9% in the coming years.

Essential oils: India is one of the largest producers of essential oils in the world. The essential oil industry in India is valued at around $1 billion and is expected to grow at a CAGR of 6-7% in the coming years.

Herbal supplements: The herbal supplement industry in India is valued at around $1 billion and is expected to grow at a CAGR of 10-12% in the coming years.

Traditional medicine: India has a rich tradition of using natural products to treat various ailments. The traditional medicine industry in India is valued at around $5 billion and is expected to grow at a CAGR of 8-10% in the coming years.

Current market size and growth projections: The plant-based industry in India is valued at around $10 billion and is expected to grow at a CAGR of 8-10% in the coming years. This growth is driven by increasing demand for natural and organic products, growing awareness about the medicinal properties of plants, and government initiatives to support the industry.

Key players in the industry: Some of the key players in the plant-based industry in India include Dabur, Himalaya, Patanjali,

Baidyanath, and Nirma. These companies are involved in various sectors of the industry such as Ayurvedic medicine, herbal supplements, and essential oils. Additionally, there are many small and medium-sized enterprises that are involved in the cultivation and processing of medicinal and aromatic plants in India.

Dabur India Limited
Himalaya Drug Company
Patanjali Ayurved Limited
Baidyanath
Nirma Limited
Emami Limited
The Himalaya Wellness Company
Herbal Hills Global
Organic India Private Limited
Kama Ayurveda
Sri Sri Ayurveda
Forest Essentials
Kancor Ingredients Limited
Synthite Industries Limited
S.A.L. Ltd
A.G. Industries
A.V. Naturals
Basic Ayurveda
Bio Organic & Natural Pvt Ltd
Charak Pharma Pvt. Ltd

Dabur India Limited: One of India's oldest and largest Ayurvedic medicine manufacturers, known for its herbal and natural health care products.

Baidyanath: A leading Ayurvedic medicine manufacturer that produces a wide range of herbal products, including medicines, cosmetics, and health supplements.

Himalaya Drug Company: A leading producer of herbal and ayurvedic products, including personal care, baby care, and health care products.

Patanjali Ayurved Limited: A fast-growing company that produces a wide range of Ayurvedic and natural products, including food items, personal care, and health care products.

The Indian Herbs: A well-known company in the herbal industry that grows and processes a wide range of medicinal plants, including herbs, spices, and essential oils.

Aimil Pharmaceuticals: A leading Ayurvedic and herbal medicine manufacturer that produces a wide range of products, including medicines, cosmetics, and health supplements.

Natreon Inc: A US-based company with a facility in India, that specializes in the extraction and isolation of natural compounds from plants for use in dietary supplements, functional foods and pharmaceuticals

Organic India: A leading producer of organic herbal teas, supplements, and personal care products that are made from sustainably grown herbs and plants.

Sesha Herbal Extracts: A leading producer of herbal extracts and essential oils, that sources its raw materials from farmers across India.

Herbal Hills: A leading producer of Ayurvedic and herbal products, including dietary supplements, personal care products, and herbal teas.

Research and Development

Overview of the institutions and organizations involved in R&D on medicinal and aromatic plants in India: There are several institutions and organizations in India that are involved in research and development (R&D) on medicinal and aromatic plants. Some of them are:

Council of Scientific and Industrial Research (CSIR)

Indian Council of Medical Research (ICMR)

Central Council for Research in Ayurvedic Sciences (CCRAS)

Central Institute of Medicinal and Aromatic Plants (CIMAP)

National Botanical Research Institute (NBRI)

National Medicinal Plants Board (NMPB)

Indian Institute of Integrative Medicine (IIIM)

National Institute of Ayurveda (NIA)

Regional Research Laboratory (RRL)

Central Institute for Research on Buffaloes (CIRB)

National Research Centre for Medicinal and Aromatic Plants (NRCMAP)

Current research and development initiatives in the field: There are several research and development initiatives that are currently ongoing in India in the field of medicinal and aromatic plants. Some examples include:

Identification and documentation of medicinal plants

Development of new plant-based products

Study of the chemical composition of plants

Study of the pharmacological properties of plants

Study of the genetic diversity of plants

Study of the cultivation and harvesting of plants

Study of the processing and preservation of plants

Study of the traditional uses of plants

Study of the economic and social aspects of the plant-based industry

Role of government and private institutions in supporting R&D: Government institutions such as CSIR, ICMR, CCRAS, CIMAP, NBRI, NMPB, IIIM, NIA, RRL, CIRB, NRCMAP play a crucial role in supporting R&D on medicinal and aromatic plants in India. They provide funding for research, infrastructure, and human resources. Private institutions also play an important role in supporting R&D by investing in research and development programs and collaborating with government institutions. The government also provides financial assistance to the farmers and rural communities for the cultivation, processing, and distribution of medicinal and aromatic plants.

The Indian Council of Medical Research (ICMR)

It is the apex body in India for the formulation, coordination, and promotion of biomedical research. It is an autonomous organization under the Indian Ministry of Health and Family Welfare and was established in 1911.

The main objectives of ICMR are to:

Promote, conduct and coordinate biomedical research in the country

Develop a national policy and strategy for biomedical research

Promote and coordinate the participation of Indian scientists in international biomedical research programs

Provide a national perspective to the development of biomedical research in the country

ICMR has a nationwide network of 27 research institutes and centers that conduct research in various areas of health and medical research. They also provide research training to students and scientists at different levels.

ICMR also plays a vital role in the research and development of medicinal and aromatic plants (MAPs). It has several research centers dedicated to the study of MAPs and their medicinal properties such as the National Institute of Medical Statistics, New Delhi, and the Regional Medical Research Centre, Port Blair, that conduct research on the ethnobotanical, phytochemical and pharmacological aspects of MAPs.

The ICMR also provides financial assistance to institutions, organizations and individuals for research and training in the field of traditional and complementary systems of medicine, including Ayurveda, Unani, Siddha, Yoga, and Naturopathy, which makes use of MAPs extensively.

The National Medicinal Plant Board (NMPB)

The National Medicinal Plant Board (NMPB) is a government body established by the Government of India in 2000, under the Ministry of AYUSH (Ayurveda, Yoga and Naturopathy, Unani, Siddha, and Homeopathy).

The main objectives of the NMPB are to:

Promote the cultivation and sustainable use of medicinal plants in the country

Develop and implement a national policy for the conservation and sustainable use of medicinal plants

Provide financial assistance to farmers and entrepreneurs involved in the medicinal plant sector

Promote research and development on medicinal plants

Coordinate and collaborate with other government and non-government organizations working in the field of medicinal plants

The NMPB also works to establish a network of medicinal plant conservation areas, and also provides technical assistance to farmers, entrepreneurs and other stakeholders in the sector.

The NMPB also plays an important role in the export of medicinal plants and its products, by providing certification and other support services to exporters.

Central Institute of Medicinal and Aromatic Plants (CIMAP):

A premier research institute that conducts research on the cultivation and processing of medicinal and aromatic plants, and provides training and technical assistance to farmers and entrepreneurs involved in this sector.

National Bureau of Plant Genetic Resources (NBPGR): An organization that conducts research on plant genetic resources, including medicinal plants, and works to conserve and utilize these resources for sustainable agriculture and horticulture.

Forest Research Institute (FRI): A premier institute that conducts research on the conservation, management, and utilization of forest resources, including medicinal and aromatic plants.

National Botanical Research Institute (NBRI): A premier institute that conducts research on various aspects of botanical science, including the study of medicinal and aromatic plants.

The Indian Council of Forestry Research and Education (ICFRE): A premier organization that conducts research on various aspects of forestry, including the study of medicinal and aromatic plants found in forests.

National Medicinal Plants Board (NMPB) : A government body established to promote the cultivation and sustainable use of medicinal plants, provide financial assistance, technical assistance and other support services to farmers, entrepreneurs, and other stakeholders in the sector, coordinates and collaborates with other organizations working in the field of medicinal plants, and plays an important role in the export of medicinal plants and its products.

XV

Schedule T- Good Manufacturing practices of Indian system of medicine

Schedule T is a set of guidelines for Good Manufacturing Practices (GMP) for Indian systems of medicine, such as Ayurveda, Unani, and Siddha. These guidelines are intended to ensure that products manufactured under these systems of medicine are of consistent high quality and safe for consumption. Schedule T lays down the standards for the manufacture of raw materials, packaging materials, and finished products. It also includes guidelines for documentation, record-keeping, and inspections. The implementation of Schedule T is mandatory for manufacturers of Indian systems of medicine, and non-compliance can result in penalties or revocation of licenses.

Components of GMP (Schedule – T) and its objectives

Schedule T of the Drugs and Cosmetics Rules, 1945 lays down the guidelines for Good Manufacturing Practices (GMP) for Indian systems of medicine. The components of Schedule T include:

Premises: The guidelines specify the requirements for the construction, layout, and maintenance of the manufacturing premises, including provision for adequate lighting, ventilation, and sanitation.

Equipment: The guidelines specify the requirements for the design, construction, and maintenance of equipment used in the manufacturing process, including provision for calibration, cleaning, and maintenance.

Personnel: The guidelines specify the requirements for the qualifications, training, and responsibilities of personnel involved in the manufacturing process.

Materials: The guidelines specify the requirements for the quality, storage, and handling of raw materials, packaging materials, and finished products.

Production: The guidelines specify the requirements for the manufacturing process, including provision for documentation, record-keeping, and batch production records.

Quality Control: The guidelines specify the requirements for the testing and release of finished products, including provision for a system of quality control, standard operating procedures, and documentation.

Complaints and recalls: The guidelines specify the requirements for the handling of complaints and recalls, including provision for a system of traceability, and documentation.

Self-Inspection: the guidelines specify the requirement for self-inspection of the manufacturing facility.

The objectives of Schedule T are to ensure that products manufactured under the Indian systems of medicine are of consistent high quality, safe for consumption, and conform to the standards laid down in the Schedule. It also aims to ensure that the manufacturing process is in compliance with the principles of GMP and to protect the consumer's interest.

Infrastructural requirements

The infrastructural requirements of Schedule T of the Drugs and Cosmetics Rules, 1945 for Good Manufacturing Practices (GMP) for Indian systems of medicine include the following:

Premises: The manufacturing facility should be located in a hygienic environment and should be constructed to prevent the entry of dust, pests, and other contaminants. The premises should be well-ventilated, with adequate lighting and temperature control. Adequate space should be provided for the storage of raw materials, packaging materials, and finished products.

Equipment: All equipment used in the manufacturing process should be designed and constructed in a way that prevents contamination of the product. Equipment should be easy to clean and maintain, and should be regularly calibrated and inspected.

Personnel: Adequate facilities, such as restrooms and changing rooms, should be provided for personnel. Personnel should be properly trained and qualified to carry out their responsibilities, and should be required to follow good personal hygiene practices.

Materials: Raw materials, packaging materials, and finished products should be stored in a manner that prevents contamination, deterioration, or damage. Adequate facilities should be provided for the quarantine and inspection of incoming materials.

Production: Adequate facilities should be provided for the manufacturing process, including provision for documentation, record-keeping, and batch production records. Adequate facilities should also be provided for the cleaning and maintenance of the production area.

Quality Control: Adequate facilities should be provided for the testing and release of finished products, including provision for a system of quality control, standard operating procedures, and documentation.

Complaints and recalls: Adequate facilities should be provided for the handling of complaints and recalls, including provision for a system of traceability, and documentation.

Self-Inspection: Adequate facilities should be provided for self-inspection of the manufacturing facility.

The working space requirements

Adequate space: The manufacturing facility should have enough space to accommodate all the equipment, personnel, and materials required for the manufacturing process. This includes separate areas for raw materials, packaging materials, finished products, and quarantine areas for incoming materials.

Clean and hygienic: The working space should be clean and hygienic, with provision for regular cleaning and disinfection. Floors, walls, and ceilings should be made of smooth, non-absorbent, and easily cleanable materials.

Separation of areas: Different areas of the manufacturing facility should be separated to prevent cross-contamination. This includes separating raw materials, packaging materials, finished products, and quarantine areas.

Lighting: Adequate lighting should be provided in all areas of the manufacturing facility, including production areas, storage areas, and laboratories.

Ventilation: Adequate ventilation should be provided to maintain a clean and hygienic environment. This includes provision for the exhaust of dust, fumes, and other contaminants.

Temperature control: Adequate temperature control should be provided to ensure that raw materials, packaging materials, and finished products are stored at the appropriate temperature.

Pest control: Adequate measures should be taken to prevent the entry of pests, such as rodents and insects, into the manufacturing facility.

self-inspection: Adequate space and facility should be provided for self-inspection of the manufacturing facility.

Storage area

The storage area requirements of Schedule T of the Drugs and Cosmetics Rules, 1945 for Good Manufacturing Practices (GMP) for Indian systems of medicine include the following:

Adequate space: The manufacturing facility should have enough space to store raw materials, packaging materials, and finished products separately, in order to prevent cross-contamination.

Clean and hygienic: The storage area should be clean and hygienic, with provision for regular cleaning and disinfection. Floors, walls, and ceilings should be made of smooth, non-absorbent, and easily cleanable materials.

Separation of areas: Different areas of the storage should be separated to prevent cross-contamination. This includes separating raw materials, packaging materials, finished products, and quarantine areas.

Lighting: Adequate lighting should be provided in the storage area, to ensure that materials can be properly inspected.

Ventilation: Adequate ventilation should be provided to maintain a clean and hygienic environment. This includes provision for the exhaust of dust, fumes, and other contaminants.

Temperature control: Adequate temperature control should be provided to ensure that raw materials, packaging materials, and finished products are stored at the appropriate temperature.

Pest control: Adequate measures should be taken to prevent the entry of pests, such as rodents and insects, into the storage area.

Labeling: All materials should be properly labeled, indicating the type of material, batch number, expiry date, and storage instructions.

Quarantine: Adequate facilities should be provided for the quarantine and inspection of incoming materials.

Machinery and equipments

Machinery, and equipment requirements of Schedule T of the Drugs and Cosmetics Rules, 1945 for Good Manufacturing Practices (GMP) for Indian systems of medicine include the following:

Adequate space: The manufacturing facility should have enough space to accommodate all the equipment and machinery required for the manufacturing process. This includes separate areas for different stages of the manufacturing process.

Clean and hygienic: The area, machinery, and equipment should be clean and hygienic, with provision for regular cleaning and disinfection. All equipment should be easy to clean and maintain, and should be regularly calibrated and inspected.

Separation of areas: Different areas of the manufacturing facility should be separated to prevent cross-contamination. This includes separating raw materials, packaging materials, finished products, and quarantine areas.

Lighting: Adequate lighting should be provided in all areas of the manufacturing facility, including production areas, storage areas, and laboratories.

Ventilation: Adequate ventilation should be provided to maintain a clean and hygienic environment. This includes provision for the exhaust of dust, fumes, and other contaminants.

Temperature control: Adequate temperature control should be provided to ensure that raw materials, packaging materials, and finished products are stored at the appropriate temperature.

Pest control: Adequate measures should be taken to prevent the entry of pests, such as rodents and insects, into the manufacturing facility.

Equipment design: All equipment should be designed and constructed in a way that prevents contamination of the product. Equipment should be easy to clean and maintain, and should be regularly calibrated and inspected.

Machinery maintenance: Adequate facilities should be provided for the cleaning and maintenance of the machinery.

Self-inspection: Adequate space and facility should be provided for self-inspection of the manufacturing facility.

Standard operating procedures

Standard Operating Procedures (SOPs) are a set of detailed instructions that outline the steps to be followed in performing a specific activity or task within a manufacturing facility. In the context of Schedule T of the Drugs and Cosmetics Rules, 1945 for Good Manufacturing Practices (GMP) for Indian systems of medicine, SOPs are used to ensure that the manufacturing process is carried out consistently and in compliance with the guidelines laid down in the Schedule.

The objectives of SOPs in Schedule T are to:

Ensure consistency: SOPs ensure that the manufacturing process is carried out consistently, by providing detailed instructions on how to perform each task. This helps to ensure that the final product is of consistent high quality.

Compliance: SOPs help to ensure that the manufacturing process is carried out in compliance with the guidelines laid down in Schedule T. This helps to ensure that the final product is safe for consumption and conforms to the standards laid down in the Schedule.

Documentation: SOPs provide a written record of the manufacturing process, which can be used as evidence of compliance with Schedule T.

Training: SOPs provide a training tool for personnel, by outlining the steps to be followed in performing a specific task. This helps to ensure that personnel are properly trained and qualified to carry out their responsibilities.

Self-inspection: SOPs provide a basis for self-inspection of the manufacturing facility, by outlining the steps to be followed in performing a specific task.

SOPs should be written in a clear and concise manner and should be easily understood by the personnel who will be performing the task. They should also be reviewed and updated on a regular basis to ensure that they remain current and accurate.

Health andHygiene

Health and hygiene are an important aspect of Good Manufacturing Practices (GMP) for Indian systems of medicine as per Schedule T of the Drugs and Cosmetics Rules, 1945. The guidelines aim to ensure that the manufacturing process is carried out in a clean and hygienic environment, and that all personnel involved in the manufacturing process maintain good personal hygiene.

The guidelines for health and hygiene in Schedule T include the following:

Personal hygiene: All personnel involved in the manufacturing process should maintain good personal hygiene, including regular hand washing and the use of protective clothing and equipment as appropriate.

Cleanliness: The manufacturing facility should be kept clean and hygienic, with provision for regular cleaning and disinfection. Floors, walls, and ceilings should be made of smooth, non-absorbent, and easily cleanable materials.

Pest control: Adequate measures should be taken to prevent the entry of pests, such as rodents and insects, into the manufacturing facility.

Garbage and waste disposal: Adequate facilities should be provided for the disposal of garbage and waste materials.

Air quality: Adequate ventilation should be provided to maintain a clean and hygienic environment. This includes provision for the exhaust of dust, fumes, and other contaminants.

Temperature control: Adequate temperature control should be provided to ensure that raw materials, packaging materials, and finished products are stored at the appropriate temperature.

Self-inspection: Adequate space and facility should be provided for self-inspection of the manufacturing facility.

Documentation and records

Documentation is an important aspect of Good Manufacturing Practices (GMP) for Indian systems of medicine as per Schedule T of the Drugs and Cosmetics Rules, 1945. The guidelines aim to ensure that the manufacturing process is adequately documented, and that records are kept of all activities and transactions that take place within the manufacturing facility.

The documentation requirements of Schedule T include the following:

Batch production records: Detailed records should be kept of each batch of product manufactured, including the date of manufacture, the raw materials used, and the results of all tests and inspections.

Standard operating procedures (SOPs): Written procedures should be in place for all manufacturing processes, including SOPs for the preparation of raw materials, the manufacture of finished products, and the handling of complaints and recalls.

Record-keeping: Records of all activities and transactions that take place within the manufacturing facility should be kept, including records of raw materials used, finished products produced, and personnel training.

Quality control: Records should be kept of all quality control activities, including testing and release of finished products, and the results of inspections and audits.

Complaints and recalls: Records should be kept of all complaints and recalls, including the nature of the complaint, the actions taken to address the complaint, and the outcome of the complaint.

Self-inspection: Adequate records should be kept of self-inspection of the manufacturing facility.

Logbooks: Logbooks should be maintained for equipment and machinery, including records of maintenance, calibration and cleaning.

All records should be accurate, legible and easily accessible for inspection

9 798889 866701

Printed by Libri Plureos GmbH in Hamburg, Germany